"HEY, THIS WAS REALLY FUN!"

A Memoir

from ***Sesame Street*** *to*

Bear in the Big Blue House

& Beyond

Noel MacNeal

Table of Contents

"But Charlie… Don't forget what happened

to the man who suddenly got everything

he always wanted…

He lived happily ever after."

— Willy Wonka (Gene Wilder)

"It's only a problem
If you make it a problem."

- *Edna MacNeal*

To Susan … who still believes in me

To Matt … who still inspires me

To Mom … who was always proud of me

I dedicate this book to you.

Thank you

INTRODUCTION

"Oh! Hi there! It's so good to see you. C'mon in!"

I wanted to start this off right and I couldn't think of a better line than that. It was what one of the (many) characters I've done would say every time he saw the viewer at home. Maybe you were one of them. He'd open the door, look right into the camera, and be truly excited that *you*, the viewer, stopped by to spend some time with him and his friends. I'm talking about a character I got to bring to life called *"Bear in the Big Blue House."* This is exactly how I feel right now. So, thank you for stopping by and wanting to spend some time with me… and some of my "friends."

To be clear, some of my friends aren't "human." But that's not to say they aren't as attractive, interesting, or full of depth as any human can be. More so, sometimes. I've gotten to know so many over the years, some I've performed and some I've even gotten to perform with — even having a "hand" in their performance. (This is the first of many puns to come so, if that one jarred you, just put this down, and continue with your life. No harm, no fowl.) But I have also gotten to know many, many people through the years, some of whom are still good friends. They are talented, creative, funny, and *never* dull. You'll get to meet some of them as we spend time together.

By the way, the character whose greeting I co-opted, *Bear in the Big Blue House*, was a show on Disney channel in the late '90s and into the early 2000s. And he lived in a big blue house which he shared with an excitable mouse, and each day his other friends — two otters, a lemur, a bear cub, a shadow of a young girl, and said mouse — would have adventures. But he always had time for them, no matter what he was doing, and especially loved seeing (and sniffing) *you*. In case you watched it as a kid or had a younger sibling who did and you ended up watching it too, or were a parent or grandparent, or babysat a kid who watched it, then you know who I'm talking about. If not, he was a seven-foot tall, talking bear named… "Bear." But that's not his *real* name. His real, "legal" name is *"Bear in the Big Blue House."* Seriously. When it came time to copyright the name — a procedure shows do to have their character name and show title belong to them so no one else can use it for their own project — well, the producers discovered they couldn't own the word "Bear." Because it's so common. It would be like trying to own the word "Christmas" or "Día de los Muertos" (Spanish for "Day of the Dead" which the Walt Disney Company DID try to copyright to link it with their movie *Coco*. They weren't able to.) But our production *could* file it as *"Bear in the Big Blue House."* So, "Bear" is actually his nickname. I'll talk more about this show and this experience later. It continues to be a part of my life. An extremely pleasant part and I'm proud it's a fond memory for so many families, and now that (as of this writing) it's airing on Disney Plus, creating new memories for families.

The other characters I've done have been wide and varied. Mostly in children's television, some in commercials, a couple of movies, and live theater. I'm proud to say that my résumé is most people's childhood memory. But I've also been able to break out of "kiddie TV" and perform on shows for grown-ups, such as *Saturday Night Live, Hollywood Squares*, and *Last Week Tonight with John Oliver*. Being on these shows was great because you didn't have a curriculum to adhere to and the characters could be cheeky to downright naughty. Which is always fun to do with puppets. Puppets can get away with so much more than a human can.

What you're going to read is my life in "the business we call show." Because children's television is part of show business: the good parts (creating characters, entertaining others, the great people you sometimes get to work with) and the bad parts (the money you're owed, not being paid what you're worth, the not-so-great people you sometimes have to work with). It's my life and the lessons I've learned as a little pink bird, a baby dragon, a ninja turtle, a precocious inner-city kid, a lion cub, a bare hand with eyeballs on my knuckles, a profane squirrel, a man-eating plant, a bear in a big blue house, and on occasion, a very big bird. Plus, all the monsters, grouches, talking food, assisting, writing, directing, producing, and appearances I've done along the way to this introduction. As I write this, I just celebrated my sixty-first birthday. (Yikes! Where'd the time go?) When you get to fifty you start to think about what you've done and what's left to do. By *sixty* I know one thing I wanted to do: write down all the stories I've told on a lot of podcast interviews and the stories I haven't been able to. And they are good ones.

So, let's start at the very beginning (a very good place to start) and how this four-decade old "dolly-wigglin'" career started. Because a grown man could make up many things.

This is not one of those occasions.

A Quick Glossary of Terms

OK – before we get into all this, I wanted to give you a heads up about some of the terms and phrases that I'll mention. Words that come naturally to me but will be a bit of a mind warp to you. And even if you've heard some of these, this is *my* way of explaining them.

PUPPET

Right. This is easy. To me a "puppet" is anything that can be brought to life with the aid of a human being. Starting with their hands, even if they are using their hands to remote control it, it's puppeteering. (There are "feet puppeteers" but that's another story.)

PUPPETEER

A person that brings the puppet to life. Some puppeteers also make puppets but, primarily, a puppeteer operates the puppet. Animating the inanimate.

ROD PUPPET

A puppet that has these sticks or thin "rods" coming out of their wrists and the puppeteer uses them to gesture the puppet's arms. You've seen this kind: Kermit the Frog; Miss Piggy; Elmo. They are rod puppets.

PRACTICAL HAND PUPPET

This is what I call a puppet that needs *two* puppeteers. The main puppeteer does the head and has one of their hands in the puppet's hand (like a glove at the end of the arm) and another puppeteer slips their hand into the puppet's other hand. You've also seen this kind of puppet: Cookie Monster; Ernie; Fozzie Bear. These are practical hand puppets.

RIGHT HAND or "ASSIST"

This is when another puppeteer will right hand (or left hand or even do both hands, whether it's a rod puppet or a practical hand puppet) or help with a prop the puppet needs. I was often the right hand for Ernie on *Sesame Street* (for both Jim Henson and Steve Whitmire). The rare occasion happened when puppeteer Louise Gold was on Sesame, and she puppeteers with her *left* hand and had her right hand in the puppet's right hand. So, I was her *left hand*! (See? Mind warp!)

When I was right handing for Jerry Nelson's "The Count" for the *Sesame Street* song "The Batty Bat," we had to "waltz" around the room. Muppet performer Richard Hunt gave me this tip: "Stick your thumb through Jerry's belt loop in back – and hang on!" And he was right! (Go on YouTube and you'll see what I mean!)

FULL BODY PUPPET

This is a puppet you wear; it covers the majority of your body. It's NOT a costume character or a sports mascot. If you can animate the mouth and use the same principals and techniques used for rod puppets and practical hand puppets, then it's a body puppet. And you've seen this kind of puppet: *Sesame Street's* Big Bird; Sweetums from *The Muppets*; Bear from *Bear in the Big Blue House*. These are full body puppets.

WRANGLER

The person who preps the puppet and makes sure it's ready for the puppeteer to use.

PUPPET CAPTAIN

It's derived from the world of dance and the term "Dance Captain," meaning the one in charge.

Right then!

Shall we?

PART ONE

"It's Only a Problem If You Make It a Problem"

My mom always believed in this. She was an extremely optimistic person. "Can you walk, can you talk, can you see? Then you've got nothing to complain about." She was always positive and it's one reason why I am who I am. But who was she?

On 20 June 1931, in Hempstead, Long Island, Edna Wilkerson was born. Her mother was Rose Pierce Wilkerson (who was sixteen – yes, *sixteen* years old, having been *married a year*. Yeah – take a moment to absorb this bit of old school math. I recently mentioned this to friends we had over for dinner and our teenage son said, with a shocked expression, "You never told me that!" Yeah, kid. You're the same age your great grandma was when she became a mother); and her father was Edward Dushane Wilkerson (thirty years old, roughly). Edna was named because her parents wanted a boy to name after Edward. So "Edna" was the closest they got. She hated her name and said that at one point in high school she changed her name to "Elizabeth." One day in class when a teacher kept calling "Elizabeth," my mom wondered who the woman meant, because she'd forgotten changing her name. (I told my mom it could have been worse – they could have named her "Edwina" and she agreed.)

Edna was an only child. He mom was a housewife, and her father was a supervisor for the United States Post Office. They eventually moved from Long Island to New York City, to the neighborhood of Harlem, and into the historic Dunbar Apartments. Edna grew up here, going downtown to Harriet Beecher Stowe High School on 67th Street and Second Avenue. After graduating, she became a hand model and dreamed of being an actress. You see, once upon a time, a beautiful young black woman, with a seventeen-inch waist she was most proud of, had a dream of performing on stage. She even attended acting classes from a young thespian by the name of Sidney Poitier, in a little room on West 125th Street in Harlem. She befriended one of the other students there, a "sad, scrawny, kid with holes in his sneakers," she told me. She'd often invite him home, where she still lived with her parents, knowing that her mother would "fatten him up" with her home cooking of fried chicken, collard greens, and made-from-scratch dinner rolls. Of course, she had no idea that this "kid" would become the much-acclaimed actor (and, as she put it, *hunk*) Billy Dee Williams. "Because, if I did," she said, "your last name would *not* be 'MacNeal.'" (Years later, Billy Dee guest starred on *Sesame Street.* When I asked if I could get a photo with him, I said, “Do you remember taking acting lessons from Sidney Poitier on 125th Street?” He gave me this look of *How the hell do you know that?* and quietly said, “Yes.” I asked, “Do you remember a young classmate named Edna Wilkerson?” His face relaxed and he said he did. “She’s, my mom.” Then he broke into a huge smile, and said, “Tell her I said, ‘hi!’”)

Meanwhile …

In the fall of 1930, my father was born. He was one of seven siblings (one of whom was nicknamed “Nuffie” and married the famous black entertainer Cab Calloway), served in Korea, and eventually made it to New York City. Mutual friends of Edna and he introduced them in the spring of 1960. Edna’s father did not like him for some reason. (Foreshadowing?) When I was planning my wedding, I asked my mom where the photos of hers were. “Oh, we eloped,” she said matter-of-factly. You see, in the fall of 1960, they drove to the Midwest to meet his family and his siblings who were still there. On the way, they eloped. They stopped off somewhere along the way and got married. So, when they reached his family, he wasn’t introducing his girlfriend to them, he was introducing his *wife*. And they welcomed Edna with open arms.

Edna and he lived outside of New York City. In January of 1961, they found out the news that would change their lives (or at least Edna’s) forever; Edna was pregnant. Edna’s mom, Rose knew the baby would be a boy (and would except nothing less). And Edna’s father, Edward, could not wait to teach his grandson how to fish.

However, …

In early September of 1961, just two weeks before the baby was born, Edward Dushane Wilkerson suffered a heart attack at home and died. With the baby so close to the due date, Edna could not attend the funeral for her father. She had to remain calm for both her and the baby’s sakes, so her husband drove her around in the car that day. After the funeral was the reception back at the apartment, with well-wishers consoling Edna’s mother. But Rose didn’t need consoling; she was too busy showing off everything she and “Eddie” had gotten for their grandson (because, again, she just “knew” the baby would be a boy).

And then …

On 15 September 1961, at 7:57AM, Edna gave birth to a healthy baby … boy. (Yep, Rose was right.) In honor of her father, who wanted to see and hold his grandchild so much, she gave the boy his first name. But for a middle name, she wanted a name that would remind people of a happy time, like Christmas.

And so, Edward Noel MacNeal entered the world.

When I Was a Kid …

Whenever I'm asked, "Noel, how did you get started in puppetry," I start my answer with "When I was a kid, there were more puppet shows on TV." And watching these shows was a part of my childhood. But of course, I did have other parts that helped shaped who I am.

I have only two actual photographs of my father. It was from my first birthday and he's holding me, wearing a white t-shirt and trousers, and wearing glasses, his black curly hair slicked with pomade. The second photo is with my mom holding the cake my grandmother made for me. She would make all my birthday cakes and I still have the brown ceramic bowl she used. Our family legend is that when Edna was a baby in a store, she reached for it. My grandmother taught me how to make the cake and I've used the bowl to teach my son how to make it. In the photo, my mom and father are smiling, and I have a cute little suit on and wondering when I can stick my hand in the frosting. We're all standing in the Dunbar apartment of Edna's parents. After her father died and I was born, she lived with her mother and her father's brother, John. That way she could look out for them, and they could help with the baby. (My mom told me that after her father died, Uncle John come to her with his bank book and said, "Here." Eddie had taken care of their home and now it was Edna's turn.) My father, still working his job outside of the city, would come back on the weekends and then head back upstate, during the week.

There are a couple other photos of me as a baby there; first and second Christmas; in my English style pram; right after a bath, smiling with no teeth. I have the dimmest memories of being there, the kind that are more like suggestions than actual remembering. And zero memories of my father. Just those two photographs.

It was during this time when I was far too young and unaware, right around when I turned eighteen months, my father had left for work … and never came back. I remember, many years later, asking my mom one morning, when I was about nine years old, "What happened to my dad?"

"He went out for cigarettes and never came back," she answered so flatly, the underlying tone was clearly *"And we will NEVER talk about this again."*

There came a point that my mom decided that we all needed to move. The apartment had too many memories for her and her mom and uncle of where father/husband/brother Edward Wilkerson had lived and died. So, my mom moved us, still in Central Harlem, to The Lenox Terrace. (Quick side note: For those of you unfamiliar with Harlem, look at most New York City maps for tourists, and it's the part above 96th Street where the map gets cut off. Yet strangely enough, subway lines, bus routes, and even streets mysteriously continue upwards.) Now get any thoughts of tenements out of your head. The Lenox Terrace is a complex of six apartment buildings with terraces and twenty-four-hour doormen. It was, at that time, the only luxury apartment complex in Harlem and Uncle John was so proud to live there, he'd invite his friends to come by, to show it off. Of the six buildings, all with a doorman, we lived in the last one that was built – between Lenox Avenue (now Malcom X Boulevard but to locals it will always be Lenox Ave – no offense Malcolm) and Fifth Avenue. We went from a three-bedroom apartment to a two-bedroom apartment, the largest units in the Terrace. Uncle John got the bedroom with the half-bathroom, and I got the smaller one next door. My mom and grandma shared the pullout bed in the living room.

We even had a terrace with a commanding view south and west, that swept from one of the towers of the George Washington Bridge, all the way left to the 125th Street Bridge. In the center facing south was all of midtown Manhattan, including the Empire State Building. All the low storied buildings gave us this view and when lit up at night, midtown was the vision of being "The Emerald City," a place so unlike the surrounding neighborhood, not just a place to visit, but a goal. There were people in our neighborhood who'd never gone below 125th St, with no desire whatsoever. But my mom wanted to make sure that I knew there was life beyond Harlem.

Growing up, I was raised by my mom, and my grandmother, and Uncle John. My grandma having been a housewife, with homemade meals every night for her husband after his long day at the post office, knew how to keep house, cook, clean, do laundry, etc. (The woman made biscuits from scratch! But then discovered the wonder of Pillsbury. For many years I was terrified of the "pop" of the tube when she slammed it on the corner of the counter to open it.) Every birthday cake I ever had growing up was handmade by her (except the frosting; that was supermarket frosting and every time I taste Pillsbury chocolate frosting from a can, I'm a kid again). I would help her make meals and I was good at it. She taught me how to cook because my mom could not and she said, …

"I don't want my only grandchild to starve to death."

I remember once my mom actually tried to cook chicken. It was a cut up chicken and she tried to roast it in the oven. And an hour later, it wasn't cooked. It was still raw. She tried cooking it in a pan on the stove. Still raw. She finally threw the parts under the broiler and set the flames to its highest setting. She pulled out the singed pan and the pieces were – still raw. And that was the last time she ever attempted to make anything. (Nope – not true; from that time forth she made "reservations.")

My Uncle, John Wilkerson, who was in his early 80s, was retired from the railroad, having been a Pullman Porter, one of the few jobs black men were allowed to have that directly interacted with white people. During the summer months, he would go downtown for errands, always dressed to the nines in a three-piece suit and fedora, mainly to get his cigars from a place near Wall Street. Tagging along with him during the summer, we always rode the subway, and it was my indoctrination to NYC's underground system at a very early age. Once, he took me to Penn Station and down to the trains where a friend of his was. I got to climb aboard one of the massive Amtrak engines and was awed by the number of dials and buttons and switches used to operate it. My little Lionel train set at home was much easier to operate.

I was an only child and so was my mom. But she realized that I needed to begin to know how to socialize with other kids. There was a pre-school located in one of the other buildings in the Lenox Terrace; "Vergie's Tot Town." (I remember that lunch was often instant grits.) My mom once told me of a time (I don't remember) that something happened with another kid, and I was upset, and Tot Town called home and within minutes my grandmother came and immediately took me home. My mother did not approve of this; whatever occurred, I should have stayed. And the next day *she* dropped me off, with instructions that, from then on, if anything happened again, to call *her* at the office. Looking back at this and a few other instances, I now know that there was a certain rivalry, even tension, between this mother and daughter, whose ages were only fifteen years apart. And her dad having doted on her, Little Edna could do no wrong in Eddie Wilkerson's eyes. Which I believe is why my grandmother had never taught her how to cook. I think it was a way to keep this special talent that her husband loved about her, to herself.

For elementary school, I went to P.S. 197 on 135th St, so close to us. But we lived in the other "zone." There are "lines" that divide school districts from one another, and NYC elementary school kids go to the public school within their "zone." And the district line cut right across the street, separating us from the convenient school. To get around this, we used my aunt's address. "Aunt Sis and Uncle Smitty" lived in the Riverton apartment complex, directly across the street from 197, but inside the "zone." So, they let us use their address and I was enrolled from kindergarten through sixth grade. When I was in sixth grade and my love of puppets was firmly cemented in me, I got to teach first graders how to make puppets for a month. I'd go and we'd make simple puppets from paper and cardboard, a skill that I'd use with my own son and, one day, write two books for families on how to make puppets, together. Of course, this love for puppets and especially the Muppets on Sesame Street did not go unnoticed.

"Nicky & Dicky" were twin brothers, sharing the same brain and a talent for teasing. When they discovered I watched Sesame Street, they'd make fun of it, and me, in front of others. I finally told my mom who gave an odd suggestion:

"The next time they do it … laugh."

"What?!?"

This was way too cerebral for a nine-year old. But she explained that if I don't let it bother me, and actually laugh along with everyone else, it won't work. I was wary of this tactic but the next day, Tweedledum & Tweedledumber started in, and … I started to laugh. And she was right! This completely threw these two troglodytes off their game, and they never bothered me again. They also never graduated 197 because at some point, they both got expelled, while I went on to eventually work on Sesame Street and meet and work with Jim Henson, himself.

It's rare, but when it does happen, it's nice to get the last laugh.

Once I graduated from 197, I'd be going to junior high, and then, high school. But the public junior highs and high schools in our zone were limited: either the school where the kid was stabbed or the school where the kid was shot. Realizing that public school was not a viable option at all, my mom began to look into private schools. The one she found was the Rhodes Preparatory School on 54th Street between 5th and 6th Avenue in midtown. We went there, so I could take an academic assessment test, which I passed. This meant I could attend Rhodes, … along with the $500 tuition deposit my mom would need to give them, within thirty days. And she didn't have it.

When we got home, we told what happened to my grandma and my uncle. Uncle John then went to his room and came back with some cash and handed it to my mom. "Here," he said, explaining he'd played "the numbers" that day (the old school neighborhood version of the lottery) and he had won. My mom counted it and … it was exactly $500.

When I first started going to Rhodes, I'd ride downtown with my mom. She was due at her job, as a secretary for a banking firm (C.I.T.) on 59th Street and Madison Avenue, by 8:45AM and I was due at school on 54th Street between 5th Ave & 6th Ave by 8:45AM. So, we'd often eat breakfast at the cafeteria within the GM (General Motors) Building on 5th Ave, directly across from The Plaza Hotel. It was open to the public (although the public didn't know it). We'd kiss good-bye and she'd head around the corner to her job, and I'd head down 5th Ave to school. Then after school, Uncle John would meet me outside of Rhodes and we'd take the subway home.

Every morning, I'd knock on his door and peek in and say "Morning Uncle John. See ya later." "All right," he'd respond. One morning, I knocked, and peeked in for our usual routine, except he was still in bed, asleep. At least, he *looked* like he was asleep, and yet, something felt a little … *off*. I didn't say anything to my mom or grandmother cause what if I was wrong? He'd be embarrassed and I would be, too. He's allowed to sleep in. I wish I could during those first school days waking up at 6:30AM to be ready to get the 7:15AM No. One Bus, "the Limited," that stopped every ten blocks.

All that day, it was still in the back of my mind, and I began to wonder if I'd see Uncle John that afternoon. I figured I'd know come 3:00PM; he'd either be there or he wouldn't. I went to classes, had lunch (not mentioning any of this to my friends), more classes, and then the bell rang. Three o'clock. I got my stuff from my locker and headed to the front door.

Just before I stepped outside, I stopped for a moment. In the next three seconds I'd know if I was right or, hopefully, wrong. I stepped outside and looked to my right at the usual spot and standing there was … no one.

"Sweetheart?"

I turned around and there, to my left, was my mom … *and* my grandmother. I walked over to them and said, "Hi."

"Sweetheart, …we …" my mom began, her eyes watery, "We have to … tell you something." But then the words couldn't come out. My grandmother however was much more direct.

"Uncle John's dead," she said.

"Oh," I said quietly.

My mom reached her hand out to my shoulder and asked, "Are you all right?"

"Um … yeah?"

"Ok. Let's go home."

We began to walk down the block and we hadn't gotten halfway when I suddenly said, …

"You know … I thought he looked kind of 'dead' this morning."

They both stopped and looked at me.

"You *knew*!?!" they both said together.

“Well, no, but when I went in to say ‘See ya later’ he was still in bed, and I thought ‘Huh - He kinda looks dead.’”

And they both smiled and hugged me, and we continued our way to get a cab home.

Rhodes had been around for seventy-five years and resided in a townhouse designed by the famed architect Stanford White, located across the street from the Museum of Modern Art. There was a dress code: boys wore blue blazers, collared shirts and ties, and dress pants, and polished shoes; girls wore starched shirts and skirts. If my mom wanted me to know life beyond 125th Street, then there was no better place or location. Every kid in that school was different; white, black, Asian, Latino, there was even a kid from Germany and one from France. My graduating class was just fifty-six of us. I made many friends there, but the one whom I’m still friends with is Danny. We met in art class in seventh grade, him asking me to draw a circle for him (it is a talent I have), and we’ve been friends ever since. Danny is the one who introduced me to Broadway. In senior year, one Wednesday, we were both done by 1:00PM. I wasn’t due to meet my mom until 5:00pm, when she got off work. He wanted to see this show, *“Ballroom,”* and asked if I wanted to come along. “Sure,” I said, “But aren’t shows expensive?” He took me to TKTS, the half-price ticket booth, in Times Square, where you could get discounted tickets for shows that day. We got mezzanine seats, and I watched my first Broadway show. It was wonderful and it wouldn’t be my last.

Danny loves to travel, to this day. In high school he was obsessed with train travel. In senior year, he, and I, and two friends planned our own senior trip for a two-day adventure to Washington D.C. And, of course, we traveled by train. (My grandmother told my mom after I left “I’m not getting a wink of sleep until that boy is back,” to which my mom answered calmly, “G’night” and went to bed.) This was so exciting for me. The furthest out of state I’d gotten was New Jersey (home of Great Adventures theme park, in Jackson, N.J.). When the Amtrak train stopped in Maryland for ten minutes, I jumped onto the platform, so proud that I’d made it this far from home.

The four of us stayed at The Watergate Hotel. Yes. It was May of 1979, so the hotel was still in its infamy, but not the tourist attraction it is today. But we thought "you can't get more 'D.C.' than staying in The Watergate!" (Years earlier I was annoyed every afternoon after school, coming home, and having *Sesame Street* and *Mister Rogers* preempted, for live coverage of the hearings. Living through history is wasted on the very young.) I had contacted the office of our congressman, Representative Charles Rangel, and gotten tickets for a tour of Congress and the White House (which you could do for many years). One highlight that Danny said we had to do was the Congressional Subway.

I'm sorry; the *WHAT* now?!?

But it's true. Under Congress is a little train shuttle that connects the House of Representatives to the Senate. This way the members and staff can just hop aboard and travel back and forth when need be. (Something so simple and efficient downstairs and yet, upstairs, so much complicated hypocrisy and red tape. Go figure.)

Danny then went from train travel to cruises. He even missed our high school graduation because he was on his first cruise. When his name was called, his mom walked on stage and received the diploma. He's sailed for years – been to Antarctica seven times - and finally talked me into going on one in early December of 1989. Two weeks, from Tahiti to Sydney, Australia, airfare, and all meals onboard, included.

"When?" I asked.

"Tomorrow."

Hubba whuh?!?

But it was a great deal and so I went for it. The next day, while as I was packing to head to the airport, my mom came by my room.

"Have a great trip sweetheart."

"Wait – where are *you* going?"

“Oh, Atlantic City. Rosemary (the concierge at one of the resort casinos and my mom’s friend) got me a free room. Love you!” and she was out the door. No “not getting a wink of sleep until that boy is home” from this lady. One of her favorite movies was *“Mame,”* based on the life of the flamboyant Mame Dennis. And my mom embraced her philosophy …

“Life is a banquet. And most poor suckers are starving to death.”

Danny and I flew from NYC to L.A., with a seven-hour layover till our flight to Tahiti. So, what could we do in that time? Why rent a car and head to … Disneyland! I had visited two years prior, but Danny of course had never been to “The Happiest Place on Earth,” and seemed to enjoy it, at least for my sake. Then we got the eight-hour flight to Tahiti, where there’s black sand covering beaches. Have you ever seen Tahiti on a map? There’s a good reason. You can’t. It’s *that small*! It’s smaller than a dot! But we landed and checked into our cabin aboard the Sea Princess, part of Princess Cruise Lines (aka *“The Love Boat”* cruise line).

I had never been at sea before, and it was … interesting. I remember the first day walking out on deck and seeing the ocean surrounding us, like a humongous blue table, and the clear sky, like a bright blue dome, over us. I had no sense of movement until I looked over and saw the ship cutting through the waves. But there was nothing around us – *nothing*! Just sea and sky. And – I had a panic attack! By this time in my life, I’d been inside body puppets of a dragon, a big bird, even a Snuffleupagus. But *this*?!? I had never known what claustrophobia felt like until that moment. And realized I was trapped for the next *fourteen days*! I went inside to the ship’s library, a beautiful wood paneled room and sat with my back to the windows and calmed down. But it was the adventure of a lifetime for me. Seeing so many islands and cultures and all due to my friend from high school. One evening we watched the sunset on deck (and by then the claustrophobia had passed), and I said, …

“I’ve never seen you so happy. You belong out here.”

Danny was (and still is) an investment banker, but these words changed his life, as he's told me. He and partners he's gotten have pursued starting their own boutique cruise line, and I've no doubt it will happen one day.

The summer between junior and senior year of high school, I hung out with Joe. During the school year we started having more classes together and we'd gotten to know each other. He even gave me a nickname: "Hey Christmas," he would call out seeing me in the halls. That summer we'd go to the theaters in Chinatown, where he lived with his family, that only showed kung fu movies. Between that, and the moves and techniques he'd learned in kung fu class, we'd try them out. (I always wanted to take classes in martial arts, but we couldn't afford it. So having my own tutor worked out.) One time in school, Joe wanted to show me this new technique he'd learned, getting into a fighting stance, rotating his hands and arms in front of him. "Try and grab me," he dared. I focused, as he rotated his arms, and realized there was a split second when there was an opening and –

"Gotcha!" I said grabbing his tie.

"How'd you do that!?!"

He and I would talk on the phone for hours about martial arts, exercises (I had gotten "The Mighty Marvel Comics Strength & Fitness Book," with superheroes like the Hulk and Captain America demonstrating exercises you could do), and the girls we liked. Yearbooks came in and we signed each other's, him using the nickname he'd given me; "Hey Christmas" he wrote and wished me luck in college. After we graduated Rhodes, we hung out a couple of times that summer, but we both were getting ready for our respective colleges. I once heard "friendship is a relationship of convenience," which I always thought was so sad. And it is sad because, sometimes, it's true. And this was 1979 so there was no Facebook or Instagram to keep tabs on one another; no texting, or facetime on cell phones, no cell phones at all. In time, we lost touch with each other. But you know it happens. It's happened to you, right? It happens when making new friends and having new experiences in new places. It just happens.

A few years later, early one morning, the phone woke me up. I answered and it was Danny.

"I have something I have to tell you."

What's wrong with his voice? I thought. I'd never heard this tone from him.

"What? (There was a pause.) Danny? What's wrong?"

He paused again and then told me Joe … was dead.

It's that moment you hear words you never thought you'd hear, or ever want to hear, that moment you try to not absorb them, because then, their meaning won't be true. You know that moment?

"No. Wait… What… What do you mean he's *dead*?" My mind was racing, trying to make sense of what he just told me.

"I'm sorry."

"No. You're wrong. You're *wrong*! Joe's NOT dead! He can't be dead!"

But it was true. And it was how it was true that was the most disturbing.

After graduating business college, my friend had gotten a job and met a girl. They dated and it was serious, and he eventually asked her to marry him. And she said no. I don't know why. Then one morning, he got up, got dressed for work, and went to her place before going to the office. She opened the door and saw him pull out a gun. And he shot her point blank. And then shot himself.

Danny and I talked a little, making sure the other guy was OK, and then hung up. And I just sat there trying to figure out what happened. How could someone I know … knew… *know* … have done this to himself. To someone else? He killed that girl. He *murdered* her. And then took his own life. He committed murder and then *suicide*. How could my friend, *my* friend, have done this? And I sat there going over it and over it, trying to figure out what went wrong.

Danny and I attended the wake. There was a large photo of Joe, his yearbook picture, hair slicked back and smiling. And next to it was the coffin. And it was open. And he was lying there, in a suit, eyes closed. I wondered if somewhere in the city, at that moment, there was another funeral home with the girl, and her family and friends, attending her wake. We joined the processional pass the casket, to say good-bye, and when I got there, I took a moment to stare at him. And I didn't cry. I hadn't cried since Danny had told me the news. Not one tear. In fact, I wasn't sad.

I was angry.

I was furious.

I wished he was alive, and I could have used some of those kung fu moves he'd taught me, on him; for me to beat the crap out of; to slam him against the wall and scream at him, "WHY!?! YOU WERE MY FRIEND! HOW COULD YOU DO THIS!?!" But that's a talent we humans have; to make a situation, especially one about someone else, about ourselves. *My* friend had done this horrific act of violence, and somehow, it was *my* fault. For the longest time, and I'm talking *years*, I had this guilt. *If* I'd stayed in contact, *if* we'd still had been tight like we were in high school, this never would have happened. I would have seen it, the depression and pain in him he obvious had in him, and could have talked to him, stopped him. If *I'd* been a better friend, two people would still be alive. But then, I realized, this was about him, not me. And maybe, if we had still been in contact, it would still have happened. But I had to stop beating myself up for something I had no control in happening. It did happen and I had to forgive myself. And I had to forgive him. He was a product of his time. A time when there wasn't the open discussion of depression, the resources to find online help, or just seeing others, famous and non, publicly admit their struggles, on social media, in case it could help others. No; you kept it to yourself, especially as a guy, … as a *man*. My wife and I have told our son to always share his feelings, especially with us. I'm proud of him and his generation, so aware and trying to be themselves. And so far, succeeding.

When I was a kid, luckily, I had someone who always believed in me, my mom. Between my wife and I, I think my son will be able to say the same thing one day.

Better Late Than Never

All right – so far – I was raised by a single mom (and my grandmother and great-uncle until their deaths), and my father left us when I was only eighteen months old. But we lived quite comfortably in the Lenox Terrace and my mom worked two jobs; one during the week as a secretary for a banking firm (C.I.T.), and the other on the weekends as an operator for an answering service (Tel-Answer), to put me through private school. I attended the prestigious Rhodes Prep School, on West 54th Street, and when I wasn't studying and cramming for the next exam, I was building puppets and watching *The Muppet Show.* (Every Monday night at 7:30pm on WCBS New York's channel two.) And my mom didn't mind at all. I was being creative, and she loved the puppets I made and the little shows I'd do for her and my grandmother.

You see, growing-up, the whole "what-happened-to-my-father" epic was not discussed. It was just one of those topics — well, the *only* topic — my mother would not talk about, because it was "too painful." She only told me the basics: his family came from the Midwest, and he had a black father and an "Italian" mother. Hence, why my complexion was light brown compared to hers and his. A year after he left, she said he called asking about me, and she made it clear that he was not going to be *that* dad; the one who drifts in and out of his son's life on a whim, setting the boy up for disappointment after disappointment. No.

"You're in or you're out."

Around a year later, she got another call, this time from a friend of his, saying that he had "died" in a car accident. And that was that.

In the spring of 2008, I got to train puppeteers for The Philadelphia Zoo's *"X-tinction"* event, that would last until the fall. It would have puppets of animals that were extinct, on the verge of extinction, and saved from extinction (for the time being). The puppets were built by The Jim Henson Company's Creature Shop in New York (the same shop that takes care of *Sesame Street's* characters and every designer there is a gifted artist), and I would travel back and forth to Philly, with the project manager. On a train ride back, he got a message from his college roommate who happened to be related to Cab Calloway. Then, he asked me, "Didn't you mention you were related to Cab Calloway?" I did. Remember? That sister of my father's, who'd married Cab Calloway? When I got home, I looked him up on Facebook and we friended each other (realizing we were "cousins'), and, suddenly, I saw all these relatives, currently living and those from the past, going back generations, popping up. People I never knew existed, directly related to me! Aunts! Uncles! Cousins! Great-Grandparents! (And may I brag, in saying, these are some *fine-looking* black folks.) I even saw pictures of my great-grandfather and great-grand-uncle as members of the John Robichaux Orchestra, the first jazz orchestra in New Orleans (and featured in Ken Burns' documentary, *"JAZZ"*).

And it turned out that "MacNeal" wasn't a "slave name" after all. I am legitimately half *Scottish* from James MacNeal, who emigrated to the United States in the early nineteenth century, from Scotland and ended up in Virginia where he met a woman named "Parthenia." They had children, including a son, James Jr., who ended up in New Orleans, and met a Creole woman named "Pelomina." They had kids, two of whom, James the Third, and his brother Wendell, were in the jazz orchestra. So many photos of so many people (with not a drop of Italian to be found; between the Creole and Scottish DNA, no wonder I wasn't as dark as my parents).

I scrolled down seeing all these faces, in color, in black-n-white, in tin type, completely beside myself with joy. This was my *family*! All of these people were related to *me*! I couldn't believe it. My new found cousins – *my* cousins – have all embraced me and welcomed me with open arms. My cousins are the best, showing me photos and sharing tales of our family's history. (Being a part of the John Robichaux Orchestra in New Orleans. Another ancestor working alongside Susan B. Anthony. And one cousin was a signer of The Declaration of Independence. Not bad, huh?)

Have you ever heard of "The Great Migration?" Most likely, no. Until recently, neither did I. (Just another example of African American history, which *is* American history, not taught in schools; but let's keep perpetuating that rhyming lie about Christopher Columbus "sailing the ocean blue.") After the Civil War and the end of slavery, Blacks began to make strides in American society, owning businesses, being elected to public office, even Congress, itself. This brief period of achievement during the Reconstruction was ended when resentful Whites, particularly in the South, drafted laws to curtail the freedoms of Blacks. These were the "Jim Crow Laws," that suppressed the rights of Black people and promoted "separate but equal" (in and of itself another lie). This caused a rift within the MacNeals, between those who "passed" (for white) and those who could not. As a result, many Black families left the Southern states and migrated to the Northern and Western United States, my family included. One brother took his family north, and the other headed west.

"What if" is a loaded question, with endless possibilities. That's why it was such a hit for Marvel Comics, taking established characters and situations and then asking … "What if?" For me, it's *"what if" my father stayed … "what if" he'd gotten in touch with me growing up?"* I could have had cousins to grow up with, memories of family events and celebrations with these relatives. But would I still be the person I've turned out to be? Maybe the answers are somewhere in the Multiverse.

I told my mom what I'd discovered, and she finally told me that she knew his "death" was a lie and that she had called one of his brothers, when we moved out of the Dunbar, and gave him our new phone number, to pass along to my father. Whether he did or not, I'll never know. I do know that my father never tried to reach out to me. Period. Being a father myself, I could not imagine leaving my son for any reason. I remember him at eighteen months; how could I turn my back and walk away from him? (He was so cute!) My mom told me that I love my wife and I her, but the love I will feel for my baby, will be like no other. And darn it, she was right. So, the fact that this guy could just walk away from his family, says a lot. It made me realize he isn't worth the mind space or the time. I have now an amazing extended family I've met and will always be in contact with.

That old saying is true – *Better late than never.*

There Were a Lot More Puppet Shows

I know what you're thinking right now:

When's he gonna start talking about puppets? The Muppets? Bear in the Big Blue House?!?

Hey, I'm getting there. But all journeys start with a first step.

When I'm asked how I got started and what inspired me to become a puppeteer, I always start off with …

"There were a lot more puppet shows on TV when I was a kid."

And it's true.

I don't know when I saw my first puppet on TV, but I do remember whenever I did see one, I wanted to see it again. One of the staples of children's TV was the series, *"Captain Kangaroo."* "The Captain" was played by Bob Keeshan, who was the original "Clarabell the Clown" on the previous staple of children's TV, *"Howdy Doody,"* whose puppets were marionettes. The Captain's home and headquarters was "The Treasure House" and every weekday morning, Monday through Friday from 8:00 am until 9:00am, on CBS, he would welcome you, and for the next hour you'd hang out with him and his friends: the local farmer "Mr. Greenjeans;" the neighbor (and I think teacher) "Mr. Baxter" (who was also African American; even as a kid I noticed this); and "Dennis the Handyman." These were the human characters. But the puppet characters were the ones I enjoyed see: "Mr. Moose," who had an obsessive habit of always dropping ping pong balls onto the Captain; and "Bunny Rabbit," who always tricked the Captain into giving him carrots. (Even as a kid I was like *He's a rabbit! Just give him the carrots!*) These were performed by Cosmo Allegretti, who was also "Dennis" and any other human extra needed, as well the costumed characters; the silent, "Dancing Bear" (self-explanatory); and "Cornelius the Walrus." He also "puppeteered" "Grandfather Clock," a tall clock who had blinking eyes and a mouth. I was fascinated by this and even tried to make one out of construction paper and shoe boxes. This was my go-to material, by the way, along with scotch tape and any type of cardboard. (Many years later I'd write a book about all the things you could easily make from cardboard, but I'm getting ahead of myself). Cosmo also did these shorts pieces that appeared in-between segments; cutouts against black to orchestral music (usually the music of Leroy Anderson, who's famous for the Christmas song "Sleigh Ride") which for a little kid like me was mesmerizing.

Captain Kangaroo ran on CBS from 1955 until 1992, first as a full hour show Monday through Friday. But then the morning news shows became more popular so, it was reformatted, including the set, into "Good Morning Captain" and a half hour version 7:30AM until 8:00AM. And then it was gone. And now a piece of TV trivia.

Another staple of TV puppetry was ventriloquist Shari Lewis. She had more than one show and had a career that spanned *four decades*. Her most famous character was the cheeky little sock puppet, "Lambchop." The one show I remember of hers was a parody of *"The Mary Tyler Moore Show,"* called *"The Shari Show."* In it, Shari gets a job at "Bearly Broadcasting" where the staff and crew are all puppets and the owner is "Mr. Bearly," and *all* voiced by Shari. It was syndicated, meaning the local NBC station could choose when to air it so, sometimes I'd catch it, but sometimes not. But when I did, I loved it.

Another ventriloquist was Paul Winchell, whose characters were traditional wooden dummies – the smart alecky "Jerry Mahoney" and the dimwitted "Knucklehead Smith." I vaguely remember the theme song to this show, "Winchell-Mahoney Time," and images of Jerry slapping a cream pie into Paul's face. (Sadly, none of the show's episodes exist; according to the Google search, Metromedia Inc., in a dispute with Paul over the syndication rights, erased all 288 episodes. Paul sued and won over seventeen million dollars. Puppetry for the win!) Paul Winchell went on to have an incredible career as a voice actor for many Hanna Barbera cartoons ("The Banana Splits;" "Wacky Races;" "Dastardly & Muttley in Their Flying Machines;" to name just three), but most famously as the original voice of "Tigger" for Walt Disney's *"Winnie the Pooh"* cartoons. (He also helped invent the artificial heart. Oh yeah. It's true. And proves puppeteers can save lives.)

With Paul and especially Shari as examples, I tried ventriloquism but just never got the hang of it. It is a true skill and artform and ventriloquists never get the respect they deserve. Usually, they are portrayed as psychos with split personalities and a penchant for killing people but blaming the dummy for it. In the comics and then on TV, one of Batman's villains is the ruthless crime boss "Scarface," who's a dummy carried around by his weak-minded, milk toast accountant Arnold Wesker. When I first started college and met Big Bird and Snuffy designer/builder Kermit Love and began working at his shop parttime, I saw an episode of the "Columbo" spinoff series "Mrs. Columbo." In this, a young ventriloquist kills his white-haired, old tormenting mentor. And the ventriloquist's name was "Noel." (Maybe it worked out for Kermit that I *didn't* learn ventriloquism. More on why later.)

My absolute favorite of all of these was a show called "Kukla, Fran, & Ollie." It originally started in Chicago from 1947 until 1957, and then new productions were created in the sixties and seventies. The show was about a misfit cast of puppets, who always try to put on a show. (Sound familiar? This series also had an influence on a young puppeteer named Jim Henson.) It, too, was syndicated, so I'd check and recheck the TV Guide to make sure to be home to see it. (Remember – no VCRs or streaming back then. You were home to see the show, or you missed it.) The only human cast member was actress Fran Allison, the amiable foil, straight-man, and aid to the puppets. And all the puppets were performed by Burr Tilstrom. His style of puppetry was traditional; there was a small proscenium stage with a background (a piece of fabric called a "scrim") that Burr could see out of, but, with lighting, you could not see inside. Ollie (aka Oliver J. Dragon) was a puppet whose mouth could move by putting your hand inside and opening and closing your hand in time to your words spoken. (It's called "lip synch.") All the other puppets were the traditional kind that you put your index finger up in the head and your thumb and middle finger are in its hands. Pretty ordinary little puppet show that happened to be on TV.

Except for two things …

NUMBER ONE – *all* the shows were IMPROVISED!

Yep. 99% of the time all the shows were improvised. Burr would decide that "it's Ollie's birthday" and it's going to be a surprise and then the props and any decorations were pulled together and … they'd just do it. For a full half hour! And it worked! You would never have known that the show wasn't scripted let alone rehearsed. It just naturally flowed together seamlessly and that's because of …

NUMBER TWO – Burr Tilstrom.

This man was the master of characterization. Burr had such distinct and clear voices and attitudes that completely separated *all* the characters. His lip synch for Ollie was far from perfect (to non-existent), but Ollie was so specific and alive, you didn't care. His talent for characters was so precise to the point where they had a life of their own. A puppet builder friend of mine would often refurbish the puppets for Burr. He said that whenever he needed to ask Burr something, he'd call, and sometimes one of the characters would answer. Like he'd call and Beulah Witch (my favorite of his characters) would answer with a cheerful "Oh, hello dearie" and then let my friend know she'd tell Burr he'd called, and then, a minute later, the phone would ring, my friend would answer, and could then ask Burr what was needed.

The *best* story I heard was from Jon Stone. Before co-creating *Sesame Street* and being a director, producer, and writer for the series, at one point, Jon was a stage manager on *Kukla, Fran, & Ollie.* One Christmas, there a was party onset and Kukla and Ollie were the hosts. At one point, someone placed a bottle of whiskey on the puppet stage. Ollie took it below to have a nip (as did Burr) and did this repeatedly, until the dragon was quite "tipsy," even slurring words. But Kukla? Kula was "stone sober." Yes. Jon said that Burr was able to clearly separate his inebriated side from his sober side. It was astonishing besides being hysterical to watch.

The puppets on TV were either sock puppets, or marionettes, or ventriloquist dummies, or the kind you could buy at a toy store. (In fact, Captain Kangaroo's "Bunny Rabbit" was a Steif puppet that had little glasses sewn on.) It wasn't until a Sunday night in 1969, that I just happened to see a half hour show on Channel Thirteen, our local PBS station. It was showing clips from a brand-new puppet show premiering the next day. And the two hosts were puppets; one had a yellow head that looked like a banana, and the other had a head shaped like a football. And their names? "Ernie & Bert." And the new show was called … well you know the answer. They showed clips both, live action and animated. And then, … I saw Big Bird. And my tiny little eight-year-old jaw dropped. It was a character, a larger-than-life puppet, that was talking as its beak was moving, and it was *walking around*! You could see him move around, head to toe! Holy Hannah! I am *definitely* watching this show! (By the way, that first incarnation of Bird was *not* the Big Bird we all grew up with. Check it out on YouTube. Seriously. I'll wait. Go and see.)

(You're back? OK – now go see Snuffy's first appearance. That first version is the stuff nightmares are made from. Go see.)

I once made a puppet of Bert out of yellow construction paper. I drew him, colored him in, and attached a stick to the back and a straw to his hand. Even I noticed that his hands moved because of the stick (or rod) that came from his wrist (which makes him and others like this "rod puppets"). I made early attempts at Oscar (with cardboard and a green bathmat), The Count (with an old white shirt, a Halloween cape, and paper plates for the head), even Big Bird (with large paper bags from the store). I caught the characters appearing on other shows; The Flip Wilson Show; Hollywood Squares; The Dinah Shore Show; and others. Then with *The Muppet Show*, it looked like some of the puppets were made from foam, so I tried that (making a Miss Piggy and a Waldorf from cutout pieces of foam and felt). Of course, it was The Muppet Show and Jim and his team having careers in puppetry that sealed the deal for me. *I want to be a puppeteer!* Which of course prompted the question …

How?

"Okay… What Do We Have to Do?"

Seeing how that guy Jim Henson and all those people with him were making a living from puppetry, I thought I could too. When it was time to pick a college, I tried to find one that specialized in puppetry. There was no Google search not to mention the internet in 1979, so I did research the old fashion way – I went to the library. (You know … the public *library*; it's like Barnes & Noble, but it's free.) And would you believe I found, not one but, *two* — two colleges, both on the East Coast?

One was the University of Connecticut, in Storrs, Connecticut (that to this day offers a four-year puppetry program, where you can get your master's degree in puppetry) and the other was Pratt Institute, in Brooklyn, N.Y., which at the time had a theater department and within that was a class for puppetry. After doing all the research, I presented my case to my mom. You remember her. My single mom. My single mom whose husband walked out on us. My working-two-jobs-to-put-me-through-private-school single mom. And I told her, "Mom, I know what I want to be. I want to be … a puppeteer." And I braced myself for the response.

And she looked at me and without any hesitation said, …

"Okay. What do we have to do?"

Wait! What!?! OH!

And I showed her both college choices. "There's this one in Connecticut and this one in Brooklyn."

And she said, …

"Okay. What do we have to do?"

Oh! Right! Okay.

And I told her the requirements and the due dates and when to expect responses and all the while she just kept asking, …

"Okay. What do we have to do?"

That's all she kept saying! She never belittled it; she never dismissed it; she never told me to have a back-up plan. She was all in.

Finally, I had to ask her, …

"And … you're all right with all this?"

And she said, …

"Sweetheart, I've been typing the same letters for the same executives for years. You can always get a job. Get a *career*."

And we hugged and then she added, …

"And if you decide tomorrow you want to be a lumberjack, then we'll figure out a way to do that."

The woman who had to put her dreams of acting on hold wanted me to have mine.

When I went for my interview at Pratt, the head of the theater department, Jordan Hott, explained that the department was being phased out. I was the last theater major that would be allowed in. After me – zip. So, I really would be in "a class by myself" come senior year. But I accepted, because of the puppetry class and specifically the teacher.

Kermit Love was a theatrical costume designer who had worked with choreographers George Balanchine, Jerome Robbins, Twyla Tharp, Agnes DeMille, and more. Kermit applied all the costuming tricks he'd learned to make for ballet dancers to puppets for Jim Henson, specifically body puppets – puppets you wear over your body. His two most famous body puppets are Big Bird and Mr. Snuffleupagus for Sesame Street. Kermit had his own workshop and staff on Great Jones Street, in Manhattan's Greenwich Village. And he also taught Pratt's puppetry class. (And NO – the frog was NOT named after him; that's just one of life's weird coincidences.)

How do I describe someone as larger than life as Kermit Love? Let's see – OK - imagine Santa Claus with the slightest edge of Rasputin, and that starts the process. A friend who also knew him described him as "not so much a mentor, but a tormentor." He loved the sound of his own voice, an affected hint of an English accent from a guy born in Central New Jersey. He knew so many famous people and didn't hesitate in name dropping. Years later, when I worked at *Sesame Street*, he came back after lunch, having mentioned that he was being taken to The Russian Tea Room (the famous restaurant next door to Carnegie Hall), before leaving. I was standing next to Debra Spinney (wife of Big Bird and Oscar puppeteer, and my mentor, Carroll Spinney, and still, to this day, one of the sweetest people I have ever had the fortune to meet), when he strode back in.

"And how was lunch?" I asked.

"Lovely," he purred, "I even spotted Barbera at her table as we passed, and we chatted."

"Barbera," I said, taking the bait. "Barbera … *Streisand*?"

"Of course," he said with both an air of "who else, you foolish boy" and a touch of pride in his knowing her. But I couldn't let it go. This was too easy.

"And let me guess, … you once told her, 'Never get your nose fixed.'"

Without missing a beat, he clapped his hands together and exclaimed, …

"That's RIGHT!"

That first semester of freshman year at Pratt I lived in the dorms, which were one of three apartment buildings next to Pratt. It was a two bedroom with four of us living in it; the senior guys each had a bedroom, and I shared the living room with another guy, a fellow freshman, named "Ed," who was a photography major. I remember one night, we were each in our beds talking about life and the universe, as young souls out of the nest often do, and he asked me, …

"Do you believe in God?"

At the time I still did and replied, …

"Yes."

"Then why doesn't he solve many of the problems here?"

I thought for a moment and said, …

"Well … God is 'The Father' right?"

"Yeah."

"Well, … would you want *your* father constantly telling you what to do?"

"Hell no!" he answered, and we both laughed.

While attending Pratt, I performed puppet shows and birthday parties for kids and got paid for it. This is the classic image that usually pops into people's minds when you say, "I'm a puppeteer." It's one of the ways my chosen profession is constantly dismissed and disrespected. We're in the same category as magicians and clowns. In December 2020, I was puppeteering at The Bronx Zoo, part of their annual "Holiday Lights" celebration. Alongside James Wojtal, Jr., who built the puppets (beautifully, as James always does), we were inside the new installation called "The Luminous Garden." This was a walkthrough for guests with large live plants beside ginormous lit-up flowers and bugs — called "lanterns," because the shapes were covered in silk. Our little alcove was the last thing for visitors to see before exiting, which was supposed to resemble a pond, with animals native to New York State around it: a bullfrog, a great blue heron, and a snapping turtle. Mine was the very large bullfrog that guests constantly called "Kermit," even though it looked nothing like Kermit; it was blue, for starters. "You think this place could afford Kermit?!?" my frog would respond. Or… "Kermit's from Sesame Street. I'm from Southern Boulevard" (which was the main avenue right outside the zoo). One evening a dad started asking the puppets if they did children's parties. "You couldn't afford me," my frog replied, hopping away, as he chuckled.

In November of 1979, I came home for Thanksgiving weekend. Because I was living in the dorms, I gave my room to my grandmother. When I got home Wednesday evening, she was feeling a little worn out, like a cold was coming on. But vowed she'd be able to make Thanksgiving dinner for us. And sure enough, she was up and prepping and cooking in the kitchen that Thursday morning. You'd never known she wasn't feeling well.

I got up early to head to the Macy's Parade, specifically where it started – the American Museum of Natural History on Central Park West. Back then, the floats were parked along the street, and you could walk right up to them, which is what I did. The Sesame float was parked along 89th Street, across from the Planetarium, and I wanted to see them off. I spied Kermit who saw me and waved me over. He and another member of the Henson Workshop were setting up the puppets for the puppeteers. Not all the main puppeteers were there – no Jim Henson, no Frank Oz, no Carroll Spinney. Other people, a couple of shop people actually, would hold the puppets out the windows and have them wave as the float rolled by. But several of the human cast were there, including Will Lee, who portrayed the genial shopkeeper Mr. Hooper.

The Macy's Parade begins exactly at 9:00AM and takes an hour for the first float to arrive in front of the store on Herald Square. That's why they have casts from Broadway shows perform in front of the store to fill the hour *before* the parade actually arrives. At the museum, each float, balloon, and marching band joined the line-up, in order, and the Sesame float was about to roll into place.

"Get on!" Kermit called to me.

"What?"

"Get! ON!" he yelled.

And I jumped onto the float just as it began to roll into place. Kermit handed me Herry Monster (a character originally performed by the incredible Jerry Nelson) and told me to quickly go inside and stick Herry out one of the windows. I did and through the sheer fabric that I could see out of, but no one could see in, I saw hundreds of thousands of people, all waving back and cheering and calling out the characters' names, and laughing, and smiling, and – I couldn't call home! There were no cellphones in the autumn of 1979! This was all happening, and I couldn't tell my mom or grandmother to watch! But I was too busy having the time of my life to worry.

After each float passes the iconic department store, it rounds the corner of 34th Street and 8th Avenue and slides into a side street for performers to disembark and the float to be dismantled. As soon as the float stopped, I got up holding Herry and Kermit opened the door. He took the puppet from me and said, …

"Off you go!" with a grand gesture to indicate that I vamoose before too many people saw what he'd done.

I arrived home to find good smells from the kitchen and the parade on TV. My mom and grandmother had it on in the background and I told them what happened and asked if they saw the float and a blue monster with large eyes and a large nose.

"That was YOU!?!?"

I told them the whole story again while we ate dinner and – well, talk about being truly thankful.

The next day was Friday and when I was little my mom would take me and my grandmother to Macy's and give us "Macy's dollars," to spend on whatever I wanted. We'd go early and leave by noon before the true chaos (that would evolve into "Black Friday") began. But mom was still working part time at the answering service and working the day after Thanksgiving meant "time-and-a-half."

I was half asleep on the couch when I heard voices from the back of the apartment. I went down the hall to my old room, now my grandmother's, and found her in bed and my mom standing over her.

"Mama, you're not feeling well," my mom said. My grandmother who never slept in was still in bed under the covers.

“I’m fine,” she insisted. But she looked more than tired. Her face was drawn, pale even (she was the lightest skinned of her four sisters, even lighter than me) and her voice was a little hoarse. I got her a glass of water, but she could barely sit up.

“I’m calling an ambulance,” my mom said.

“No!” my grandmother said, trying to yell, her voice cracking.

“Grandma,” I began quietly, “If they come, they can just check you out and see what’s wrong. They can even tell us what we could get from the drugstore. It doesn’t mean they’ll take you to the hospital.” My grandmother was deathly afraid of hospitals. Aunt Sis was taken to the hospital a couple of years earlier and never came home.

“But let them come and just take a look at you, O.K.?”

And she nodded her head.

The paramedics soon came and helped her sit up on the side of the bed and checked her out. She was too weak to stand let alone walk, and she was dehydrated. They determined that she should go to the hospital.

“No,” she said.

They couldn’t make her go but would need her to sign a waiver saying that it was her decision to not go. She was clear headed enough to understand their questions and when they gave her the pen and held up the waiver, my mom tried to stop her. With the last ounce of reserve strength she had, my grandmother, without even looking up at my mother, pushed Edna’s hand out of the way, snapping, …

“NO!”

The paramedics packed up and left. My mom was so annoyed, but I told her I’d look after her and call to let her know how she was. My mom left for work, and it was just me and my grandmother.

Later that morning, I was watching something on TV in the living room, when I heard sounds coming from the hall. I got up, turned the corner, and there was my grandmother leaning against the wall. She was just in her nightgown, barefoot and a few feet from the bathroom. "Are you trying to get to the bathroom?" I asked and she nodded. I put my arms around her to help her, but suddenly, I could feel her weight; she couldn't walk, and I was holding onto her to keep her from falling to the hard floor.

"Grandma!"

I spoke. I was trying to gently lower her down on her back. I was looking down at her face and she was looking right up at me, her breathing ragged.

"Grandma!"

I said again. I managed to gently lay her down, my hand cradling her head. And she was still looking at me and her breathing … her breathing was … wait … is she breathing?

"GRANDMA!!!"

I slowly pulled my hand out from under her head. She was lying there, eyes open. I listened for her heart. Nothing. I ran and got a hand mirror and held it to her mouth and nose. Nothing. I waved my hand in front of her face. I gently shook her.

Nothing.

I ran to the phone and called 911 and then waited in the living room. I didn't call my mom yet because I wanted to see what the paramedics would say, even though I knew. I just wanted confirmation. You know when you don't want something to be true, so you wait, you stall, until someone else tells you? That was me at this moment. The paramedics, different from the ones earlier, came and I pointed down the hall. I stayed in the living room and then they came back in and confirmed what I knew. They asked to use the phone to call the coroner, who would have to come and take the body. Because that's what she was now – "the body."

I called my mom's job, Tell-Answer and one of my mom's co-workers picked up. I asked if Edna was available, and she said just a minute and called out to my mom to come over.

"Hi sweetheart," she said.

How do I do this? How do I tell her?

I was trying to hold it together myself to keep from babbling. I'm alone with a dead body in the hall.

"Hi … um … so … I had to call 911 again … but … it was too late."

I heard my mom gasp, the phone on her end hitting the desk, and someone in the background exclaiming, "Edna!" followed by muffled sobs. Then, …

"O.K.," she said, "I'll be home as soon as I can."

I got a sheet from the linen closet in the hall, to drape over my grandmother. I looked at her one last time and very gently closed her eyes, kissed her forehead, and placed the sheet over her. The coroner had not arrived yet and my mom was on her way, and I prayed they wouldn't come at the same time. Our living room window was on the entrance side of the building, and I planted myself in the window to keep watch over who would show up first. It was the same window my grandmother would sit in knowing what time mom and I would come home from work and school. We'd see her in the window and we'd all wave to each other. I saw a van pull up near the building entrance and two men get out and retrieved a gurney. The coroners had arrived. I let them in, and they proceeded down the hall while I went back to the window, just in time to see a cab pull into the driveway; it was mom.

I headed to the front door which was next to the hall and opened it. I saw my mom get off and head towards the apartment which was at the end of the hall. I looked back and the coroners were still busy as my mom got closer. When she got to me, I said, …

“Look at me. Just … Look ... At ... Me ...” as I walked backwards inside with her eyes on me the whole time and passing the hall, without looking down it.

I lead her to the dining area, which was around the corner of the living room, with no view of the front door, and sat her down. I got her a glass of water and then went to the coroners, who were ready to leave. I signed some papers and they left. I went back and sat with mom and told her everything that happened. Her eyes were full of tears, but she took my hands and said, …

“She loved you so much,” she said, “And she wanted a grandson so much, I could never have brought home a girl.”

What she meant was that the last image my grandmother saw, the last person who was there with her, wasn’t a paramedic or a doctor or a nurse.

It was me.

PART TWO

You Always Remember Your First Time

No, I'm not talking about *that*. Get your mind out of the gutter.

During the summer months, Kermit offered me a job, my first job *ever*, at his studio to help build "Big Birds" for the touring *Sesame Street LIVE* shows and refurbish the Bird for the TV show. The body would need to look new again, all clean and fluffy, for the TV show. And the way to do that is with feathers. White turkey feathers dyed yellow. And the way to put them on is to steam the spine with a hot iron so that the feather curls. Then, with a hot glue gun, you dab a drop at the end and, while wearing rubber tips on your fingers, you press the feather, with the scorching hot glue, to the body.

One. That's one feather! Ah-ah-ah! (Cue the thunder & lightening.)

Did I burn my fingers with the hot glue? Take a guess.

But the birds for the live touring shows had feathers that were machine sewed onto light nylon fabric (each piece I had to cutout first), then ironing the spine for it to curl, and then machine sew them all onto long ribbons, that were then machine sewed directly onto the body and neck of Bird. I lost count how many sewing needles got broken. Oh, and it was summer and no air conditioning. Fun times!

Towards the end of one day, as I was cleaning up the many loose tuffs of feathers from everywhere on my body. As the guys were leaving, Kermit asked if I was free for dinner. I said "yes," and we went to the bar nearby, Phoebe's, where we each had a burger and fries and talked puppets, and Muppets, and what I wanted to do. I said I'd love to work with Jim and be a "muppeteer." We walked back to the shop, and he asked that I could come upstairs; he wanted to see how my puppeteering skills were. Upstairs, he pulled out a little red furry puppet with huge white eyes and an orange nose. (This would years later beknown as "Elmo," or, *Sesame Street* director Jon Stone jokingly called it, "The Little Red Menace"). I put it on and held it up in front of the huge mirror. Kermit proceeded to have a chat with it, standing behind me to see what I was doing in the mirror, and I actually made him laugh (though I my voice was nowhere near to what this character would eventually have). I was proud as I brought the puppet down, commenting that my arm was tired and shaking it out

"You need to build up muscle," Kermit said, placing his hand on my upper arm and taking a step closer to me.

"I do push-ups, but I guess I need … to …" but I didn't finish my sentence. Because Kermit, still holding my arm, was leaning his face into mine – to try and kiss me. I leaned back, but he placed his other arm around my waist pulling me in, to try again.

I stepped back hard enough to release his grip on me. I put down the puppet and without looking at him, said, …

"Thanks again for dinner."

And I quickly left.

I walked to the bus stop and, as I waited, my mind was reeling. I tried to piece together what just happened. *My teacher, my boss, … a MAN … came on to me, made a pass at me. He tried to KISS me – twice!* And I had to go back to work the next day. What would it be like? Would I even have a job? I began to think, *Should I have – NO! First: the man is in a committed relationship. And second, if I were gay, I sure as hell wouldn't want to do it with* him*! His age is somewhere between God and dirt!* I got home and immediately took a shower, to also wash off the day's sweat and feather fluff (and you'd be surprised where it can end up), and I was angry. But also embarrassed. Because I was eighteen in the summer of 1980, and college was the first time I'd been around non-straight people. Because on TV and in the movies, they were depicted as either a joke or depraved or both. The people I met at Pratt, who were "out," were nothing like that. They weren't hitting on me or enticing me. They were my friends. So to have this relic try to do this to me … I didn't tell my mom, not my friends, no one.

The next morning, I woke up, got dressed, and headed back to the shop. When I arrived, the other guys were there, and so was Kermit. They all said good morning to me, and I headed straight to the backroom to start my feathering for the day. All that day, Kermit never came into the back area. The day came to an end and Kermit said his good nights, before heading out to get the bus home to upstate. So, … I guess I still had my job? And I finished out my work that summer and Kermit nor I ever mentioned that evening to each other, ever again. (It wasn't until many years later that I found out I was not the first young man the old letch had tried this on.)

My first real professional puppeteering job wasn't on *Sesame Street*. It happened before I landed there. My first *real* professional, paying, puppeteering gig came while I was still in college, the summer between junior and senior year, 1982. During the summers, I had worked at Kermit's studio in Greenwich Village. His shop was quite reasonably called Great Jones Studios, because it was on Great Jones Street, the four blocks of Third Street between Broadway and the Bowery. Number Five was near the alley, one of the few to exist in Manhattan, and the studio was on the second floor. Once buzzed in, you'd climb the rickety stairs, go through the front door, and step inside what looked like a toymaker's attic. Costumes and puppets hung on walls, a couple from the ceiling, posters of past ballet and puppet productions, and fabric, thread, and notions were scattered about. And that was just when you first walked in.

My usual summer job of feathering Big Birds for the touring shows, and re-feathering the Bird for the actual show, had gotten done early. Kermit had called me and asked if I could stop by the shop; he wanted to talk to me, run something by me, in person. I arrived at the shop and walked up to the landing and saw the project his staff was working on. They had built six puppets for a series of commercials for "Magi Bouillon Cubes": two foxes dressed as hunters; two Japanese samurai; and two rabbits. Two puppeteers were needed for the commercial and Kermit asked if I'd like to be one.

"Yes," I replied, smiling. "Thank you."

"Good," he said. "And your passport is up to date?"

"My what?"

"Your *passport*." (Emphasizing the "t.")

"Why would I need a *passport-t*?" (Echoing his "t" emphasis.)

"To go to Paris, of course!"

At this point I thought the old guy had finally lost it.

"Why would I go to Paris?"

He sighed, exasperated. "Well, do you want to be in the commercials or not?"

"Yes – Wait – (finally piecing it all together) The commercials are … in Paris? *France*?"

"That's what I just said, isn't it?!" I caught the guys smiling, trying not to laugh out loud.

Jim Kroupa was part of this first professional puppeteering gig of mine. I first met Jim at Pratt. The first puppetry class I attended freshman year was the class Jim was in, for his senior year. Like me, he was a "theater major," but really a "puppetry major." Jim lived in the dorms and each year produced a puppet variety show, for the whole school to come see. He invited me to be a part of his last one that fall, again, because this was his graduating year. I was one of many birds for a rendition of "Rockin' Robin" and a fish, among many, with music by Saint Sains. Jim is an incredibly talented builder, and when it comes to mechanics for puppets, he's the master. Any rig, any mechanism needed for a puppet to blink its eyes, or flick its wrist, any special effect, he's the go-to man. He teaches a puppet mechanism class for the O'Neil Puppetry Conference in Connecticut each year, and each year it's the first to sell out. Jim is also one of the funniest guys I know, with a deep appreciation for The Three Stooges. And ever since meeting him that night for my first puppetry class in September 1979, he and I have been friends ever since.

It was July and the commercials would be in August, so I had to get a passport - fast. And I did. My first passport. For my first trip to Europe. On my first plane ride. A lot of firsts. I even had to buy my first suitcase. Seriously. We could never afford to travel anywhere, so this was my first suitcase, and it would last me for years. (I teared up a little the day I finally had to throw it out.) The day of the flight, my mom rode with me to the airport.

"Why?" Kermit asked her at the terminal.

"Because I want to see my only child board the plane," she answered, not tolerating Kermit's attempt at humor. I was 20 years old but would always be her little boy. (As a parent now, I get it.)

Kermit, Jim, and I boarded and took our seats (in coach, but I didn't care); Jim and I sat next to each other, and he gave me have the window. Kermit sat a couple of rows in front of us. It was a night flight, but the sun hadn't set yet. I could see the last rays of the sun turning the sky a deep, warm orange as the plane pulled away from the gate. I was beyond excited. I could not believe this was happening — my first *flight* to my first *professional puppeteering* job, … in PARIS! My mom said, "You may not know how your career will go, but you'll always remember how it started." I heard her words in my mind as I caught sight of her waving from the terminal, as the plane made its way to the runway.

I don't know if you remember the first time you flew on a plane. My son has been on a plane since he was three months old, so for him it's been a part of his life. But for me, at 20, this was huge. I'd always seen characters in movies and on TV flying in a plane, but it's not the same as real life. Because in real life as I looked out the window, as the plane suddenly accelerated, the pressure pushing me back against my seat, the ground slipping away from under us, it suddenly dawned on me — *Oh. My. GOD. We are going up into the AIR?!? Over buildings? The highway? The ocean? THE OCEAN?!?! We're FLYING over the OCEAN?!?* I wasn't panicking, but this was quite the catharsis for me, realizing that flying meant "*flying*."

In high school, I had taken two years of French. I could have taken Spanish, and living in New York, that would have made more sense. But my mom told me she had taken French in high school, so I thought "great - convenient tutor right under my roof." Oh, how wrong I was. My mom had *taken* French, but she had remembered *none* of it. So, I took French for two years and hated it, just passing it, with the underlying resentment "When am I ever going to use French?" *Oh, mon ami*

— *La vie aime vous jouer des tours.* (*Oh, my friend — Life loves playing tricks on you.*) I packed one of my French books with me, for catching up on the plane, and the polite phrases came back to me.

The thing about the French, at least the ones in Paris who have to deal with tourists, is this: if you just try to speak French, they appreciate the attempt and will immediately stop you from further butchering their beloved language and speak English themselves. But if you're *that* "American" who thinks *"if I say it in English LOUDER, they'll understand,'"* that's when they will just speak French, forcing the privileged tourist to point to the menu, or even worse, mime what they want. Years later, when I was in Paris with my wife, we witnessed this. First, I used my little French and the waiter then spoke English to us. Then several tables over a group of middle-aged Yanks waddled in and planted themselves, loudly chatting. The waiter came over, they spoke loudly to him, in "American" (because it wasn't even close to English), and he didn't flinch or give then any assistance. He just stared at them and then cocked his head to one side to convey he didn't understand. We were both amused by and ashamed of our fellow citizens.

The River Seine divides Paris. The parts are called, with Gallic simplicity, Rive Gauche et Rive Droite (the Left Bank, and the Right Bank). We were put up in a hotel on the Left Bank, the Hotel Lenox, in the 7th arrondissement ("neighborhood"). It was a lovely little hotel, by today's standards, described as "boutique." And with history: in 1920 James Joyce and his family lived there. With no elevator, you had to climb the stairs to rooms. Mine was in the back with a lovely view of the alley but, quiet.

My first encounter with European culture came in, of all places, the bathroom. I had to pee. When I entered, I saw two toilets: one that had a seat, and next to it, one that did not. "Oh," I thought, *"it's like a urinal but not attached to the wall. O.K."* And I peed and then went to flush it. This is when I discovered what a bidet is, because instead of the water swirling *down,* a thin geyser shot *up* — and nearly got me! *"Never using THAT again,"* I swore to myself and used the toilet, as I was accustomed to back home, for both my needs.

One thing that would occur when walking the streets of Paris with Kermit is that he'd describe a building in detail before we even got there, and then, turning the corner, there it was, exactly as he'd mentioned. With his history in ballet costume design, Paris was, of course, where he'd lived. He even pointed out the apartment, or garret, he once lived in, at the top of an old building.

The commercials, three of them, were being shot at a studio just outside of the city. We had to be driven to and from there each day. We would be shooting for less than a week — five days. I would learn later on that this was pretty leisurely for three commercials. But this was my first job, and it was also with the French. The first day we got to the studio it was at 10:00 am. I helped Jim set up the puppets on a nearby table reserved for us and looked at the sets. All three were raised up four feet so that we could just hold up the puppets and be able to stand. One was having lights added. Then suddenly at 10:30AM, lunch was called. *Really? Now? At 10:30 in the morning?* Yes, and we were taken along with the director, assistant director, cinematographer, client, and assistants to a nearby restaurant. We were seated at a large round table, handed menus, and the house wines were brought out. Again, before 11:00 am. We ordered and ate and sat and talked about the shoot, a few of the French smoked cigarettes, and this all lasted for over *two hours*. We even had desserts. And more wine.

When we got back, we began with the first commercial and kept shooting, non-stop, until we finished it — at 10:30 pm. The only time Jim and I got breaks was when they were reloading the camera or adjusting a light. Usually on commercial shoots back home, everyone gets a break or two, crew included, for about 10 or 15 minutes to take a bathroom break or get a snack at "craft services" (I loved craft services in "the before times" before COVID; craft services was this bounty of free food, laid out and routinely refreshed). If it's especially long, then we'd all get a dinner break. But nope; not here. That nice long lunch obviously was to sustain us for the next 10 hours. The next day and the day after, I ordered more substantial meals to hold me over. Luckily, the next two days were not as long, and we managed to wrap before 7:30 pm.

It was on one of these "early" evenings that Jim and I decided we wanted to go out. Kermit had accompanied us before, but this evening we wanted our own time, and not to be regaled with more Parisian tales and critiques of how Paris had changed, the quality of its food as we were digesting it, or the service of the café we happened to be in, etc., etc. Before we even left the studio,

Jim and I made a plan; when we'd get back to the hotel, trudging up the stairs, we'd tell Kermit that we were both tired and going straight to bed. We'd say our "bon nuits" and, as we continued up the stairs to our floor, would wait to hear Kermit close his door from below. And it worked. Perfect. We each headed to our rooms and then met five minutes later, in the lobby.

One thing I learned about Jim Kroupa is that there is no food he won't try. Back in New York, the man introduced me to sushi and would order the weirdest pieces. I, being skeptical, would look and wonder *who thought that THIS piece of a fish, that resembled phlegm, would taste good?* But I was young and still going to live forever, so what the hell. And some of those pieces really do taste good. My favorites are still eel sushi and sweet shrimp — fried shrimp with its head also fried, separately, antennae intact. I've had fun freaking friends out, who've never seen it, let alone ever want to try it, by sticking the head on my finger and "puppeteering it" (it's begging not to be eaten and then popping it into my mouth)! Never gets old.

This night we met our mutual friend, Rob, who happened to be visiting Paris, as part of a summertime European tour. We found a café and on the menu was the one thing Jim wanted, no *needed* to try: "escargot." Even my limited French knew what that was… *snails.* Yes, that's right; *snails.* Again, who on Earth looked at this thing crawling across the dirt and thought *"you know what — I bet that would taste good — but not the shell, just the snail's slimy body itself. Magnifique!"* When the waiter came by, Jim immediately ordered it for an appetizer, then looked at me. "Come on," he cooed with a smirk. It's such a thing guys do to each other — "I dare you to do *this*," "I bet you *can't* do that," and we fall for it because it's what we guys do. We wind each other up, and then, let the fun begin.

"Sure," I sighed at the waiter, and he left. When he returned, he brought two plates, two sets of "tongs" and tiny forks, and a basket of freshly cut French bread (or as the French call it … "bread") and set them on the table. I stared down at my collection of six snail shells, the butter and garlic running out of them onto the plate. I had to admit they did smell good, but get a grip Noel, — it's a plate of cooked *SNAILS*! Still in their shells! I looked at Jim who was using the tongs to clasp the shell and the tiny fork to scoop out the meat (again, the snail's whole body), and pop it into his mouth. *Well, now or never*. Either way it was going to be a story, so I figured might as well make it a good one. I picked up the tongs, clasped a shell, scooped out the snail, popped it into my mouth, and let it slide down my throat and — Jim was watching me for a reaction.

"Damn it," I quietly growled, "it's good."

Jim and Rob laughed, Jim giving is signature, hearty, cackle I'd get to know for many years. And they really were delicious in fact but, what few things aren't delicious being cooked in heaps of butter and garlic?

Once the commercials were over, we had a day to ourselves, so Jim and I met up with Rob and the three of us walked through Paris, from Notre Dame to the Louvre, and even climbed to the top of the Eiffel Tower. It was an amazing day, with my limited French still coming in handy.

The three of us met Kermit for dinner and sat outside, which is what one does in Paris. Except one does not expect an elderly homeless woman to wander by, stop at your table, look you in the eye and declare, slamming the house wine bottle on the table, "*Votre beauté devrait boire du champagne, pas cette eau grasse.*" "Your beauty," Kermit translated, chuckling, "should be drinking champagne, not this swill." She resumed her stagger down the street as Kermit, Rob, and Jim had a good laugh. If I was wishing for a Parisian maidan to find me attractive, remember… be careful what you wish for.

That weekend instead of flying straight back to New York with Kermit, Jim and I decided to change our reservation and fly home Sunday and spend the weekend – in London! This was my first trip to Europe, and I was going to make the most of it! We took the quick flight from Paris to London as the sun was setting over the English Channel. We stayed at the Rembrandt Hotel, directly across from the Victoria & Albert Museum and down the street from Harrod's, London's famous department store. We never went into the museum but did shop at Harrod's. Jim wanted a tweed jacket with elbow patches. It looked cool, so I got one, too. We walked around London, went to see a production of *Guys & Dolls* at the National Theater, that was spectacular, and a ridiculous musical called *Mr. Cinders,* written in the 1920s before the concept of having the songs propel the plot became a standard. (God bless you Richard Rodgers & Oscar Hammerstein.) I remember two characters who suddenly broke into song about playing tennis. And that's it. They were done and it had nothing to do with the rest of the show, which was very forgettable.

In college I never liked beer. Of course, college beer is never good outside of it being cheap. But Jim and I had lunch in a pub, and I tried Guinness. The day was raw and chilly even though it was summer, but I came to learn that raw and chilly was a standard British summer back then, and this beer was rich and creamy and… warm. Yeah. Brits find our drinking cold beer appalling. But this was different. That dark brown ale warmed my insides to help brace myself for more walking along the cold London streets. Since then, of all beers I've tasted, Guinness is still my favorite. It's a meal in a glass.

Puppetry would have many more trips to foreign countries planned for me, but this trip, this first professional business trip, will always stay with me as one of my favorites. And I'll always remember my first time.

"He's Puppeteering the Kid!"

I attended Pratt Institute in Brooklyn as a theatre major. That was the only way to take the puppetry class taught by Kermit Love, the designer and builder of Big Bird, Mr. Snuffleupagus, and other over-sized Muppets for Jim Henson.

Kermit had also been a costume designer and had worked with and knew everyone. I mean *everyone*. The man would name-drop constantly, and you wondered if some of the tales were true, until you realized they were. Even the *Sesame Street* Muppets he worked on bore the imprint of his life in theatre, specifically ballet. Big Bird's feathers were inspired by the tiny, feathered skirts worn by the dancers in the Ziegfeld Follies. For Carroll Spinney, the original puppeteer of Big Bird, who was only 5'10", to achieve Bird's 8'2" of height, platform cork shoes, inspired by those Kermit had designed for the entertainer Carmen Miranda, were glued inside Big Bird's orange feet.

I started on "The Street," in September of 1982, after it moved from its West 81st Street studio to one on 55th Street and Ninth Ave. One lunch hour, Kermit and I were walking down West 57th Street and Edward Villella, the legendary ballet dancer, was walking towards us (and wearing a buckskin-fur jacket only the 1980s could have conceived of).

Kermit yells, "Eddie!" And of course, Villella stops, smiles, and they embrace, before I get introduced to "Eddie," who then continued his way to Lincoln Center.

One of the high points of attending Kermit's class at Pratt was getting to see a dress rehearsal of *The Nutcracker*. Today, practically every dance company, major and minor, does some version of *The Nutcracker*. It's *the* money-maker, often raking in what a dance company will need to sustain itself for the rest of the coming year. But the reason for its popularity is due to one man: George Balanchine. Balanchine had seen performances during his youth in his native Russia, and when he came to America and created New York City Ballet, he decided to introduce this unique story to American audiences as a Christmas treat. And the rest, as they say, is history.

I remember the rehearsal I got to see. We were sitting in the red velvet seats of the orchestra section of New York State Theater at Lincoln Center. They were rehearsing the scene after the mice and the toy soldiers battle. The beautiful backdrop of glistening snow covering the trees sparkled in the light as the young boy, still wearing the Nutcracker mask and uniform, triumphantly strides forward and — *whoosh*! — the uniform "vanishes" (due to the yanking of the strings attached to them) and the "Nutcracker Prince" gestures that the spell upon him has been broken and —

"No! No! No!" cackled this creaky little voice from several rows in front of us. Everyone, including the prince, stopped to watch this little silhouette stand and head towards the side entrance leading to backstage.

And then, onstage, there he was.

George Balanchine, himself, walking across the stage, and taking the boy by both shoulders, and walking him backwards, to where he started from. I couldn't hear him but saw him motion to the boy to watch, demonstrating the choreography, himself: striding forward, and then, the gesture. It was amazing how this old man suddenly had this regal presence in just a few steps and with the slightest wave of his arm. But then he goes back to the boy, takes him by the shoulders and, in the same cadence as he did, walks the kid towards the front of the stage, and then, taking the boy's arm, does the gesture for him. "Oh my God," I said *sotto voce* (translation: "a quiet voice") to a fellow classmate, "He's puppeteering the kid!"

When I entered Pratt, the theater department was being phased out. When I was scheduled to graduate in 1983, I would be alone. And as successful as a one-man show can be, a one-student theatre department seemed a little too daunting (and depressing) at the time. By the end of the summer of 1982, however, Kermit offered me the job of being his new assistant … on *Sesame Street,* to prep Big Bird on camera.

The term used today is "puppet wrangler," but I liked using the phrase "puppet valet." (Hey, you're allowed to be pretentious when you're in your early twenties.) The job meant making sure that Big Bird was neat and clean for the camera — no loose or twisted feathers. And if there were any, you yanked them off (but saved them as "souvenirs" for a kid visiting the set). If there was any kind of prop or costume element, I would make sure they were ready for Big Bird (except hats — Kermit always insisted "no hats" because they would end up crushing the feathers that make up the head). It also meant helping Big Bird on and off his performer.

See, "Bird" is actually three separate pieces (the head, the neck, and the round body) that can be slipped onto the puppeteer and rest comfortably on the shoulders. The puppeteer's right arm goes up the neck into the head, where the hand opens and closes the mouth and eyes, while the left arm slips into the left "wing." And there's a very thin string (called monofilament or fishing line) that goes from the left wing's wrist up to a ring just under the beak, and then down to the right "wing," so whenever the left wing moves, it counter levers the other wing to move. Neat, huh? (The Jim Henson Company would end up using this same time-tested technology for a character on a show called *Bear in the Big Blue House,* but that's a later story). But I wasn't just taking care of the Bird: I was also taking care of Carroll Spinney.

Carroll Spinney was the original performer of both Big Bird and Oscar the Grouch. He was their voice, their spirit, their souls. Carroll did them since day one. He told me that on the days when he wasn't feeling particularly perky, it was great to be Oscar. And on the days when life was good, it was a joy to express it with the Bird. From the first day I met him, Carroll was the most gracious and sincere man I have ever known. It's always gratifying to finally meet your idols, but when they turn out to be nicer than you imagined them? When they exceed your expectations, it's remarkable.

Carroll would always thank me when I would take Bird off him or handed him Oscar, ask me how my day was going, little things that might not occur to others, but were part of Carroll's nature. Never in his entire time as two of the most recognizable and most beloved characters of children's television did, he ever felt the need to exhibit any "power" or demonstrate who was "boss;" that was not him. And to the end, he was amazed at how blessed he had been with his career. (Carroll wrote his own memoir, *The Wisdom of Big Bird ... and the dark genius of Oscar the Grouch*, as well as being the subject of the acclaimed documentary "I Am Big Bird." I encourage you to check out both. You won't be disappointed.)

Once Big Bird was doing a bit with guest star Tony Danza. They were to play tennis. I put the Bird on Carroll and then handed him the prop. Big Bird says, …

"Thanks for the bat, Noel."

I replied, "It's a racket, Big Bird."

"I know," Bird responded, "Sometimes I feel like I'm stealing the money."

<RIM – SHOT!>

Carroll was living proof that sometimes one of the nice guys can finish first.

"NOW, It's a Buy!"

My job as the wrangler wasn't just putting the Bird on Carroll and handing him Oscar. I also helped take care of the other Muppets, such as the Count and Telly Monster. That meant I got to sit in on production meetings. These are when the different departments of the show (except the writers) sit down and go over a script, segment by segment (called "bits"), to see what's needed and what isn't. I remember that first meeting. I sat there next to Kermit, who introduced me to everyone, with my pile of scripts in front of me. The producers were there, as well as the director, Jon Stone.

Jon Stone is the other major factor that shaped and evolved *Sesame Street* in the early years. Think of him as the Ringo of the group. Without him, the band never would have had that consistent beat. Sure, the Muppets got all the attention, but why did they always *look* good on camera? Jim Henson collaborated with Jon on various projects and the two were close friends. Jon, who'd worked on *Captain Kangaroo*, was brought in to help develop the show from the get-go. He was not only the primary director but, over the years, also became a writer and a producer. He was gifted with a keen sense of the visual and how to tell a story and appreciated the tongue-in-cheek humor of Jim & company.

And Jon was also in charge. Oh, there was an executive producer and a producer and an associate producer, but from that first meeting, I definitely got the impression of who was really beating the drum.

Back in 1982, *Sesame Street* was still an hour-long show, with the "Street story" and the inserts (such as Bert & Ernie or any animation about the number 3 or the letter R) cut into them. Similar to commercials during a show, the "sponsors" were numbers and letters. That's why the shows always ended with a character saying, "*Sesame Street* was brought to you today by the letters ___ and ___, and by the number ___." As the pages were turned, I was shocked at the number of bits that were cut and why — it was too long and didn't get the lesson across; it was too complicated prop-wise; too many characters that didn't do anything productive to move the story along; and so on and so on and so on.

I began to wonder if there would be any show left to shoot! But the most egregious was when a bit was rejected because the producers and the director simply didn't like it. *Wait... didn't you read it? It was funny! Really.* Nope. When Jon took his pencil (which he would keep stuck in his thick grayish beard — imagine Zeus wearing a safari vest and a plaid shirt and you get the image) and slashed a line through a bit, that was that. There's probably an encyclopedia of four decades' worth of never-produced bits archived somewhere at the offices of Sesame Workshop (just ready to be released to your local Barnes & Noble for the next anniversary celebration).

I've gotten to perform many background characters on Sesame; I've been every Snuffleupa-relative (Snuffy's mom, dad, grandmother, cousin; mailman; even his personal trainer, "Arnold Snuffleupa-nager); various chickens, grouches, cows, horses, you name it. I've also held up an established character for crowd scenes (such as Oscar or even Big Bird). But the most memorable time I held up a character is not only a favorite story to share, but one I've used when training other puppeteers. Specifically, when you're part of a group scene, you have to stay up and stay alive, because the scene is not about you. You're in a group and need to be a team player and help make the scene as good as possible. Case in point …

Sesame is known for having guest stars come on. For this bit, "The Gospel Alphabet," we got to work, with none other than, Patti LaBelle. (The other time I got to work with her was when she guest starred on *The Puzzle Place Holiday* VHS tape.) It starts out with "Little Chrissy" (named after gifted Sesame composer and heck-of-a-nice-guy, Chris Cerf), as Patti begins to croon the ABCs. Various characters enter and settle in to listen, and sway to her melodic voice. Then, it breaks out into a full-blown gospel revival session, with clapping, dancing, and singing, ending with everyone looking to Patti for that final glorious close. In fact, why don't you watch? Go to YouTube and type in "Sesame Pattie Labelle Gospel." I'm holding up "Bert" (one of my favorite Sesame characters). I'll be here when you get back.

<humming; whistling>

You're back! Great. Now, for the story.

I'm holding up Bert and have him enter, and he sways with the music, listening in rapture to Patti, right near "The Count." It's a wide shot and one long take which goes from her singing straight into the frenzied dancing and right the end: no cuts. We play it back and everyone sees it and loves it. "It's a buy," meaning the take is good and we can move on. "No," I call out and that's when I bring up Bert … who's *missing ONE EYE*!!! Here's what happened: as the gospel rhythm kicks in, it's a free-style, free-for-all of dancing in place. There are monitors all over the floor for us to watch. And that's when I noticed Bert's left eye was … *GONE*! I look up and sure enough, he was suddenly a cyclops. What happened was … you know that pointy collar on The Count's cape? Well, it had gotten behind Bert's left eye and FLICKED it off! I can't bring him down because it's a wide shot with everyone in frame. Also, it was so tightly packed, I couldn't even if I wanted to. So, that's when Bert starts to rock-n-roll in *profile*. But – *oh no* – he has to now *turn around* and look at Patti for the end! So that's when I literally WHIP him around so fast, he's a yellow blur, to see the back of his head looking up to her. Then, carefully, hiding behind a character, he turns and nods in approval with everyone, in profile. The whole take was so good, that to save it, we did "cut aways;" shots of various characters, mixed in with close ups of Patti singing.

Now, it's a buy!

Sesame Street has evolved over the years but, still prides itself on being socially conscious and tackling issues prevalent to its young audience — marriage, the birth of a baby, adoption, and in recent years, divorce, incarceration, military deployment, autism, and racism. I was involved with the one that started it all and the most poignant issue that *Sesame* felt the need to deal with. And it wasn't their choice.

Will Lee was the actor who portrayed the affable shopkeeper Mr. Hooper, whose name Big Bird could never pronounce correctly ("Thank you, Mr. Booper" being one of many malaprops that spanned a decade). Mr. Hooper was also one of the most popular of the human cast and the most recognizable at the Macy's Thanksgiving Day Parade. In November of 1982, he wasn't feeling well before the parade, but still wanted to do it because it meant so much to so many people. That Thanksgiving Day was rainy and performing in the parade only worsened his condition.

On December 7, 1982, Will Lee died of heart failure. I attended the memorial along with the rest of the cast, crew, and staff, and was amazed at the depth of his career in show business, including being blacklisted in the 1950s. The service, of course, ended with a clip from *Sesame*, of Mr. Hooper singing about life as a young boy, working in his father's store.

We finished out the season, with scenes involving Mr. Hooper being re-written for other cast members or completely cut. The producers decided to give themselves time and wait until next season to figure out a way to deal with the loss of one of their major characters, and one of the most popular. During the hiatus, scenarios were proposed and rejected. To completely ignore it and go on as if he never existed would be insulting to not only Will, but to the audience, young and old. The idea of Mr. Hooper moving away seemed a cheat and too easy. Then came the thought: what if *Sesame Street* actually explained to everyone that Mr. Hooper *died*?

At the time, no other children's show had ever attempted to do such a concept, and everyone knew it. They would spend the time to fully flesh out the sensitivity needed to deal with explaining death to kids.

According to the breakdown of the script, early within the show and long before the moment to address Mr. Hooper's passing, Gordon (Roscoe Orman) is on the street when he sees Big Bird walking towards him, backwards, with his head between his legs.

"Big Bird?" Gordon asks, "What are you doing?"

"Oh," replies Big Bird, "I'm walking backwards with my head between my legs."

"Why?" Gordon asks.

"Just because," counters Big Bird.

"Just because?"

"Yep, just because," and Big Bird then continues on his way, Gordon joining him. A quick cute bit with Big Bird doing something that's silly and makes absolutely no sense. (Hold that thought.)

Now it's time to tape the bit to explain what happened to Mr. Hooper. Jon Stone was directing, and when he would normally have to yell for quiet in the studio during the reading, not a sound was heard. We all had seen and read the script and everyone, both in front of and behind the camera, were bracing themselves.

Big Bird arrives in the arbor with hand-drawn pictures of everyone, the last, he proudly holds up, is of Mr. Hooper. (These drawings were all hand drawn by Carroll, an accomplished artist and illustrator.) Everyone is moved until Big Bird announces, "I can't wait to give it to him."

With uneasy looks to each other, Maria (Sonia Manzano) says, "Big Bird, don't you remember? Mr. Hooper died. He's dead."

"Oh, yeah," Big Bird says, "Well, I'll just wait until he gets back."

Susan (Dr. Loretta Long) says, …

"Big Bird, when someone dies, they don't come back."

"Ever?" Big Bird asks, as the reality starts to hit him. The scene continued with the others reassuring Big Bird that they will take care of him. After a moment, he angrily asks, …

"Why do people have to die? Give me one good reason."

This is when Gordon steps forward and as gently as possible, says, "Big Bird, people die — just because."

"Just because?"

"Yes. Just because."

Big Bird sighs and as he gazes at his picture of his friend, says, "I'm going to miss you, Mr. Looper." "That's *Hooper*, Big Bird," Maria adds as the cast pat and comfort Big Bird.

Cut.

All you could hear were sniffles and the blowing of noses, as tissues were passed out. The scene was shot again, and we all watched it to make sure it all worked, and it did. The cast hugged one another, proud of this accomplishment, as well as their characters being able to publicly say good-bye to their longtime friend.

The show aired on Thanksgiving Day, 1983. It was more than a success. It was applauded by the press, heralded by fans, and lauded by the Academy of Television Arts and Sciences (the Emmys) as one of the ten most influential moments on television. Everyone at *Sesame* was overwhelmed by the response. They had taken not just one of the most difficult subjects to deal with emotionally, but one of the most difficult issues of life to even talk about and presented it to young minds in a loving and caring, yet straightforward way. And it worked.

Sesame Street has been committed to children and families since the very first episode aired and continues to be a positive part of so many families, worldwide. Their desire to help make the world a better place is evident, and I am immensely proud to be a part of this remarkable show. In fact, as I write this, I'm now a director for the series and for the social impact segments on the YouTube channel.

Not bad for a kid from Central Harlem who started off hot gluing feathers to a big bird.

Are the Stars Out Tonight?

February of 1985 was the taping of the primetime special *"Night of 100 Stars II."* The ratings success of the first one in 1982 to benefit The Actor's Fund was enough to warrant a sequel. The bulk of the three hours show, of more than one-hundred stars of TV, the movies, and even sports (A listers and B listers of the mid 1980s), consisted of each one walking out on stage, taking a bow, and … that's it. Seriously. Go to YouTube and check it out. And this time among the stars gathered would be The Muppets!

The rehearsal and taping were done at the famous Radio City Music Hall in Manhattan, home to the world renowned Rockettes (who of course made an appearance on the special). I got to be asked to puppeteer in the opening number, a salute to NYC. There was a cutout bus with Fozzie, in the driver's seat, and the other Muppet Show Muppets would ride in as it was rolled onto the stage, all of us singing and swaying to the tune of "New York, New York." When we were upstairs and given a room to hang out in, we shared it with a few other stars. It was a large office that had Rock Hudson and Jimmy Stewart among others, and as we sat with Jim rehearsing the choreography with our bare hands (right, left, right, left – Muppets *always* start on the right; don't ask why) and lip synching, we noticed a very bewildered Matt Dillion staring at us, his mind not able to completely grasp what these people were doing with their hands. Weeks later, game show host Bert Convey would appear on "The Tonight Show" and holding up his hand, said to Johnny Carson, …

"You know what this is? It's Kermit the Frog naked!"

(And this is a joke I have always used when doing puppeteering demonstrations at bookstores, libraries, and schools. Thanks, Bert.)

There were several segments to the special, so rehearsal ran about six hours with staggered meal breaks; you couldn't have all two hundred plus performers all getting dinner at the same time. That's when I passed the line for dinner, with various people waiting for their food, when I saw … Cab Calloway. Now, if you remember, I mentioned that an aunt, one of my father's sisters, married Cab Calloway. So, he was my uncle, by marriage. And I had always heard this and knew of him. And I even went by Sesame the day he came to do inserts with The Two-Headed Monster and The Count. He even sang his famous song "Heigh Di Ho." And now here he was, "Uncle Cab," in front of me. I thought of all this as I walked by and then I stopped and turned back around to meet him.

"Excuse me, Mr. Calloway," I began, "I know you're online for dinner, but I just had to say that – you were great on 'Sesame Street.'"

"Thank you," he said with a broad smile.

"Bon appetite," and I walked away. Because that was not the time to bring up "Oh, and by the way, I'm your long-lost nephew you never knew existed." Let the man has his meal. And I still have no regrets.

Also in the opening number was Carol Channing who was joined onstage by Big Bird to sing "I Love New York in June." Once that segment was done so were the Muppets – except for Carroll who had to be Bird at the very end of the show, and Jim, because there was another segment coming up where he walks out (arm in arm with two Rockettes, with other celebrity gents, and bow when introduced). Kermit Love was "wrangling" Caroll, but he warned me a couple of days before that he might want to catch the last bus back home, upstate where he lived. So, he asked me if I'd mind staying to dress Caroll for the finale. I said "OK," and he said his goodnights to me, Caroll and Debbie (Spinney who had also come) and took off. I had not realized when agreeing to stay that the taping that had started at 7:00PM would not wrap until *2:00AM the next morning.* The Muppet segment was over, all the other puppeteers were released but now I was stuck there for the next *seven hours*.

But what an incredible seven hours it was!

Two rehearsal studios had been turned into "Green Rooms," the lounges TV shows use for guests to hang out in until it's time to go onstage. (One of the oldest stories is that back in 1599, the Blackfriars Theatre, in London, included a room backstage, where the actors waited to go on, which happened to be painted green, and thus called "The Green Room." Another is when the original *The Tonight Show* was in New York, the room for guests to wait in happened to have green walls.) And in these rooms was every star of the mid 1980s you could think of, mingling, talking, introducing each other, because a lot of them were fans of each other's work. I'll always remember seeing Michelle Lee (from TV's "Knotts Landing") open her small purse and pull out this Nikon camera with the longest telephoto lens. It was like Mary Poppins's evening purse containing this thing. And she walked around taking photos and getting combo shots of people (like Christopher Reeve and Jane Seymour, who hadn't seen each since working on the movie "Somewhere in Time.")

The only refreshments being served was water and soft drinks, no alcohol. The producers (Dick Clark being the all-mighty, all-seeing executive producer) didn't want these evening gowned and tuxedo clad celebs getting tipsy and falling into the orchestra pit. So, people, mixed and mingled around. Jim who was also there came over to me and said in an old man voice, …

"It's 'The Never-ending Cocktail Party.'"

I chuckled because it was true. There was something odd in thinking of this purgatory for celebrities, an endless eternity of small talk, stone cold sober.

Jim then asked me who some people were, and I joked, "You tell me; you had half of this room on 'The Muppet Show.'"

"Well," he said gesturing to a group of ladies across the room, "Who's that?"

"Oh, that's Linda Evans."

"And her?"

"That's Heather Locklear."

"And her?"

"That's Catherine Oxenberg. They're all on a show called '*Dynasty*.'"

"And him?"

"David Hasselfoff from '*Knight Rider*.' On the show he has a talking car. And – oh!" I said pointing at actor William Daniels, across the room, "He's the voice of the car."

For the next few minutes, he continued to ask who other people were and I suddenly realized I was educating Jim Henson in pop culture. Having watched WAY too much TV I knew everyone in the room. (And yes, I did watch "Dynasty" – no shame.) And for the record, Linda Evans was more beautiful in real life than on TV). Having a hunch that Kermit would skip out and want me to take over, I had brought a small journal of blank pages to get autographs. And I did. I would walk up to someone and ask, and they were all obliging and then they'd want to know who I was, and I would explain what brought me to "the Never-ending Cocktail Party" (thanks for the joke, Jim). I talked to Bob Newhart who told me that the secret to comedy was "take your time" and let the audience appreciate the setup. I talked to Harry Anderson (of TV's "Night Court") who wanted to guest star on "Sesame Street" (but sadly never got the chance to).

My oldest and dearest friend Danny (whom you'll remember I've known since 7th grade) and I went to see a Broadway show the previous fall called, "Harrigan & Hart." Written by Cy Coleman who composed the highly successful musical "Barnum" (my all-time favorite musical starring Jim Dale and pre-TV and film star Glen Close), this was the musical tale of the legendary vaudeville duo. And it got the worst reviews, scathing in fact. And Danny and I saw it the day after it opened. Two days later, it closed. And one of the leads was Mark Hamill. Yes, "Luke Skywalker" himself, Mark Hamill.

And here he was right in front of me.

I asked Mark for his autograph, and he obliged and then I mentioned seeing the show, to which he apologized. I said I did enjoy it, but that when I saw it, it was the day after it opened, and it seemed that "you all weren't waiting for applause after each song." And he said that was correct. Being onstage with live audiences you do get a sense of the crowd and that night, the audience I was in had this vibe of "OK I read the reviews – *prove* how bad you are." So, they really were trying to just get it over with. But that was how cool and open Mark was, to actually say this. I've admired his voice acting work since then (his "Joker" – OMG!) and his return to that "galaxy – far, far, away."

There were so many people there talking to one another until I noticed three guys over to the side who nobody was talking to. They were Perry King, Joe Penny, and Thom Bray, the stars of the NBC series, "Riptide," about three Vietnam vets who now solved crimes. And they stood there like you do at a party, looking around the room but not knowing anyone but you were invited so you have to stay. (And since their show was on NBC and Night of 100 Stars was on NBC, they were obliged.) And I actually felt a little sorry for these guys. So, I eased over and as humbly as I could, asked, …

"Excuse me. I don't mean to bother you all but … could I get your autographs? I can't tell you how much I love your show." (Which was true – I couldn't tell them because I'd never seen it; only the promos for it during an episode of "Night Court.") And they beamed. They were more than happy to, and we chatted, and they could not have been nicer.

The two autographs I treasure the most are from the two men I admired the most. I asked Carroll to sign my book, and he drew Big Bird smiling and saying, "To my other self" (due to all the times I got to fill in as Bird for him). And not to be outdone, I asked Jim who was more than happy to sign my book with a flourish and a "Kermit" drawing included.

Finally, it was time for the finale and Carroll and Debbie, and I made our way to his dressing room backstage. In those days, we tried not to have people see Carroll with just his legs on and not in Bird. We'd have a huge three-fold screen on locations to hide Bird when he was just sitting on his pole. So, Carroll got completely into Bird, and I lead him onstage (to what was left of the audience). There was a riser that the stars now had to stand on and sing "The Best of Times is Now" from the musical "La Cage aux Folles." Bird was to be at the top in the back ("tall guys in the back" as they say). As I lead him up, we had to carefully pass a few stars on the way up and once on top, Bird turned around and his huge soft tail, gracefully brushed over Jimmy Stewart's entire face.

Now, Bird was in place, and the other stars were in place, there's the call to standby cause they're about to roll and … I can't get down!

There were too many people to get through, all packed together; it was too high for me to jump down from the back; and they're counting down and if they see this "nobody" it will ruin the take that everyone has waited for *hours* to do so – I crouched down, low, staring at the back of sequined gowns and black tuxedo legs, with Bird's toes to my left. Everyone sang along to the music track, me included. (Hey, I was there, and it was something to do.) And then – we were done! A wrap! The stars cheered louder than the few people still sitting in the audience. But it was a once (OK this was billed "Part Two" but still) in a lifetime experience. What an incredible day… and night … and very early morning.

The Best Thing that Could Have Happened to You

As the wrangler on *Sesame Street,* I was in charge of "the Street days," when Big Bird and the other characters were used for the Street stories. But then would be the week of "Muppet Inserts," all those segments in Bert & Ernie's apartment or The Count's Castle or on a "limbo set;" an area for any set to be put up, even just the white cyclorama and lit blue. For those days, I was not needed because the Henson Workshop team came in to take care of the puppets. The head of the Henson Workshop was a woman named Caroly Wilcox. Caroly designed and built many characters for *Sesame Street* and *The Muppet Show* (including the African Masks for the song "Make the World Go Round," with Harry Belafonte; my favorite episode – and I've heard it was Jim's favorite, too). Even though I wasn't needed, I'd still occasionally come in to watch the taping of some bits, eventually puppeteering in them, particularly ones with Jim (Henson) & Frank (Oz) in them. I got to wrangle and perform on the Sesame movie *Follow That Bird,* but before any of this, I got to puppeteer on the show… due to Caroll Spinney.

In the olden days, Sesame was an hour long show and the Street stories were the bulk of the hour. Monday through Friday, the morning would be one show and after lunch (and God willing), the afternoon was a whole new show, often with different casts involved, human and non. And there was the schedule created by associate producer Arlene Sherman (who was also in charge of all those memorable animated segments featured on the show). One day, there was an afternoon bit with Oscar and his pet elephant "Fluffy." Fluffy is just the trunk that would come up out of the trashcan; the joke being that Oscar's home had a zoo down there, along with the pool, grand ballroom, and more. (Think of Doctor Who's TARDIS but with trash – "It's messier on the inside.") At that time, Brian Meehl was still a principal puppeteer for the show (as "Barkley the Dog," and the originator of "Telly Monster") and once the morning show was done, he left, because he was not scheduled for the afternoon show. But Brian did Fluffy so when it was time for the bit … no Brian. "Where's Brian?" Arlene asked me (as if I was keeping him in a drawer beside my wrangling tools). "He left," I said. "Well, we need someone to be Fluffy," she said with an annoyed tone. And then Carroll Spinney who was next to me said, …

"Noel can do it."

Arlene and the director for the bit, Lisa Simon (who was also a producer) looked at me and said, …

"Ok."

I could not believe it. I got next to Carroll behind the trashcan, we rehearsed it, then tape was rolling, and when it was time, Oscar ducked down and, with the trunk halfway up my arm, raised it up to have it give a big kiss to Maria on the cheek. "That's a buy!" And that was that. But I thanked Carroll so much. He didn't have to do it, but again, shows a kind and sincere heart this man had.

In time I started to do more puppeteering on the show, having proved that I could do it. At one point during a show that had a lot of characters, and the shop was called in to help, Caroly actually offered me a job in the workshop. I thanked her but said that I really loved performing (and got the sense that I was not taking this generous offer seriously). Earlier in the summer of 1985, Jim Kroupa, and I started doing commercials for "Snuggle Fabric Softener." The product that was so popular in France ("Cajoline") was being introduced to the U.S. and Kermit's shop built the puppet, "Snuggle Bear." Jim lip synced the head; I did the arms (whose wrists could bend with a mech built by Jim). There's a sequence that required Snuggle to do something and Kermit told the client "No." The director came over and told us what was happening, and I said, …

"But we can."

And I did the motion with the arms, and he went back and told the clients and the agency, and we did it and everyone was thrilled. Everyone except Kermit. And because it was *my* idea, I got the silent treatment for the rest of the day. But apparently this grudge would last.

In late summer, it was about two weeks from Sesame going back into production. For me, September always felt like the beginning of a new year, more than January. School always started and it's the month of my birthday, the day that literally starts *my* new year. One day, the phone rang, and Caroly was on the other end. She wanted to call to officially tell me that my services were no longer needed, but how she appreciated everything I had done.

"What?" I said quietly, completely dumbstruck. "I'm … fired?"

"Well, …" but she stopped herself from saying "yes" but instead said, …

"Kermit didn't tell you?"

"No," as I could feel my face getting hot.

"Oh," she said. "He told me he was going to speak to you first."

"But" I said carefully, "Instead, he had you so his dirty work."

Kermit and Caroly did not get along. There was a pause because Caroly was also shocked and taking in the fact that she had been played.

"Well," I said, "Thank you for telling me." And I hung up.

I was shocked and sad and … angry. I picked up the phone and called Arlene Sherman and Lisa Simon and told them how much I loved working on the show, and thanked them for being so gracious, but that Kermit just had me fired. And yes, they too were shocked, but told me that they would make sure I had work. Since Arlene was in charge of puppeteer casting (back then), she told me she'd put me into scenes, both on the Street and the Muppet inserts. And she did.

The first day of the new season, I was called in to assist for a character, for part of a scene. I saw the new wrangler who took my place, and I walked over and introduced myself.

"Hi. I'm Noel," I said reaching my hand out to shake.

"Oh, hi! I'm Mark," he replied taking my hand.

Mark Zezotek was a builder for the Henson shop and one of the nicest and funniest guys I've ever known. I wanted to make a point of introducing myself and even saying if he had any questions, I'd answer them. Which he appreciated, since Mark had said Kermit told him that I might be standoffish, even rude, given Mark now had my old job. I did confront Kermit about having me fired, who not only denied it, but then drove Caroly under the bus saying it was all *her* idea. (Did I mention if you combined the look of Santa with the temperament of Stalin, you'd get Kermit Love?)

The very first Muppet insert I ever puppeteered in for the show was with Grover. It takes place in a supermarket, and I am the cash register attendant. And now - Time for another YouTube moment! Go and type in "Sesame Grover Supermarket." I'll be here when you get back.

<Humming the Sesame theme>

You're back! Cool!

OK – now for the backstory.

That first half of the bit would have been in a wide shot before a cut to everyone rushing over to the next register (which I was also the cashier for). I had one line … *just one line*… "This register closed. Next register over THERE, please. Thank you." And when it came time for my line to Grover … I blew it. But not just blew it – I flubbed the line, added an expletive, to which Grover (played by the one and only Frank Oz) responded with "Say what now?" So, to save what we just did, director Jon Stone did a "pick-up" – a shot from a different angle, or in this case a close up of my character saying the line. Then it cuts back to the wide shot. Bit saved and I got a close up, and a heck of a way to officially start my Sesame puppeteering career.

Those days of feathering the Bird during the hot summer months were long behind me, but I still got to puppeteer with Jim for those Snuggle commercials. And I got more puppeteering bits on Sesame. And the kicker? Kermit, who at this point was beginning his retirement phase, saw me once on set with a character and actually said, …

"My firing you was the best thing that could have happened."

And… well … he was right.

"It's Time to Meet the Muppets"

As a kid, I loved the Muppets. I watched *Sesame Street*, *The Muppet Show*, and any time the Muppets were guests on a show or had their own specials (like *"The Great Santa Claus Switch"* which needs to be remade; it's so good). The day after I graduated high school, my mom, my grandmother, and I went to the Ziegfeld Theater in Midtown Manhattan and saw "The Muppet Movie." I sat there entertained and happy and knew deep down somehow, I'd get to work with them someday.

Having been a theater major at Brooklyn's Pratt Institute and meeting the designer and builder of Big Bird and Mr. Snuffleupagus, and then being offered the job of his assistant on Sesame Street, was a nice, if not a downright extraordinary way of getting my foot in the Muppet door. Because that is where I met Jim Henson. I'll always remember shaking his hand and having this jolt run through me. I was meeting the man that inspired me to be here and to be a puppeteer. Ironically, Jim never meant to be a puppeteer himself. It was a means to an end, in his case, getting into TV. He created the local Washington D.C. TV show "Sam & Friends" when he was *nineteen*! The reason the Muppets did a movie was because Jim wanted to get into making movies (which led to "The Dark Crystal" and then "Labyrinth"). Years later, in an interview, he actually said …

"I don't think anyone sets out to become a puppeteer."

Yes, they do! I DID!!! Thanks to YOU!!!

On Sesame, I would often be right hand to Jim's Ernie or a background character in a bit with Kermit the Frog. Once, when I was his right hand for Ernie, lighting needed to make and adjustment. Jim brought Ernie down and stepped back to sit on one of two nearby apple boxes (the wooden boxes used on T.V. and movie sets). And of course, me still in Ernie's right hand, went along for the ride. As I sat next to him, my mind was racing:

Noel ... you're sitting next to Jim Henson. JIM! HENSON! Say something! Most puppeteers would give their right arm to be this close to him. Of course, if they DID give their right arm, they couldn't be a right hand for – FOCUS NOEL!

That's when I remembered a tip my mom would use to start a conversation with someone: if they are a parent, ask about their kids. And that's exactly what I did.

"Jim? How are the kids?"

And that's when this proud papa starting telling everything Lisa, Brian, John, Cheryl, & Heather Henson were up to.

But I also got to work alongside, and learn from, Jim outside of "The Happiest Street on Earth."

I got to be a puppeteer for "Muppet Meeting Films," a series of two-to-three-minute videos for corporations to motivate, inspire, and satire their business. There was one for AT&T, where Jim's business suited character, "Leo," had a line Jim said and when the take was over, the person from AT&T gave him a note; it's funnier to make it plural. Jim had no idea how this plain, bland line about earnings projections could be funny at all, let alone funnier, by making the one-word plural. That night I told my mom how my day went. Having started in the typing pool and becoming a private secretary within the C.I.T. banking corporation for twenty-five years, I mentioned what happened and recited the line with the plural. She laughed. Practically cackled. And I asked why was this so funny. And her answer made it clear that this was a prime example of an "inside joke," a bit of humor only a select few understand and live through.

When Jim needed to video tape a pitch for his newest concept, I got to be involved. "The Jim Henson Hour" was a show that would be a collection of different stories and segments each week. (The most memorable segments of this hour were "The Storyteller," starring John Hurt as the lead character who would, well, tell stories each week to us, the viewer; and his faithful sidekick, a talking dog played by Jim's son, Brian). The pitch was a twelve-minute-long video of Jim in the "workshop," explaining what the show would be like and have to offer to families each week. It was an original show mixing the realistic creatures of the Creature Shop with the more traditional looking Muppets from *The Muppet Show* (because when you hear the name 'Jim Henson' you think of Kermit). After Jim says "See ya soon," (cause it's gonna sell and it did) he leaves through the door that has one of the door knockers from his movie "Labyrinth," hanging on it. As soon as the door closes, the knocker comes to life asking "Well guys? What did ya think?" to which various creatures, furry and otherwise pop out to chime in their approval. And the puppeteer and voice of the knocker? To quote a famous pig, …

"Moi!"

In the summer of 1985, I got to be an ensemble puppeteer for the new CBS Saturday morning show, *"Little Muppet Monsters."* The previous year, the animated show *"Muppet Babies"* based on the infant versions of Kermit and the gang used in the movie *"The Muppets Take Manhattan,"* was such a ratings hit that CBS decided to expand the time and add this new show. The main characters were three juvenile monsters, Molly (the girl), Boo (the boy), and Tug (the older brother-ish character), who would put on their own makeshift show in the basement of the Muppet House. Boo was an artist, and his drawings would become animated – produced by the same animation house that drew the Babies.

The "puppet captain" (ah … there's that title, but in this case well deserved) was Muppet performer Richard Hunt. I first met Richard on Sesame when I was the wrangler, and he was … rude to me. He'd make these little sarcastic comments until the day came when I had had enough. After a bit was done, as I walked over to get the puppets, Richard, lying on the floor next to Jerry (Nelson) tosses his at me to catch. I mumbled "Jesus Christ" under my breath, and, turning to walk away, Richard yells to me, …

"Hey!" I turn around and he says, "If I didn't like you, I'd be nice to you."

I walked back over, leaned down, and said, …

"Then you must f*%king love me, Richard."

And … he laughed. It was that loud, hardy from the gut, genuine, laugh I'd come to know from him. And after that we were fine. Oh, he was still sarcastic, but I knew why.

Richard performed "Tug" but also figured out puppeteering setups, as well as the casting of the secondary characters. And what was wonderful about Richard in this role was that he consciously wanted each of us in "the chorus" to have a chance to shine in an episode. My chance was the episode called "The Great Boodidni" when Boo finds a talking magic book – played by yours truly - and high jinks and chaos ensues. I memorized the script and worked on a deep voice for it. It would be shot the next day. The night before, I and Jim Kroupa and Pam Aciero, who were also puppeteers for the show, all went out for dinner and drinks. Many drinks. (I vaguely remember several Irish coffees.) I went to bed with quite the happy buzz and woke up the next morning … fine. I braced for a headache, but nope. No hangover. Besides it was my big day, and nothing was going to stop me.

I got to the studio, and practiced with the puppet, and we shot the entire episode. Once that was wrapped, we immediately began to work on the next episode. And I felt proud and loved every minute of it, and the pressure was off, and – Ow. OW. OOOOWWWW … And *that's* when the hangover kicked in. (Did I mention one too many Irish coffees the night before?)

After a summer of *Little Muppet Monsters*, that fall, I and the rest of the cast were invited to be a part of the CBS primetime special, *"The Muppets – A Celebration of Thirty Years"* to be taped in Toronto, Canada. *"Fraggle Rock"* had been shot in Toronto, so all those puppeteers (who'd also worked on the movie *"Sesame Street Presents – Follow That Bird"* the previous year) were also part of the puppeteer team. Because this special was going to have a LOT of Muppets on camera.

The set was a ballroom with dinner tables, all raised several feet to make it comfortable to stand and puppeteer. It was deep with rows and tiers so that different groupings of characters could be together. I got to hold up a variety of Muppets, including my favorite bird from *Sesame Street* (when Carroll wasn't needed). One scene was to be a reaction shot – a cut to a small group of random characters reacting. It was me and a couple of other puppeteers way in the back while all the way up front scanning the monitor was Kevin Clash, having just joined Sesame and starting his reign as (all together now) "Puppet Captain." We held up the puppets to set the shot when behind us we heard, …

"Mind if I jump in?"

We all turned, and it was – Jim! Jim Henson, himself, with a bunny on his hand. Oh my God! He wanted to come play with us! This was too much. We all squeezed together even more, and we all held up our puppets, and laughed, and reacted to whatever was to be edited before this. And because we were so far in back, everyone up front could not see who was doing what character, just the characters on the monitors. When it was played back, we all saw it on our monitors, Jim included, and we all laughed at how silly it was, particularly Jim's little bunny. (One rule I found out was that Jim and the original performers believed in the theory "upstaging;" make your character stand out.) The assistant director yelled out that we'd do it again. We put the puppets back up and did it again and Jim's bunny was even sillier. We heard "CUT" and then, heard, …

"The bunny is doing too much! Who's doing that bunny?!?"

And that's when, stepping onto a box, Jim Henson let his head rise up over the table to show exactly who was responsible. And everyone laughed.

The special was shot over several days – several very *long* days. But when we wrapped, we got to go back to the hotel. But not just any hotel. We were all staying at the (original) Four Seasons Toronto. It's the hotel Jim would stay at whenever he was in town during the seasons of *Fraggle Rock.* It was also where Richard Hunt stayed, who had to shuttle back and forth between Fraggle (for his character "Junior Gorg") and his puppeteering duties on *Sesame Street.* It was a stunning hotel, dripping with luxury and comfort. After a long day of "dolly-wigglin'" a bunch of us were in one of the hotel elevators and we decided to get a well-deserved drink at the bar at the top of the hotel.

"Nah," Kevin announced, "I'm goin' to bed."

"Oh, come on. One drink," we all said.

"No!" he declared, "I'm tired," and got off at his floor.

The elevator opened to reveal the bar at the top floor of the Four Seasons, and it was beautiful, with a stunning view of the Toronto skyline. We were also surprised to see so many other people from the shoot enjoying drinks, and even noticed Jim was there. And then suddenly, a cake with candles was brought in, heading straight towards Jim. OMG! It was Jim's birthday, and this was a surprise for him! I wasn't the only one who had no idea this was planned and thrilled to be there for this moment. After we all sang happy birthday and he blew out the candles, we all toasted Jim, who thanked us all for a good day.

Back at the studio the next day, we were all talking about what a great evening it was, and Kevin was nearby. And when we got to the part about the surprise birthday party for Jim, …

"What?!" Kevin cried, "Why didn't ya call me?!?"

"Oh, we would have, but …," I said, the smile beginning to curl on the corners of my lips, "You were so *tired*."

Even he had to laugh.

In the last few years, I've had Muppet opportunities come up and they've all been fun and have run the gamut.

One December, I got to assist Steve Whitmire, who had taken over Kermit after Jim had died in 1990. Kermit recited "The Night Before Christmas" before the start of the Radio City Christmas

Spectacular. It was my second time on that famed stage, and I enjoyed working with Steve, who also appreciated my help. When he was Ernie on Sesame, he always asked if I could be his right hand, so he asked if I was available for this. Steve is a dedicated puppeteer and a true artist. His creativity will continue in whatever he puts his mind to.

For the TV movie, *"A Very Merry Muppet Christmas: Letters to Santa,"* I got to be "Sweetums." Not just be in him but *voice* him, too! And *sing*! I always loved Sweetums because he is of course a body puppet – big, cumbersome, you get very sweaty inside; in other words, I'm home – and because he was one of Richard's characters. But I became part of a long line of "Sweetums" performers. There was Richard who cemented the character. Then John Henson, Jim's son, played him for appearances. Now, it was my turn, and it was fantastic. And when I got an email in 2017 about a live version of *The Muppet Show* to be performed at the acclaimed Hollywood Bowl and being asked to be Sweetums again, I was floored. I couldn't stop smiling and started practicing the voice, again.

For *"The Muppets Take the Hollywood Bowl,"* the Muppet guys (Matt Vogel, Eric Jacobson, Dave Rudman, Bill Barretta, and Dave Goelz, himself) would be dressed in black, wearing black hoods and on "rollies." Imagine sitting on a small throw pillow with four office chair wheels and that's a "rollie." They're used on *Sesame Street* all the time and for this it would be more practical than trying to constantly hide the guys (and other puppeteers). Of course, being Sweetums, I had the ultimate hiding place. The first day we did a walk-thru to figure out entrances and exits. After the opening number, Kermit (beautifully performed by Matt Vogel) welcomes everyone, until Sweetums enters, galumphing across the stage, Kermit calls him over, they have an exchange, me doing my best imitation of Richard's voice, and Sweetums sets off to "help." When I exited, the person in charge of The Muppets for Disney at that time scurried over and said to me, …

"Matt does Sweetums now."

"Oh?"

"And he'll pre-record the voice."

"Oh, …" I replied quietly, letting it all sink in and then said…

"O.K."

Of course, I was disappointed. It wasn't mentioned in the email to me so I thought I'd have the chance to do it again, since the shows would be live. But I had agreed and committed to doing this, even before this clarification, so I carried on. Matt did pre-record the voice and I did learn the lines and worked out the timing of having it played back to lip sync to. And it all worked perfectly.

Now as a result of this moment of "sucking it up" and being a professional and moving forward, I got to be a part of this amazing experience and then got invited to re-create my job (along with all the other puppeteers from the Bowl gig) for *"The Muppets Take the O2,"* London's version of Madison Square Garden, only bigger. And again, another unforgettable experience. The guest for the Bowl shows was comedian Bobby Moynihan (of *Saturday Night Live* fame), who shared wonderful tales of SNL, as well as being game for anything the Muppets threw at him. For example, when we did the Hollywood Bowl, the second act's opening number was, the now classic Muppet version of the QUEEN classic, "Bohemian Rapsody." At one point, Sweetums must chase Bobby around the stage. But I had a better idea: what if Bobby and Sweetums ran through *the audience*? It would be such a surprise to the folks that this song was now happening inches in front of them. Of course, LA was also going through a heat wave, with a heat advisory. The daytime temperature for rehearsals hovered over 100 degrees, with a heat index of Hell's front porch. *Yes Noel, during the mid-day rehearsals, let's run around during a heat advisory into the open-air audience area, with zero shade. Brilliant!* But it was my idea, and I was prepared for it (hydrate, hydrate, hydrate) and it worked. The audience at the Bowl, and then at the O2, loved it. For one Bowl performance, Sweetums saw a bottle of champagne guests had (because you can have food and drink brought to your table at the Bowl), grabbed it, and headed back backstage. To the shock and delight of the patrons.

After the O2, everyone scattered to the four corners of Europe. Susan and our son came with me, and we headed up to Scotland, specifically, Arisaig House. Susan had been there for research for her fourth book in her historical-fiction *"Maggie Hope Mystery"* series *"The Prime Minister's Secret Agent"* (from Penguin Random House; available at your local bookstore; yes, this is a not-at-all-shameful plug) because the manor house had been used for training SOE (Special Operations Executive) agents during World War 2. But it was also beautiful there and the only way to get there, by rail, is a train that goes over a via duct bridge. A certain via duct bridge. And if you've ever seen the "Harry Potter" movies, you know *exactly* which bridge I'm referring to. (And you should have seen me whip out my smartphone when the conductor announced it.) The grounds of Arisaig House were lush and green and as I leaned against an old stone shed, I gazed at the Highland mountains. This was the first-time direct MacNeal descendants had returned to Scotland. And I smiled thinking how that nineteenth century immigrant would have no idea that his future kinfolk would be back, thanks to a frog and a pig.

“Of Course, You Can Think Backwards!”

For a couple of years, in the early 2000s, Sesame Workshop would send me to their “co-productions” in other countries to work with the teams there. Now, a “co-production” is a production of *Sesame Street* that is co-produced by Sesame Workshop and the production company of that region. The productions have a basic curriculum, quite similar to ours — learning letters, numbers, shapes — but these productions also have curricula tailored for their children. India’s *Galli Galli Sim Sim* had hygiene and the need for clean water; Japan’s *Sesame Street* had learning about empathy and displaying emotions; Pakistan’s *Sim Sim Hamara* had ways to learn tolerance; and so on. According to their own website, they are “from Asia to Africa and everywhere in between.” It truly is “the longest street on earth.”

One place I got to go to was Jordan. There, I was to be part of two conferences: one with the team from Palestine, for their Sesame, and one with the team from Jordan, for theirs. The first one was with the team for the Palestine version of Sesame*, Saharaá Simsim*. This version had existed in 1996 as an Israeli-Palestinian version and was now coming back solely a Palestinian production. For this trip, and the short time between the two conferences, it was easier for the Palestinian team to come to Jordan. We stayed at the Marriott Dead Sea. Yep — a Marriott on the banks of the Dead Sea. This way, our meetings would occur in one of the meeting rooms. The Palestine team was small: four writers, two producers, the director, the executive producer, the Sesame Workshop producer/project manager, the Sesame Workshop vice president for global production, and little ole me. The Palestinians were proud that they now had a chance to create their very own version of *Sesame* for their kids and their main theme was “identity” — who you are in your family, your neighborhood, and your country. They wanted to empower their kids with a positive self-worth and show non-violent ways to resolve negative feelings.

Not only is the *Sesame* curriculum tailored for the specific region it’s in, but they also get their own original Muppets, often reflective of animals or characters those children would recognize. The previous production of *Saharaá Simsim* had two original hand puppet characters: “Kareem,” a slightly vain rooster, and his best friend “Hanin,” a brightly colored and playful monster. They would be used for the "street segments," a set representing architecture of the region and where the Muppets would interact with humans (that all the majority of co-productions have). My role was for working with the team about the writing for the show. You see, we here in the U.S., having been exposed to the humor of Jim Henson and The Muppets on *Sesame Street* and *The Muppet Show*, we take "schtick" (the Yiddish word for a specific style of comedy) for granted. It's what makes Sesame "Sesame." But other countries don't have this advantage, which is why I was sent. And these writers had never written for a children's television show, let alone one with Muppets.

"There are three rules to writing for Sesame," I said. "One — make it funny. Two — make it funny. Three — repeat rules One and Two."

I showed them examples of bits that worked, emphasizing the fun and "funny," while at the same time teaching. I then gave the writers an assignment: come in the next day with an idea for a story, pitch it (as you would in the writer's room) and, if it's good, it could be considered for the show. The next day, the writers came, and we started off with one story pitched by this young guy. Through the interpreter, he described it:

"We see the Sesame puppet answer the phone and in a split screen, we see his puppet friend who is in the Gaza Strip. It's hard for the Gaza puppet to hear his Sesame friend due to the bombing in the background. The Sesame friend writes a note and ties it to a dove and lets it fly up out of frame. A second later, you hear a gunshot, and on the Gaza side, feathers fall onto the head of the Gaza friend."

I took a moment to fully absorb what he just described, and then, through the interpreter, I answered, "A world of 'no.' I understand what you want to say, and I respect that you want to say it, but *this* is not the way to do it on *Sesame Street*." I realized that unlike American kids who get shielded from harsh realities as much as possible, Palestinian children are introduced to death and dying from the time they're born. So, I did understand what this guy wanted to try to convey. Which is why I asked the other writers how this could be turned into a story for their Sesame. It ended up being this:

The two Muppet characters see their human friend is sad. They ask why and the human says he hasn't heard from his friend, who lives in the Gaza Strip, for some time and is worried about them. The Muppets decide to try and help their friend feel better and dress up as clowns and try to do tricks to make their friend laugh, including making balloon animals, which of course they can't, and end up flying around. Their human friend thanks them for trying to help and tells them they have given him an idea. They draw a picture of the three of them for the human's friend, tie it to a balloon, and let it sail over their wall towards the Gaza Strip.

"You watered it down!" the writer said. And through the interpreter I responded, …

"You're damn right I watered it down! This is *Sesame Street*!"

Sesame Street is a haven for kids and even when the outside world intrudes (the death of Mr. Hooper; the hurricane destroying Big Bird's nest), we reassure our viewer that everything will be okay thanks to the people around you — your family, your friends, and your neighbors.

I'm proud to say that the bit did end up being used for the show. (However, that writer did quit after the conference.) The Palestinian conference lasted around three days, and everyone agreed it was a successful start to their *Sesame Street*. I then headed back to Amman, Jordan to stay and attend the conference for the Jordanian team at the Grand Hyatt Amman.

In one of the hotel's larger conference rooms, I walked into a crowd of people. Whereas the Palestinian team was small, the Jordanian team was not. Their team for *Hikayat Simsim* was the size of a baseball team, coaches and managers included, except it was the executive producer, several producers, the director, and the entire writing team of around ten people, plus assistants. They didn't have just one interpreter for this conference, they had *two:* one voice assigned to interpret us to the team and the other voice to interpret the team to us. And we all wore earbuds to hear them interpret in real time. *This* Sesame had some serious bucks.

Remember how I said we take "schtick" for granted and how the Palestinian writers had never written for a children's show? Multiply this by ten and you get the idea of what I was working with in Jordan. I'd show them the same examples of bits and the same rule of "make it funny first" and none of the writers, the majority younger than me and just out of school (one was an architect), not one of them asked any questions. But man did they take notes. During a break, as I was getting coffee, I chatted with one of the writers, who was an older gentleman. I mentioned, "I was hoping for you to ask questions" because that was why I was there. And he said that in Jordan schools you *don't* ask the teacher a question unless it's a very good one. Otherwise, you are judged for wasting the teacher's time and — SMACK — you get hit! Now I understood. And that's the fascinating aspect of going to other countries — discovering their culture. After the break, I welcomed everyone back and addressed the lack of questions saying there are no dumb questions.

The executive producer was the first to actually ask a question.

"Noel," he asked, "What if you have a really good ending, a so-so middle, and no beginning. What do you do?"

"Well," I said, "you figure out how you got there. Like 'reverse-engineering.' You think backwards."

And then, the young architect-turned-writer raised his hand and asked the producers, …

"Am I *allowed* to think backwards?"

The Sesame Workshop project manager said, "Let me answer this, Noel." They turned to the writer and yelled, …

"Of course, you can think backwards!"

And everyone laughed.

When I spent two weeks in India, I worked with the writing team for *Galli Galli Sim Sim.*

This version of *Sesame* had existed for two seasons but was now being relaunched and co-produced, not only by Sesame Workshop, but also by Turner Broadcasting India. And it would be the first co-production with entirely original content. Other co-productions have their street characters but also have access to the vast library of Muppet inserts, to be dubbed into their languages. But the *Galli* team, after seasons of this, found that the humor of Bert and Ernie bits, and others, didn't translate (as in the jokes didn't make sense to them). So, it was decided, no more dipping into the library. There would be a *new* format. The start of each show would have the "street story," centered around their Muppets and human characters. Then the segment "Elmo's Word of the Day" would be shot against green screen with their Elmo. And finally, "The Adventures of Grover and Toto," with Grover and his sidekick monkey named "Toto." And these segments would be shot on location — in the real world. And scenes were to be shot in Hindi and then in English.

In New Delhi, there was the two-day conference announcing the new segments, the enhanced curriculum that would include teaching the importance of clean water and preserving nature, and the binder containing all this information. And not just a "binder." This thing was so thick with charts, graphs, and goals you could use it as a weapon to whack someone. The original Guttenberg Bible is a pamphlet compared to this thing. Which was actually a problem.

The first day I began work with the writers in the writer's room, I held up the binder and said, "See this?" And then I let fall out of my hand onto the floor with a loud THUD. "Forget it. There is no way on earth you will get to *all* these points in this timeframe and this number of episodes. You'll drive yourselves crazy." I then told them, for this first season, pick the *one* thing above others to teach, then two more in order of preference. They picked clean water followed by hygiene.

The writers were so diligent and dedicated to the show that they began to second-guess themselves. For example, they were so concerned about getting Grover exactly right because they loved the character so much. I wrote to Eric Jacobson (who took over for Frank Oz) and asked what advice he could give to them. Eric is the most meticulous performer I have ever met, so he would definitely know Grover's mindset. He wrote back that they should think of *their* Grover as a cousin to *our* Grover. Same family (hence why they look and sound alike) with the same characteristics: never uses contractions; never admits he doesn't know what he's doing; never gives up; and always proper and formal in presentation.

"Oh!" they exclaimed. "He's Punjabi!"

I'm proud to say I also rescued a character from extinction. The character "Aanchoo."

"Aanchoo" is a practical hand puppet. (Remember? The main puppeteer doing the head and left hand and a second puppeteer as the right hand. Think of Ernie or Cookie Monster). Whenever she sneezed, she would – *POP* - disappear. Flighty and sweet, but this was her main thing. And the writers didn't know what to do with her and thought the best idea was to dump her. I said that this was an opportunity to have "accidental chaos," meaning someone who doesn't mean to cause trouble, but it happens whenever they are around. Since she could obviously do magic, she would be perfect for this role. Remember Aunt Clara from the classic sitcom *Bewitched* (which they'd all seen)? Aunt Clara tries to help and means well when using her magic, but it always goes wrong. Always.

The writers were concerned about having a character who performed magic and that it wasn't grounded in the real world. (Well, they have a seven-foot-tall talking lion, but fair enough.) I explained that our Sesame also has magical characters, from The Amazing Mumford (originated by the amazing Jerry Nelson) to Abby Cadabby (performed by the incredible Leslie Carrara-Rudolph), but magic *never* solves problems; in fact, there are times it makes things *worse*. And that's what Aanchoo could do: be the character who sets up the problem, and the non-magic characters have to use their brains, even cooperate, to figure out a solution. We came up with a story focusing on sources of clean water, with a touch of cultural exposure thrown in:

There's a heat wave and the Galli is scorching hot. The two kid Muppets, Chamki, a little girl, and her best friend, Googly, a boy monster, complain how hot it is, when Aanchoo suddenly pops in. She says she knows a spell to bring cold weather in, but instead makes appear the one animal you would never see in India: a penguin! And before she can send the penguin back to Antarctica — AAACHOOOO! — she disappears! Now, Chamki and Googly must help the penguin stay cool (clean water to make ice cubes) and learn about what the penguin needs to survive (aka learning about someone else's culture). Perfect.

The writers also introduced me to real Indian cuisine. I told them how my wife and I love Indian food back in NYC and showed them a menu online, from one of our favorite restaurants. They were appalled at the prices. "This is 'street food!' They're charging you this much for 'street food'!?!" After that, their homemade lunches included extra portions to share with me.

In March of 2004, Sesame Workshop asked me to join Kevin Clash (aka the originator of "Elmo") to help audition and train the puppeteers for the revamped version of the show – in *Japan*. There were going to be two new characters – two monsters; one named "Mojabo" (with a slightly grouchy attitude); and "Teena" (carrying on the sweet and friendly vibe of "Zoe" back home) as well as the three staples of our show - Elmo, Cookie Monster, and Big Bird. Kevin wanted to concentrate on the training of the hand puppeteers so, I was in charge of training the eventual performer of their Big Bird.

The whole trip with auditioning and training would be two weeks and this was the trip of a lifetime. I traded in my business class ticket for two coach tickets so that my wife, Susan, could go with me. The flight from New York's JFK to Tokyo was a solid fourteen hours and change, non-stop. When we landed, we were taken to the Hilton Tokyo, where we checked in and were exhausted. The two educator advisers for the project contacted us, wanting to take us to dinner later. Since it was 2:00PM we needed to nap, to be fresh for the evening. Just a nap - for an hour or so. We both laid down and suddenly this sound woke me up from a deep sleep. I bolted up to see the room was completely dark and it was night outside. (Has that happened to you? You wake up from a sleep so deep and you have no idea where you are?) *What time was it!?!* I discovered that the sound was the telephone, and it was the educators, who were downstairs in the lobby. I told them we'd be down in ten minutes, and we splashed water on our faces, and headed out. They said the restaurant was just across the street, but we looked and only saw an office building. We followed them into the lobby, into an elevator – where were they taking us? Well, we learned that land in Tokyo is, extremely scarce. The city is so densely populated that you can't build out so, … you build *up*. We got off the elevator, in this office building, to find a mini mall. The entire floor was made up of shops, with the restaurant we were going to (which was delicious and had a stunning view of the city).

Reading up on the culture and phrases for our trip, Susan and I got to use all of it. Tokyo itself is one of the most fascinating and unique cities I've ever been to. It's not just clean, its immaculate. Not one piece of litter anywhere. And their subway; well-lit stations with easy-to-read directions in English; no litter; no *smells*; people actually waiting until you got off to get on! For this born and raised New York City boy it was a dream come true. On the streets there were vending machines for whatever you needed; from coffee to umbrellas (to… um … "personal items"). Taxi drivers have a handle next to them to open the passenger doors for you and you sit on lace covered seats.

This was just the beginning to this extraordinary trip. The norms and cultural expectances were amazing to experience. Of course, I was there for work, and I got to have fun with the one group vital to these co-productions: "my people."

The puppeteers.

"Don't Forget to Have Fun!"

The next morning, Susan and I went down to breakfast at the hotel. We stepped up to the podium and bowed to both attendants and said, …

"Ohayou gozaimasu" ("Good morning")

Both attendants smiled while simultaneously taken aback.

We were seated and ate and when we left, we said to both of them, …

"Gochiso sama deshita" ("It was a feast")

They were both, again, pleasantly shocked that two Westerners had taken the time to learn and use such a Japanese phrase. We found this would be the case everywhere we went. Our time studying the guidebook was paying off.

I left for the studio, which was within walking distance of the hotel. The first day, I had to cross one huge intersection and waited along with many other people going to work, including young male office workers dressed in black suits and ties (called "Salary Men"). They were particularly antsy about wanting to cross the street; fidgeting, even jumping, waiting for the light to change. But here's the thing – they could have crossed the street. We *all* could have, because there were absolutely *no cars* at all, in either direction. None. Back home, I'd have just walked across, but here, I didn't. The Japanese follow "the rules" and adhere to what is proper. And the rules say you wait until the light is green to cross the street. And I didn't want to be "that Westerner." So, I too waited and then the light turned green, and the "Salary Men" bolted across the street, racing to their respective buildings.

When I got to the studio it was in an older building, on the second floor. Before entering, I saw the cubbies with "indoor shoes" and took a pair, putting my "outside" shoes in a cubbie. The Japanese don't believe in tracking in the outside indoors, so they take off their shoes before entering and put on their indoor shoes – which are different from their "bathroom shoes," which were also available. (Speaking of bathrooms there were two; a "Western bathroom" and a

“Traditional bathroom.” The Western is the one we all know and have at home. But the “Traditional” was … a small room with a sink and next to it was a stall, with no door and - a hole in the floor. Yep. You squat! I wanted to try it and I made the mistake of glancing down between my legs and … *OH! MY! GOD!* And, let me tell you: I have come to the horrifying realization that you are *never* meant to see what comes out of you. When I was I India, I visited “The Museum of Toilets” – I am not making this up – and India came up with the idea of sitting comfortably. (Thank you, India.)

For two days Kevin and I auditioned potential puppeteers, keeping track of who was “getting it” and who wasn’t. Surprisingly several older Japanese puppeteers did not “get it.” We worked with them and really wanted one of them to work but, given the time restraint we had, and the fact that these gentlemen were so ingrained in their ways, it didn’t happen. Once again though, non-puppeteers did work. At the end of the second day, we had our cast, especially Big Bird, and it was close. It was between one guy and one *girl,* and we both thought how interesting it would be to have a female Big Bird. But in the end, it went to Satoshi Tsurouka, who nailed it.

For the next couple of days, Kevin was in one room with the hand puppeteers and Satoshi, and I were in another. Everything was setup for us – a camera for recording, as well as providing the video feed to his monitor strapped to his chest. I loved working with him, and we got along great. He’s a voice actor and I mentioned that flipping channels in the hotel room, I saw an anime about tennis, with all the action and editing of a *Dragonball Z* episode, but with tennis.

“‘*Prince of Tennis!”* he said through the translator, “That’s me!” (Meaning *he* was the voice of the lead character).

(Here’s a quick bit of trivia: the new Muppets built for this production had five fingers, not the usual four. Why? Because in Japanese culture, the number four is unlucky; it’s their number thirteen. Even in elevators there was no fourth floor. But there was a thirteenth!)

I got to not only train Satoshi, but to be his wrangler, too. (“Back in the saddle, again.”) Michelle Hickey, who is the wrangler for Sesame (and one of the nicest people I will ever know), was brought over to train the wrangler(s) for the show on how to prep the puppets, even how to handle the puppets, especially Big Bird. Michelle wears a glove on her hand, so that when holding the Bird by his open mouth, to lower him or lift him, your dirt and oil won't ruin the fleece of the beak. So, when wrangling Satoshi, I wore the gloves. (Which I never did when I was the wrangler on the show or the Sesame movie "Follow That Bird." Did my dirty hands lead to this innovation? I still wonder.) Satoshi worked hard to incorporate my instructions, while still being in character. He also knew he had to start training more, especially his right arm. We recorded the basics – walking in and exiting while keeping eye contact; dealing with a prop; and bits of scenes with me, being the human cast member. All this through the translator and my miming skills (of which I have none). By the last day, Kevin and I had the whole cast do a song, one that would have each character enter, sing a line, and then be there watching the next one enter and sing, until they were all together in a lovely group shot. That's when we taught them, in order to get the group shot, you set up where everyone needs to be for that final lovely look, and then, exit just enough out of frame for the entrance. And it worked! They were great … and exhausted. Because it was an excellent exercise in not being the main focus of a scene, but being part of a scene, while still looking "alive."

Mizuka Kamijo ("Meez") worked for the production as a coordinator. On a day off for all of us, she was kind enough to show us *her* Tokyo. After being treated to a bunraku (the traditional puppetry style of Japan) performance (which was so long we were told it's OK to take a nap during it), she took us to "Kaiten Sushi" or "Conveyor Belt Sushi." You sit at a counter and a conveyor belt in front of you passes with various dishes. You take what you want and then the plates are counted at the end, to add up what you owe. She took us to a supermarket with so many food products we never see here, like shrimp flavored potato chips. We did karaoke (cause how could we NOT do it in the birthplace of karaoke) and ended the day at this little coffee house, that gave me one of the most beautiful foam designs on top of my coffee I've ever seen.

If you ever have an opportunity to go to Japan, do it. It's amazing and fascinating and everyone we encountered were friendly, even total strangers. Whenever Susan pulled out a map to get her bearings, someone would come up and assist her (because it was quite obvious, we weren't locals). When she and I went to see the "Sakura," which are the cherry blossoms, in a park, a family asked if they could get their picture taken … with us in it! The culture, the food, the history is incredible, but it's the people that made this trip unforgettable. After Kevin grilled everyone one more time to remember everything that was taught, I followed up with a phrase I had memorized with the translator's help, …

"*Itsumo tanoshinde kudasai*" ("Remember: always have fun")

"Are You Going to Connect with Your Ancestors?"

Of the seven continents I've visited, thanks to the Sesame Workshop co-productions, the one *continent* I've been to the most is the *continent* of Africa. (I'm deliberately repeating the word *"continent"* to aid my fellow Americans' geography skills.) On the *continent* of Africa, I've been to three *countries*: South Africa, Nigeria, and Senegal. Two of them were on purpose and one by accident.

The first time I was to go to Africa was for the South African co-production *Takalani Sesame*. I was going to work with the puppeteer who played "Kami," a playful young female monster, characteristics most young Sesame characters have except for this one distinction: Kami is the first and only Muppet to be HIV-positive. For years, with the AIDS crisis that swept the world, South Africa suffered from stigmas and falsehoods associated with the disease. Around the time I went, the youth spokesperson for the national South African AIDS awareness association, devoted to educating young people on the truths and myths behind AIDS, resigned, because they contracted the disease and thought washing in a hot shower would get rid of it. Kami was a major step in educating not only children, but their families, about someone being HIV-positive.

I boarded the South African Airways flight with the Sesame Workshop producer/production manager and settled in to the fourteen-hour non-stop flight. Correction: the fourteen-hour flight that included a stop in Senegal to refuel. It was a standard procedure for this flight: land in the middle of the night, refuel in less than an hour, take off, and continue. That's what was *supposed* to happen. Here's what *actually* happened...

Our evening South African Airways flight, that departed JFK, landed in Senegal, and they began to refuel, and we sat.

And sat.

And sat.

And sat.

And this is now going much longer than anticipated. We find out that there's an issue with one of the engines and we all must deplane, taking any carry-ons with us. Since the producer and I were flying business/first class (thank you Sesame Workshop), we and the other upfront passengers were herded into the airport's departure lounge, while the other passengers were led to the normal gate area. And there we sat.

And we sat.

And we sat.

And the sun was starting to rise.

And we sat, until we were told that a part was needed for the engine and was being flown in. In the meantime, all passengers were to be taken to a hotel to freshen up and have food. Then, after a few hours to literally wander aimlessly around the hotel, we all got back into the vans and headed back to the airport where… guess what?!?

We sat.

And sat.

And sat.

And sat.

All. Night.

We sat all night because the wrong part had been delivered. And we would have to wait another day for the right one to be delivered and then installed. This is when I began to rally my fellow passengers to not only tell relatives and friends and business colleagues what was going wrong, but to also go on social media and let the world know, too. I went on Twitter and shared South

African Airways handle, but also tweeted the BBC, CNN, and MSNBC, letting them know what was going on, and sharing pictures.

As dawn broke on our second day, we were herded back into the vans and back to the hotel, where rooms were set aside for us to shower and even nap in. (Of course, this was for us in business/first class. As miserable as this experience was, it was worse for those in coach.) As I strolled around the pool and garden, I was approached by a camera crew and reporter — from BBC World News! Jackpot! They interviewed me and several other people and told us that it would air in a few hours. We all texted and tweeted and let the word out.

It's amazing how social media can work in your favor. If we hadn't notified the rest of the planet that we were stuck in Senegal with no immediate departure, we'd all still be there. But suddenly, after the story broke, South African Airways told us that a whole NEW PLANE was arriving to take us to South Africa. We got back in the vans, back to the airport and waited until — yep — another plane had arrived! All our luggage was transferred to the new plane and just shy of midnight, we took off, everyone cheering and applauding. (Years later, through DNA testing, I would discover part of my African ancestry was from Senegal. Oh, the irony.) When we landed, we were each given a letter from South Africa Airways for, *not* a refund, but a *discount* on a future SAA flight. And the letter went on to say, in the most passive aggressive way, that the plane they brought had those passengers thrown off in order to get it to us. I've no doubt those poor souls are *still* waiting somewhere for an SAA plane to come get them.

We were staying at the Hyatt Regency Johannesburg because it was walking distance to the rehearsal studio, located in the nearby mall. The Sesame producer wisely decided we deserved the concierge level to make up for our "delay." They also appreciated how I never once complained about the situation. I remember Susan asking me with a wry smile before I left,

"Will you connect with your ancestors?"

"Only if my ancestors want to connect with me at the bar of the Hyatt Regency." We both laughed.

Seriously, I did appreciate the fact that as an African American I was now back in Africa. "The Motherland." Before I left, I read up on South Africa to understand any customs or cultural differences that could come up during the training session. One such local custom I read about was "The Handshake." In the travel guide, it was described as hands slapping together, shaking, and then pulling back to create a "snapping" sound, with the fingers. But it cautioned that the visitor should not instigate it; it's a local thing, and only a local should do it to you first, as a sign of respect.

Since I had lost two days, stuck in Senegal, I only had three to train with Kami's puppeteer. That first day, now Saturday, I went to the rehearsal studio. There were two guys: one for the camera and one for audio. The sessions were to be recorded, not only to play back to show her and critique her performance, but for the *Takalani* producers and Sesame Workshop to see. I walked in, introduced myself, and put my hand out. The guys took my hand and gave me the usual handshake.

The next day was the scheduled day off and I wanted to go and discover Johannesburg. I went to the concierge desk and saw brochures for safaris, which I dismissed. I didn't want to do something so touristy. I have Walt Disney World's Animal Kingdom back home for that. Then I saw a brochure for local tours of Soweto, the district created for apartheid, to separate blacks from the white settlers. It also included a tour of Nelson Mandela's home and the Hector Pieterson Memorial and Museum, both located in Soweto. Perfect. The reservation was made, and a local man showed up with his minivan. It was him, me, and an older British couple staying in the hotel. And we were off.

As he drove along the highway to Soweto, he pointed to our left at the skyscraper skyline of Johannesburg.

"See all those buildings? There're empty."

Wait. What?!? A skyline the size of midtown Manhattan and ALL those buildings are empty?!?

It was a shocking statement to hear, but he explained that when apartheid (which means "apartness" or "apart-hood" in Afrikaans) ended on May 4, 1990, literally, the next day, corporations left. And left behind all those corporate offices. But he also added that not all the buildings were abandoned; some had squatters from other African nations, who'd come to South Africa to start a new life. But with little to no work available to them, they live in squalor, in buildings with no heat or electricity or running water. And the proof came at the end of the day as he drove us back to the hotel, and, as the sun set, none of those buildings were lit up.

We arrived in Soweto and as he drove through the streets, I saw houses that ranged from shacks to ranch style, some with concrete walls built around them, to a few that were mini mansions. Literally. They were the size of townhouses, but the façades had arches and columns. Imagine Disneyland's Haunted Mansion looking the same on the outside but scaled down to a two-bedroom, one-and-a-half bath. And the wires! Wires crisscrossing over the streets and through houses. "For sharing electricity," our driver told us, because the infrastructure of Soweto hadn't improved highly since the end of apartheid in 1990. And this was 2007!

We stopped and visited the Nelson Mandela National Museum, or "Mandela House," as it's known, a red-brick one-story house where Nelson Mandela lived, and now a national treasure. It's just up the road from "Tutu House," the home of Archbishop Desmond Tutu (whom I had the fortune to meet when I was a performer for one of Sesame Workshop's gala fundraisers in New York and he was the special guest; and the man was — I am not joking — adorable. And danced — *danced* — onstage better than any Muppet ever could!). You can still see some bullet holes and chipped brick from hurled Molotov cocktails thrown at the outer walls of Mandela's home. Inside, the rooms felt cramped with some of the original furniture, along with displays of photos, citations, awards, medals, and even the championship boxing belt given to Mandela from Sugar Ray Leonard.

The Hector Pieterson Memorial and Museum is named after the young schoolboy who was shot and killed during the Soweto Uprising of June 16, 1976. It was the protest of thousands of high school and primary school children opposing the mandate of having Afrikaans (the language spoken by the original Dutch settlers of South Africa) taught to them. Hector was singing the government banned liberation anthem, "*Nkosi Sikelel'iAfrika,*" when he was shot and killed by an angry white officer, and the museum is two blocks away from where it happened. The whole facility is dedicated to that day and the many young people (around 200 of them) who gave their lives in the cause of freedom.

During our travels around Soweto and to the Mandela House and The Pieterson Museum, there was one sight that shook me and still does, to this day. I have never told anyone, not even my wife or my friends what I saw. But I will now.

We drove by an empty lot near the side of a hill, with garbage strewn all over the bottom of it. It was a pit for people to toss their garbage into and, not even in bags, just thrown garbage onto the grass. But then I saw two little girls, one at the most maybe nine years old and the other no older than five, rummaging through the garbage. Why?

"They are looking for food," our guide told us, "Because their families have thrown them out." These words hit me like a gut punch to my stomach.

The AIDS stigma in South Africa has most of the population believe that you can contract the disease by touching or even breathing the same air as a person who is HIV-positive. These girls had the disease and their families abandoned them. Threw them out. Like garbage. They never looked up towards us. They just kept searching for something to eat as we continued to drive on. My eyes welled up then and I have tears now, as I write this. This was why I was here and why Kami was so important. (And it bears repeating – I am so proud to be associated with Sesame Workshop.)

The next morning it was back to the studio. I walked in and shook hands with the two crew guys, and they asked what I did on my day off. Enjoy the hotel? Lounge by the pool?

"I went to Soweto."

There was a pause.

"What?" they asked. I could see they were genuinely surprised at my answer.

"I went to Soweto. I wanted to see it and got a tour and visited Mandela House and The Pieterson Museum. I loved it."

Just then, Kami's puppeteer arrived, and we went to work. Including working with one of the human cast members and instructing him, when the moment came to comfort Kami, to actually *touch* her, *hug* her, the way he would comfort any child. This was absolutely necessary to show.

At the end of the day, I packed up, turned around to the two guys, and said, "G'night. See ya tomorrow."

"Noel!" I heard one of the guys call out.

And that's when they both dropped their equipment, ran over to me, and extended their hands. I extended mine, and they both shook my hand — with "The Handshake."

Lights! Camera! Action!

I've gotten to puppeteer in movies, starting in 1983 with my first movie I worked on, for only one day of work. I would be Big Bird for the wedding scene of *"The Muppets Take Manhattan,"* the film directed by Frank Oz. It was shot on a sound stage in Long Island City, a neighborhood in Queens, New York, at Variety Scenic Studios, that also built the elaborate set; a huge chapel with pews, a center aisle, and stained-glass windows. Several of the walls could be removed to set up different camera angles, which is normal for custom built sets. The big difference with this one was that the whole set was raised five feet off the floor. Why? So that the puppeteers could comfortably stand and hold up the Muppets. And for this scene there were a *lot* of Muppets! Which requires a LOT of puppeteers; everyone and their grandmother was called in for this scene. And only ONE DAY to shoot it.

I and Bird were to be in the back, in the last row with the other Sesame Street characters, on the groom's side. Because Kermit, once upon a time, was part of Sesame Street. (At a puppetry conference at Boston's M.I.T. a couple of years later, Jim pulled out Kermit and Frank pulled out Cookie Monster, who proceeded to chide Kermit for abandoning his friends to go do *The Muppet Show,* become a big star, and "not have time to do alphabet," etc.) Because all the characters were to be "seated," I would only need the top half of Bird, just the neck and the head, and maybe a wing. I put on the monitor, got into position, and rehearsed with just my hand up over my head, as the other puppeteers around me were also doing. It was a shot that starts off with three bears walking in and as the camera follows them it stops to see the Sesame gang all excited for the wedding, one of those delightful character crossover/cameos fans love (and us, too). We rehearsed a couple of times for the camera to get the timing with the bears. Now it was time to shoot it. The puppets were brought over and so was Bird and …

My jaw dropped to the floor.

They brought the WRONG BIRD!

Let me explain.

Remember - Big Bird is a body *puppet*. Not a costume; a body puppet, a puppet you wear. That's how Carroll was able to perform him.

But there's *another* Bird.

This *other* Bird is used for photoshoots and for many years, the Macy's Thanksgiving Day Parade. And it's not a body puppet, it's not a puppet to perform. This really is a costume of a body puppet because, you don't put your hand up through the neck and move the head, and mouth, and animate the eyelids. Oh no, my friend. Oh no. This head is attached to the end of a metal structure, a deformed shrunken "Eiffel Tower," that is attached to – a *football helmet*, with a chin strap that is tightly snapped into place. Yes. One of those cheap early eighties helmets you'd buy at Woolworths (it was a store; Google it). But the head couldn't move; you'd have to rotate it into position, and that's where it would stay, cause if you leaned over to have Bird look down, you'd snap your neck from the top-heavy weight. I remember using this Bird for the Macy's parade, wearing it for two straight hours, and all this top-heavy weight on my head and neck, and I *hated* it. And now this Muppet monstrosity was being handed to me. *To perform!* For a *MOVIE*! For a pivotal scene! That will last *FOREVER*!

I immediately had to figure out how to perform the scene we just rehearsed, using this feathered statue. And I did. I had the head tipped down to have Bird look at the others around him, held onto the tower with one hand, so that his head would move left to right, without the whole neck moving, too (like a feathered hoop skirt). And I used my other hand to pull on the lower beak string to give him some, *any*, lip synch. When the scene was shot, there was a break to set up the next scene, and I went over to the Muppet area and asked the shop why the heck was the photo/parade Bird brought? They said that was what they were told was needed, that Bird wasn't doing much.

Wasn't *doing much*?!?

The next scene is THE SONG!

That he HAS TO *SING*!

With EVERYONE!!!

Oh … And did I mention there's *CHOREOGRAPHY*!?!? Of course, there was!

The typical Muppet choreography always starts on the right. Meaning the puppet leans to the right and then the left, and then back to right, left, right left, in time to the beat, adding little touches like a "bounce," or "double time," or throwing the head back for a long note, etc. For the song's chorus, with so many puppeteers of various skill levels, and to get the shot done, the choreography was "simple." And in order for Bird to do *exactly* what everyone else was doing, I held onto the bottom of the neck with one hand, yanked at the mouth string with the other, and turned my own head and leaned my body in time to everyone else. And I'm proud to say it worked; more than once, because you rarely get the scene shot on the first take. Go check out the scene on YouTube or whatever streaming service now exists and see.

My next movie experience was much better. In the following summer of 1984, I worked on the film *"Sesame Street Presents: Follow That Bird,"* Sesame's first full length movie. We shot it in a studio outside of Toronto, Canada. Yep, I was on my way to spend three months in *Canada*. I found my passport, dusted it off, pulled the suitcase out of the closet, and packed. I remember just before landing, looking out the window, and seeing Lake Ontario, and being shocked at how big it was. I knew it was a "great" lake but didn't realize "great" meant "mini ocean."

I (and Caroll and Debbie Spinney) lived for three months at The Royal York Hotel across from the train station and next to the harbor in Downtown Toronto. The Royal York (now the Fairmont Royal York) was once the largest hotel in North America, able to accommodate over one thousand guests. My room was at the end of an incredibly long hallway, and I half expected the twins from *The Shining* to greet me, when getting off the elevator. We would get driven to and from the studio, and any location sites, from the van that came for us and, during my days off, I would walk around and explore Toronto.

I loved the Toronto of 1984. My first impression was it was just like New York but "nicer." It had skyscrapers, a diverse population, a mass transit system of buses and subways, just like NYC. The exception was it was clean, I mean *no litter at all*; everyone was so nice (not to say we New Yorkers aren't nice, we're just always busy getting from point A to point B, which leaves no time for idle chit chat); the subways were immaculate, and the trolleys – yes, *trolleys* – were so much fun to ride on. I kept thinking of *Mister Rogers Neighborhood* and imagined riding to "The Neighborhood of Make-Believe."

Follow That Bird starred, yes, you guessed it, Big Bird. It's about how a do-gooder society, "The Feathered Friends," who feel the need to place birds with their own kind – bird families. As the movie opens, we see them and their leader, "Madame Chairbird," discussing this poor case of a young eight-foot-tall yellow bird living all alone "with no other birds around." I was the wrangler for Carroll and his stand-in for certain scenes, and even puppeteered for a couple of silent background characters. But I got to puppeteer and *voice* Madame Chairbird! I could not believe it and still don't know how it happened, and whose decision it was. I can only guess that Jim (Henson) somehow had final say in it, which makes me blush thinking about it. The day we did the scene, I had gotten such a head cold and ingested so many meds, I could not replicate the voice now without a doctor's prescription.

We shot on location all over the surrounding Ontario area, including a farm. Being the City Boy that I am I had never been to a farm in my life – the closest was the Central Park Zoo's Children's Zoo, and that was themed to storybook characters and Noah's Ark. During the night shoot in a hayloft, Big Bird sits and sings about his friends and missing them. Going up and down and hanging out in the loft creates a lot of dust. So, the next day I discovered I'm allergic to hay dust. So allergic that I had to go to the doctor, because I was having severe shortness of breath, even from walking, and was diagnosed with bronchitis *and* asthma. I was terrified I'd have to go home but, I got over it quickly with meds and still was able to do my job. I've also steered clear of any hay ever since.

On the sound stage was a replica of our Street set back in New York.

Sort of.

The normal set had painted floors, with the street, curb, and sidewalk all painted. But this set had an actual curb and I and others had to get use to stepping off the curb, almost falling a couple of times until it sank in. Oscar's trashcan was also slightly different because they painted and banged up a Canadian trashcan. The same was true for the fire hydrant; they painted it the black and grey colors of NYC hydrants, but the shape was different. But only we noticed this and if you are too busy concentrating on that, then the movie isn't working.

There's a scene in the movie where the Sesame Street gang go off to find Big Bird who's run away from his adopted bird family, The Dodos. Ernie and Bert are flying a bi-plane and Ernie turns the plane upside down to sing the song "Upside Down World," much to Bert's shock. Jim (Henson) and Frank (Oz) came to perform this, and I still am gobsmacked at how it was set up. There was a rig, built outside the studio, with a piece of the plane flipped over and a platform attached to the side for Jim and Frank to lay down on. And was suspended *fifteen feet in the air*, with the camera raised up, to shoot Ernie and Bert, flying upside down. Jim Henson and Frank Oz, the two most famous puppeteers ever, were suspended *fifteen feet in the air*! WHY?!? Green screen! Blue screen! But *noooooooo*. They actually built this, and Jim and Frank actually did it. (But since he performed the song "Rainbow Connection," in *"The Muppet Movie,"* submerged in a tank underwater, while puppeteering Kermit, for Jim, this was nothing.)

The best moment of the entire film is near the end. Once Big Bird is found and back home, Miss Finch, the ostrich like bird who was relentlessly tracking him down, comes to take him back to "The Dodos." But Maria tells her that Big Bird is loved and does have a family on *Sesame Street.* And not just birds; monsters, people, cows, grouches, dogs, honkers, you name it. To prove all this, the camera rotates around to show this crowd on *Sesame Street.* Except …

They didn't hire enough extras for the background.

So, they asked all of us, *everyone*, to be in the shot, and fill the frame. It became this wonderful moment showing all the people who helped create the film, and when the camera rotates around you see – monsters; and a cow; a dog; and the husband of Sonia Manzano (who plays Maria); and Carrol's wife, Debbie Spinney; and the grips; and the prop department; and Muppet wranglers; and the accounting department; even a very young and very skinny *me*; and even my mom! Yep, Edna MacNeal, who came to visit, ended up in *two* scenes in the movie!

A few years ago, I took my young son to see it, screened for the thirtieth anniversary at NYC's Museum of The Moving Image, and he loved it. The message that the people who love you, are your family, still rings true, now more than ever. Tony Giess and Judy Friedberg were two of the best writers *Sesame Street* ever had, and ever will. One premise for a film was Big Bird dreaming he's elected President of the United States and when an evil organization pushes him off Air Force One, it's when Big Bird finally learns to fly. But instead, they wrote this touching, sweet, sincere movie that rings true to the message that *Sesame Street* still promotes today:

Family. Friendship. And love.

In mid-August of 1988, Jim Kroupa's company, Three Design Studio (with partners Matt Stoddart and John Orberg, along with their employee Phillip "Kip" Rathke) were hired to create the practical puppet elements for the fantasy movie *"Little Monsters,"* starring Howie Mandel and a child actor named Fred Savage. It was being shot in the Dino DeLaurentis Studios (now the EUE/Screen Gem Studios) located in Wilmington, North Carolina. The premise of the movie is that Fred and his little brother (played by his real-life little brother Ben Savage) discover that monsters *do* live under your bed; that the darkness underneath is a portal to the monster world. Puppeteer Pam Arciero and I were hired to come down to help puppeteer the effects, such as disembodied hands, and clothes that move by themselves. And we flew down for the two weeks we'd be needed.

The workshop was in the same building as the production offices, an old used car lot showroom. And the guys had it completely setup for building the effects, even bringing down tools and supplies from NYC. Pam and I came by to check things out and practice with one of the rigs for the scene that was coming up in the next few days. Then, one morning, the guys called and asked if they could see us before we headed to the offices. Pam and I met them outside the motel we were all staying in, and – their faces. The expression on their faces. There was no color on any of them. They looked shocked. Pam and I braced wondering "Who died?"

"It's gone," they said.

"What's 'gone'?" I asked.

"Everything. It's all gone.".

"What's all gone?" But they told us.

Earlier the four of them went to the offices and when they got there, the facility was all but burned to the ground. There had been a fire sometime during the night and the entire building was engulfed. All the rigs they'd built, the supplies and materials, the tools, everything in the shop, was gone. And not just their shop; the offices for paperwork and some costuming had also been destroyed in the blaze. There was practically nothing left.

Needless to say, we all got the day off. And it would be several days until the guys and anyone else from the production would be allowed to go in and salvage whatever was possible from the site once it was deemed safe. The production went on hold for the next few days until the decision to continue was made. Luckily, the insurance from the production company had kicked in and more than covered the cost of everything lost in the fire.

Production cranked up again, filming scenes that didn't require the puppetry effects, to give time for the guys to rebuild. The new shop was set up in one part of a small sound stage not being used on the studio lot, and Pam and I had new duties; "shop runners." Whatever supplies and materials they needed we would drive around the area and find it, or the closest to it. And keep in mind this was 1988 – no cellphones and no internet to check places online. There was no "online." We would have to call the store from the number in the Yellow Pages and ask, and then, drive there, and then, find a pay phone, and then, call the guys and confirm with them. Other stuff that could not be gotten locally was shipped down.

The other task Pam and I assigned ourselves was to go in search of new/better lodgings for all of us. She and I realized that our "two weeks" stint was going to last a lot longer – it would end up being two *months* – and the little motel was not going to cut it for that long. We drove around and finally found a place, the Silver Gull Motel, whose rooms included a kitchen, with full size refrigerators, microwaves, stove burners; it was practically an apartment … with balconies! And the best part – it was on the beach, near Johnnie Mercer pier. And with six of us moving in at the end of their season, we even got a break in the rate. Perfect. Huzzah for haggling!

Once everything was set up again, Pam and I also helped out in the shop when we could. And then we *finally* got to go on camera, with the effects we were meant to do over a month ago! All the effects the guys created worked perfectly and everyone was impressed, especially Howie and Fred, who were so easy and fun to work with. (One day I was video recording in the backlot, and I came upon Fred and his siblings, who joked "no paparazzi," and started chasing me away.) We enjoyed the beach, while the warm weather lasted, with the one day off per week we had, and I even had to go shopping for clothes at Kmart, cause my shorts and t-shirts were not going to work in the increasingly cool weather. I even bought a skull Hawaiian shirt for Halloween, which I still have. For the perky and pastel hued 1980s, *"Little Monsters"* was kinda dark and deep, and now considered a cult classic. Who knew?

In the summer of 1992, I got to puppeteer on the third live-action Teenage Mutant Ninja Turtle Movie entitled, *"Teenage Mutant Ninja Turtles Movie III."* So clever. The tagline on the poster was "The Turtles are back … in time," referencing that the four bros would travel back in time, to feudal Japan, to save their friend April. The first two movies were successful, thanks to the magic of the Jim Henson Creature Shop, bringing the Turtles and their mentor, "Splinter" the Rat, to life. The new cutting-edge technology of remote-controlled facial expressions for the characters with never-before-created remote stations was what made the characters believable in the real world. So, I was thrilled to be working on it … except … The Jim Henson Creature Shop wasn't asked back. Instead, another company was hired. To recreate The Jim Henson Creature Shop animatronic rigs; their own versions of the same tech the Creature Shop had previously invented.

I got flown to Portland, Oregon and drove up two hours to the town of Astoria. There was a studio for all the interior sets but, locations in the nearby mountains would be the setting of the Japanese village, being constructed. Because luckily, due to the lack of actual time travel, Oregon easily subbed in as feudal Japan.

It takes five people to be one Ninja Turtle. There's –

The Puppeteer … who uses the remote-control system to animate the Turtle's face.

The Actor … stuck inside the glorified rubber suit that's the Turtle's body and the head, with the servos and wires grinding into his ears.

The Martial Artist … who does all the actual choreographed fighting for the scenes.

The Stunt Double … because for this movie the Turtles had to ride horses – and fall off them.

And finally…

The Voice Actor … who, after all the scenes and principal photography is shot, just gets to sit in a recording studio, with multiple Perrier waters, and dub his voice over all the lines for that Turtle.

I was familiar with the characters and knew about the one I was assigned to – "Raphael" or "Raph" as he was often called by the others. He had an edge and not one to be over sentimental, even sarcastic, but with a generous heart. In other words, I was type cast.

The other Turtle puppeteers were ones I knew and worked with: Jim Martin, who was given Leonardo, and who I've known since working on the TV series *"The Great Space Coaster;"* Rick Lyon, who worked with The Muppets and would later on, create the puppets for, and co-star, in the Tony Award winning Broadway musical "Avenue Q"; and Gordon "Gordie" Robertson, who puppeteered on *Fraggle Rock* and I'd met and worked with on *"Follow That Bird."* For Turtles, Gordie was also our "Puppet Captain" (there's that phrase again) and would be the liaison between us and the effects shop, and the rest of the production. In between figuring out, programming, and practicing with our animatronic stations and the heads, he'd have us, in the early days, do "acting exercises" as a group, which I found, well, odd. I wanted to play around and work out the facial expressions for Raph's head, not sit around and play games like "Continue the Story." But his philosophy was that we should all create a bond with one another; the Turtles have it, so should we. And he was right. I did not know him well, and he didn't know Jim or Rick at all, so in time, we appreciated the moments we would do the games. But the real bond I had was yet to come.

The best part of working on the film was meeting and working with *my* Turtle actor, Matt Hill. Matt is a Canadian actor, voice actor, and has since also become an advocate for social change and a motivational speaker. But when I first met him, through a group game Gordie had begun with us and the other Turtle actors, I looked at Matt, with his curly blonde hair, looking like he'd lost his surfboard, and I thought, "Who *is* this kid?" After the game, Gordie then had us all pair off with each other, and get to know each other, and our Turtle. So, Matt and I headed outside to meet "Raph." I had a notebook with me, and he and I sat on the hood of one of the two rental cars the puppeteers had and began to talk. We talked about who we were, where we were from, and how that could relate to Raph and his personality. And we *clicked*. It was kinda like that moment in a first date when you just know you and this other person have something; a connection; a genuine bond, that doesn't have to be forced. That's what happened with Matt and me. And together we gave Raph the heart and soul needed to make this gruff guy likable, mainly thanks to Matt's talent and his Solomon patience inside that damn suit. And we've been "Turtle Bros" ever since.

I have one more story to share from this film, and I love this story, even if I'm not the brunt of it. But first some context.

The animatronic stations were quite similar to The Jim Henson Creature Shop's, especially in the setup. The station was a rectangular metal box that, when closed, was about four feet tall. This was so that they could be mobile. Remember, unlike the first movie, this one had location shoots in the neighboring mountains, so they had to be portable and placed on an "apple box" (the industry term for a wooden box 20" X 12" X 8" in diameter). With the lid off there was, as I called it, an "electronic oven mitt," a foam mitt that you could open and close to animate the mouth and that rested atop a small tower that you could move forward and backward, and all hooked up with wires. This was to give the mouth expressions allowing the lips and corner "muscles" to move and give exact(ish) articulation when the Turtles talked. To its left was a panel that had a knob that controlled the eyes and the eyelids. To the right side was a panel that, when popped open, a tray slid out that had a small laptop computer on it. Now, the computer is what you used to program in specific moves for the eyes and mouth. If you ever played a fighting video game like "Tekken" or "Mortal Kombat," all those combos you use for strikes? That was all preprogrammed so that you could use them. Same theory here.

Now for the story.

We each had our stations and our heads, and, in the rehearsal room, each head was on a long table, about seven to eight feet away from its respective station. From left to right there was Rick's and Donatello's head (aka "Donny"); then Gordie's and Michelangelo (aka "Mikey"); me and Raph; and finally, Jim's and Leonardo's head (aka "Leo"). These were elaborate and complicated pieces of machinery that had to work. And every now and then there would be a glitch, or something would not quite work. But Donny's head was the best, followed by Gordie's, then mine, and then – if a puppet could actually be cursed, it was the head of Leonardo. Poor Jim constantly had issues with the head, and it would be taken back to the shop and replaced with the backup head (which all the Turtles had) to work with. Then one day, the two technicians from the shop proudly paraded in the primo Leo head, all fixed, issues gone, promising there wouldn't ever be a problem again. They set it down on the table and told Jim to turn it on (aka to synch up with his station). Which he did. All Jim did was flip the switch.

Immediately, the head violently shook for three seconds, and then, every orifice opens wide; the eyelids, the lips, the mouth exposing all the teeth, and – and I kid you not - a *bolt* from the back of the mouth shoots straight out the mouth, across the room, and hits the front of Jim's station, landing on the floor. The two guys say nothing; they silently pick up the head and carry it back to the shop, while Rick, Gordie, and I are in hysterics, tears in our eyes. At the time Jim did not see the humor, but since then, he has. I love Jim Martin. He is one of the most sincere and dedicated people I have ever met as a puppeteer, as a director, and, especially as a friend, and would work with him, again, in a heartbeat. (I'd just make sure to duck when near his animatronic puppet.)

NBC's "The Wiz – LIVE"

Me & Fynnias

Believe

Taking a break

In Arisaig, Scotland

Bear & Big Bird

Best bros part one

Best bros part two

Boo at the Zoo Spider

The Carnival of Extraordinary Animals at The Bronx Zoo

Chillin

Roscoe Orman as Sesame Street's "Gordon"

Christmas Sweater

Christmas with Mom

In a cornfield

Stayin' fit

It's us!

With Jim Kroupa

Me & Bear

Me & Leon at Shea Stadium

LWT Desk

Maggie Hope series

Matt Hill as Raph

Me & Fynnias

Me on the Balcony

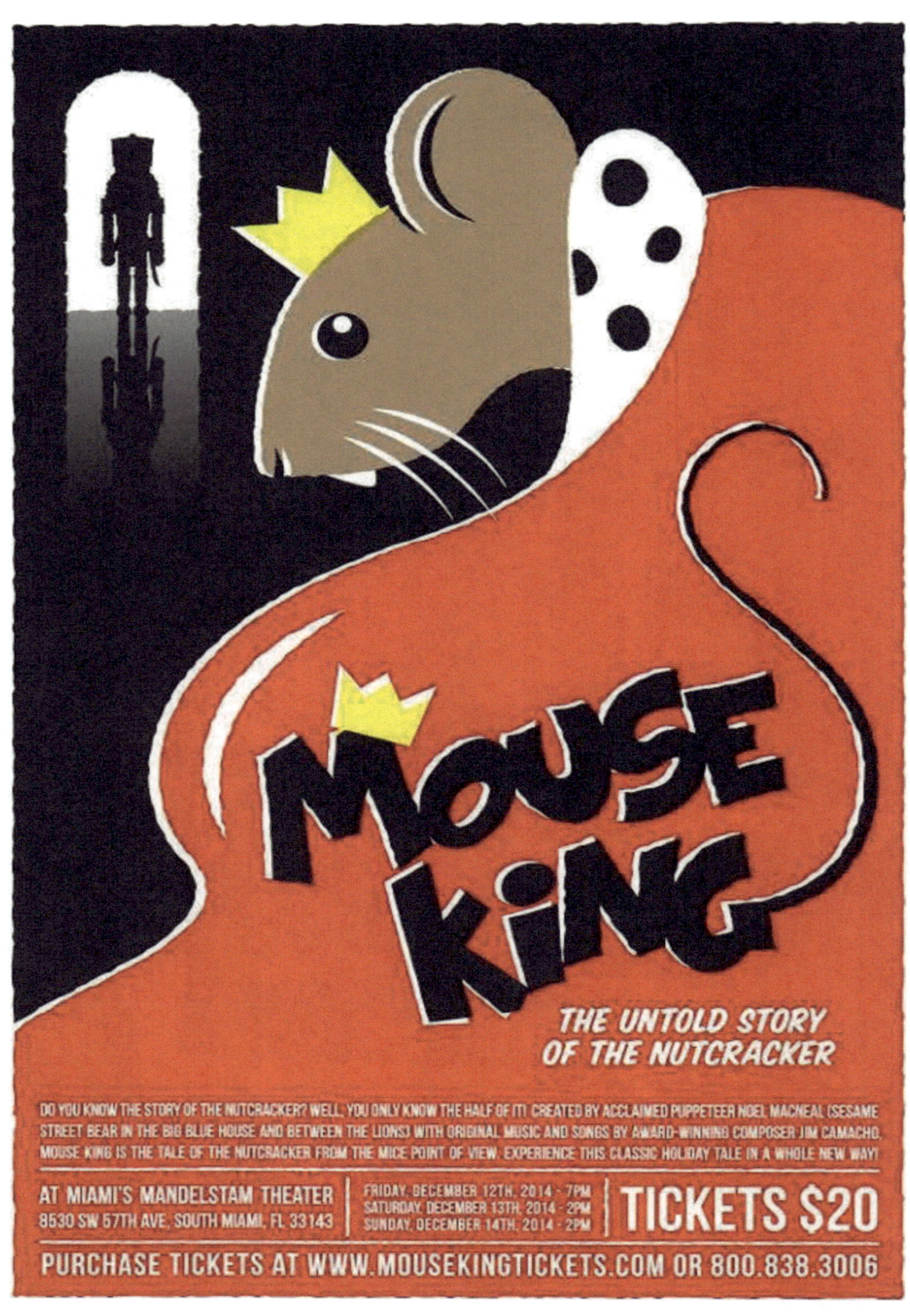

MOUSE KING poster

Me & Kako

Me & Magellan

Noel Street

Paris

Programming toys

With Caroll Spinney

With actor Rob McClure

As a Seagull

Wedding Day

With Susan

Mom

Noel MacNeal

"... But, remember what happened to the man who got everything he ever wanted ... he lived happily ever after."

—Willy Wonka

Likes: the Muppets, winter, cheesecake, cartoons, my friends at Rhodes, autumn, vacation, soft ice cream, good music, puppetmaking
Dislikes: homework, muggy days, crowds, loud people, boring books that are assigned
Will remember: all my friends and the teachers I've found particularly "human" (Mr. Moore, Ms. Orlando, Miss Rodrigues, Mr. Sullivan, Mrs. Berne, Miss Bogart, Miss Conter, Ms. Cohen, Miss Hall)
Would Rather Forget: the difficulty in getting a change in schedule
Achievements: Rhodes Reporter, Yearbook '79, Art awards '74-'78, David A. Riddle Debating Award, Drama Club, Science Fair '74-'78

Yearbook

PART THREE

"Picnic Time!"

In the summer of 1989, I began working on a show for Nick Jr., the new preschool block of shows for Nickelodeon. Previously, there was the three-to-four-hour block of shows under the heading of *"Pinwheel."* The shows were all acquisitions from other countries (but mostly Canada). But *this* new show was going to be the first *original preschool* series produced by Nick, with money coming from the profits made from their original tween series, the game show called *"Double Dare."*

"Eureeka's Castle" had an all puppet cast set in the music box of a giant. (If you have never heard or seen this show, really take a moment to absorb this concept.) The lead character was the young wizard-in-training, "Eureeka" (delightfully played by Cheryl Blaylock), who had a big heart towards her friends, which compensated for her magic not being the best; before there was Hogwarts and Hermione Granger, there was Eureeka. (The puppet also had these "curly horns" coming out of her blonde hair; imagine a croissant cut in half and jammed into your hair and that's the look I'm talking about.) Her friends that resided in the castle along with her were: "Batly," a spoiled, self-absorbed bat (played to the hilt by my friend, the incredibly talented Jim Kroupa, whose shop, 3 Design Studios, built all of the puppets - and the puppet was physically modeled after a Nick Jr. executive, who was more flattered than insulted); the bratty "Moat Twins, Bogg & Quagmire" (played with mischievous glee by Brian Meehl and Pam Arciero, respectively); "Mr. Knack" (also played by Brian Meehl), who had an interesting accent, and wore, what looked like pajamas and an aviator's hat (to which Muppet performer Richard Hunt once asked him, "Who's the East Indian aviator?"). Also in the castle cast were "The Mice:" the octogenarian "Sir Clank" (played by Jim); "Emma," the over-eating mouse (played by Pam); and roving rodent reporter (say *that* five times fast), "Kate" (played so wonderfully by Lynn Hippen); who all lived in a suit of armor. Oh yeah – and *my* characters; "Magellan," the very large (the size of Big Bird) "baby" dragon, who had a little dog-like pet, named "Cooey" (played with such mischief by Lynn); and my other character "Webbster," Batly's grumpy pet spider, who'd growl and spit when speaking (think Looney Tunes' Tasmanian Devil).

The head writer was a chap who used the moniker "Jovial Bob Stine." I'm not kidding. A great easy-going fellow who, unfortunately, had never written for puppets before. We'd have read-throughs during lunch, where we'd read the upcoming scripts and discuss what props would be needed and how it could be shot. I and the other puppeteers always made suggestions to have the scene be more visually entertaining (aka funnier). Sometimes they'd be excepted by the executive producer, but sometimes not, especially when we knew we were right and that it would work. That's when we all decided that from then on, we'd just do the gags on camera; we'd wait until we were on set, even rehearse the script as written, but once the cameras were rolling, we'd do the gag(s) we knew would work. So odd how some people in a visual medium such as television have to first *see* it in order to *get* it.

We shot the show in the summer of 1989 at a studio on 42nd Street, off Ninth Avenue, in Manhattan. The studio was large enough to accommodate the main castle courtyard and all the separate sets: Batly's belfry; the Moat chamber; Eureeka's lab and connecting kitchen; and Magellan's lair. There was also a side area for when the characters had their band and sing, and the even rarer human performers, who would come to sing. I guess whenever the Giant turned the ginormous key, this is where the music came from. Or maybe he just kidnapped traveling musicians.

There were lots of songs, too, from "The Fishtones," the statuary fountain of three fish who'd sing in harmony (and voiced by music director Peter Lurye, who would years later be the music director for *Bear in the Big Blue House*). Two puppeteers for three fish; one puppeteer for the center and the second puppeteer doing the other two. Eureeka and Mr. Knack had practical hands so they would, when possible, get a "right hand" but, Brian liked to just do the head for Knack and let the second puppeteer do both, since Knack was always handling props. I quite enjoyed doing Knack's hands; they could never be too outlandish. (And Brian had this habit with Knack of crossing his fingers of his left hand and jabbing them downward, as Knack spoke. We finally pointed it out to him, and he had no idea he was doing it, let alone why. Maybe to be lucky enough to get the bit in one take?) Magellan, however, could have *three* people for the complete illusion;

me inside; someone outside doing his right hand; and a third puppeteer for his tail (that seemed to have a mind of its own).

One gag we often did was Batly crashing into a scene and him rising, unfazed, with a triumphant "I meant to do that!" (Ah … catchphrases. More on that later.) To do this, there was a second Batly that was full body and wired to pose him in any position. Someone like myself would hurl the "stunt double" and, as soon as it "landed," Jim would pop up the puppet. Batly would fly through the window into Eureeka's lab, but also fly out of it. Which we had to stop. Why? Because at that time The Walt Disney Company released, onto VHS, their classic animated film *"Peter Pan,"* and suddenly parental groups were concerned that kids might start flinging themselves out windows to "fly to Neverland." So, Nick Jr., too was concerned, and Batly could no longer fly *out* the windows. But flying *in* through a window and land with a crash and a groan? Oh yeah, that was still OK.

Eureeka was my first time as a principal puppeteer with a lead character. Since he was completely similar to Big Bird, I used every trick Caroll ever taught me. I wore a monitor on my chest with the mike attached; my right arm went up through the neck into his head; and my left arm into his left arm. All the sets were raised five feet to allow the other puppeteers to stand and perform. But Magellan had to be taller than the other characters. So, I had to walk along and stand on platforms and runways, clamped together, with boards screwed in along the sides for my feet to feel and to keep me from falling - and crushing my fellow cast members. (I would do a similar set up again for another character, who would own a big blue house, but I'm getting ahead of myself.)

For the second season of Eureeka's, I asked and got accepted as a writer for the show. I wrote several scripts for the show and was always surprised when props and costumes were actually made for the bits. (Again, this was my first time as a writer, so I was impressed.) I even got to co-write the holiday special *"Christmas at Eureeka's Castle"* (along with Brian, Jim, and "Jovial Bob"). What was wonderful about the series is that it had no curriculum to adhere to (other than making sure not to encourage children to leap out of windows). A few of my favorite scripts involved Batly and Magellan, but one still stands out. Magellan always tries to get Cooey to do tricks, who always refuses. So, he creates a circus to inspire his pet and Batly gets roped into showing how to do the tricks first. This bit had all of us involved; me as Magellan, Lynn as Cooey, Jim as Batly, and Brian, Pam, and Cheryl tossing and catching "stunt Batly" (and "stunt Cooey"). When it's time for the last trick, "fetch," Batly hands the stick to Magellan, who's so eager, he doesn't realize Batly is still hanging on and flings it, sending his best friend flying across the courtyard. After this first-time experience as a series writer, I knew I wanted to do this again and add this skill to my resumé.

In May of 1990, we were back in the studio for season two, and one day, Nickelodeon president, Geraldine Laybourne came by to visit. The show was a ratings hit, and critics loved it. I remember seeing her and we talked just before we wrapped for the day, and she was so excited with big news; Nick had just signed a creative deal with Jim Henson. She was thrilled and we speculated about the kinds of shows and projects Jim would dream up for Nick. With his imagination the possibilities would be endless. This was the evening of May 15.

The next morning, we were all on set getting ready for a bit to do when our audio engineer came in to give us our mikes and said, …

"Hey puppeteers. Jim Henson died."

We just looked at him.

"What do you mean Jim Henson *died*?!?" we asked.

"Just heard it," he said adjusting the cables around us.

Just then, a five-minute break was called, and we were told that the executive producer wanted to see all of us in the green room. We all went in, and he came in looking concerned.

“I have some bad news to share with you,” he began, “I just found out … Jim Henson has died.”

“We know,” we said, his face looking confused hearing this and us explaining the audio engineer just blurted it out.

He was annoyed that we had found out that way, but not because he was the one that wanted to do it; and our audio guy didn’t mean to just blurt it out, either. It just happened that way and didn’t take away from the shock we were all feeling, especially for Cheryl, Pam, Brian, Jim, and me. We all knew Jim, worked with Jim, and to suddenly hear this, and wrap our heads around it was, well, a lot. For us the break lasted longer than five minutes, but then we all went back into the studio and finished out the day.

On May 21st, we all got the morning off to attend the memorial service for Jim at The Cathedral of St. John the Divine, on 112th St in Manhattan. It’s a stunning structure whose exterior is yet to be completed. (My nickname for it is “The Cathedral of St. John the Unfinished.”) Inside, however, it is glorious with its soaring columns and vaulted ceiling. The highlight is the round stained-glass window in the front. The memorial was to be a celebration of this extraordinary man, who requested, in the event of his death, that it not be a sad occasion; thus no one wear black.

“Darn,” my mom said, “I have this perfect little black dress.” She was not the only female I knew who lamented this.

My mom and I entered the Cathedral just as the organ began to play “Rainbow Connection.” I saw my mom’s lip quiver and, arm in arm, we found seats. The whole service was lovely with readings and music (and you can view it on YouTube) and when it was done, I got my mom into a cab home, and then met up with the other puppeteers, and we made our way down to the studio. We were sad, but also empowered; Jim had inspired all of us and he’d want us to go on and inspire others.

The first half of season two was shot in New York; but the second half would be shot in the new (still being finished) Nickelodeon Studios at the (still being finished) Universal Studios in Orlando, Florida. After we wrapped season two part one in June, my mom and I went to Disney World for a couple of days. While down there I arranged for us to visit the new Universal Studios that had just opened. We got a tour of the new Nick Studios and then were escorted around the park and onto rides … a few of which still needing work. For example, the JAWS boat ride would have been a bit more terrifying had the water not been crystal clear and you could see ALL of the tracks and hydraulics and shark parts, taking turns to rise and lower and lunge for the boat. It's now part of the park's past – in its place is an area called "Diagon Alley" (inspired by some book series, I think – "Harry … Something" – anyway…).

In October of 1990, we all (plus our director Hugh Martin, who is one of the best in the business) headed down to Orlando and stayed at "The Vinings," a temporary housing complex complete with full kitchens, a tennis court, and a pool. Being Florida, of 1990, my apartment's furnishings were straight out of an episode of *"The Golden Girls."* I've never seen so much whicker and ratan seating. The apartments were sixty minutes away from Universal (but only fifteen minutes away from Walt Disney World). Our sound stage was huge and all the sets that fitted in the NYC studio, now had room to spare at Universal. There was a whole half of the space we never used. Above us, along the wall was "The Tube;" the glass walled hallway tourists used to go on their guided tours of the studios. Orlando, at that time, was going to be the "Hollywood of the East," with movie and television productions to be shot there. To compete with Disney, who'd built The Disney MGM Studios (and it will always be The Disney MGM Studios to me), Universal Studios was built; just like Disney's, it was half theme park, half production studios. They had the game show "Double Dare" shot there and now it was our turn.

Jim and I had fun with the tourists. Upstairs, the control room and audio room were next door to each other, with a clear glass backwall that tourists walking by could see what the director, assistant director, producers, and audio were doing. They knew who each person was because the chairs had the titles written on the backs. Once, during a rare scene that neither of us were in, Jim and I went upstairs to the control room. We each sat in a "PRODUCER" chair, each with a wad of single one-dollar bills in our hands and, as a tour went by, with our backs to them, we started to casually toss the money over our shoulders. On set, we had "production assistants" who got whatever was needed, for a scene or in the offices, wearing t-shirts with the letters "PA" printed on the back. But there was also the "*faux* PA," who worked for the park, with a mike to tell the tour guide and guests up in the tube what was happening on set. Once, just as we broke for lunch, a tour was coming through. I stood next to the "PA" who introduced me, and I said, …

"You all are just in time. We have just begun the highly complicated process called … 'Lunch!' What happens now is I, and everyone, else goes to … *lunch,* for the next hour. So, if you what to see what happens *after* lunch, come back in an hour. In the meantime, … you can ride JAWS – oh - wait that's not working. Well, there's KONG – nope; that's down too. Well, … enjoy your day at Universal Studios!"

Our day would end when the park's day ended at 6:00pm. But if we wrapped a few minutes early there was one ride, *the ride*, we loved going on. We'd make the call and ask if BACK TO THE FUTURE was still open. This was one of the original rides that opened the park and still, to me, one of the best rides ever created. The premise was Biff has stolen the DeLorean and Doc Brown (played by Christopher Lloyd) needs your help to get it back. Luckily, Doc has his prototype six-seater DeLorean already for us. You put on the 3D glasses, the car rises up and – you're off on a rollicking trip through time (courtesy of the four-story screen in front of you)! We'd call over and, hearing "we're closing in five minutes," race across the park, running past and around the last straggling guests, and make it just in time, completely out of breath. But worth it.

We did the Christmas special while we were there, plus two more and … that was it. I remember, on the last day of production, doing a song Magellan sings, "Gee, It's Great to be a Dragon," and Brian said, …

"You know Noel, this is probably the last time you'll be Magellan."

And he was right.

We wrapped Eureeka's, came back to NYC, and the show ran in reruns, first in its original hour length, and then trimmed down to thirty minutes. The show ran in reruns for over ten years and as of me writing this, the first season has been streaming on the Paramount Plus streaming service. I loved working on Eureeka and working with such talented people. I learned a lot from the experience and have taken those lessons of comradery and team-playing with me. It was fun, silly, and nice to know that people still remember it, fondly.

Oh!

By the way … that guy, “Jovial Bob?” He also continued to be a writer after the series wrapped, but of books for children. And using his real initials – R.L. Stine. Yeah – *THAT* R.L. Stine; of the “Goosebumps” and “Fear Street” series. From what I hear, he’s doing OK.

"We're Going to *The Puzzle Place*!"

In the fall of 1993, I auditioned for a part on a new children's series for PBS. It was a series of multi-ethnic humanoid puppets, all kids in age and appearance, that had been shopped around earlier, but no one was interested. But then in 1992, after the Rodney King verdict and the Los Angeles riots that resulted from it, local PBS station KCET Los Angeles was interested. They contacted the production company behind the project, Lancit Media (who produced *Reading Rainbow*), and said that they would co-produce it, all 65 episodes. KCET felt that a show for children showing diversity, learning tolerance, and friendship was desperately needed.

The show was called … *The Puzzle Factory*.

Then it was called … *The Puzzle Works*.

I auditioned for the character named "Leon," a smart, wise-cracking, fun-loving seven-year-old from New York City. I went to the Manhattan offices of Lancit Media and put the puppet on. Leon was a rod puppet, meaning the rods were attached to his wrists, but there was this cool mechanism at the end of one. I could ride the lever up and down with my thumb and his eye lids would pop open or lower to give him this half-lid expression. He was brown skinned with dreadlocks, and I loved him. But knowing it was just an audition, I had fun and promptly forgot about it once I left.

A few days later I got a call from the executive producer. She told me that they would love for me to be Leon.

"Thank you," I said, "It seems like kismet, though, seeing what 'Leon' spelt backwards is."

There was a pause and then…

"OH MY GOD!" she exclaimed.

The one stipulation of the agreement with KCET was that it had be shot in their studios. In Los Angeles. So, in January of 1994, I'd be heading to Los Angeles. Except on January 17, 1994, North Ridge was hit with a severe pre-dawn earthquake, whose aftershocks were affecting all of Los Angeles. KCET's studio would have to be inspected and then cleared for safety, which meant production was postponed over a month.

In late February, my mom had a friend who owned a limousine service and arranged with him to take me and three of my costars — Alice Dinnean ("Julie"), Carmen Oshbar ("Kiki"), and Allison Mork ("Jody") — to the airport, since we were all on the same flight. Of course, I didn't tell them a limousine was picking them up, so it was most satisfying for me and my mom (who naturally came along — a ride in a limousine? Do you have to ask? This *is* Edna MacNeal we're talking about.). She told us, "You don't know how this will all end, but you'll always remember how it started." Sound familiar?

After a week at the first place the production set up for us (which now included Peter Linz as "Skye" and Jim Martin as "Ben"), Alice took on the task of finding something much better. And she succeeded. We got furnished apartments at The Oakwoods, joked about on *The Larry Sanders Show* as the place newly separated or divorced men transition to. It was also March and overrun with kids and their stage moms, because it was still "pilot season," the month when Hollywood commissions pilots for possible TV series. I got a studio apartment with a murphy bed. (For the second season, which lasted three months, I upgraded and got a one-bedroom with a balcony.) The aftershocks were free. Sitting one evening on the couch and suddenly feeling like a giant hand smacked the wall behind me, I learned to sleep with my shoes next to the bed, and a flashlight on the night table, in case I had to evacuate in the middle of the night. But the shocks faded as time passed, so that by the end of the six months of living there, no hint of them.

The Puzzle Place was shot at the studios of KCET Los Angeles along Sunset Boulevard, near Los Feliz. Every morning we'd each drive the cars provided to us to the studio. Except one morning I couldn't. I had upgraded myself to a 1994 Ford Mustang convertible. (Hey — when in L.A., baby!) I had it less than a week when I got in, turned the key and… nothing. Absolutely nothing. And my knowledge of cars and engines had run its course — *"turn key, car start; turn key again, why car no start?"*

I called a cab and got to the studio and told the production what had happened. I gave them the keys and they contacted the car rental company, which apologized (and I found out that not only do cars have a "battery," but sometimes they just die) and was told they would replace it, even bring it to the studio. However, they no longer had convertibles, so they would give me an upgraded car for the same rate. "Ok," I thought, "But what's more expensive than a convertible?"

I was handed the keys and walked to the parking garage and beheld my new wheels. Oh. My. Gods. A 1994 white Cadillac Sedan Deville. With a pale blue leather interior. I went from a blue convertible to a boat, because that's what it felt like driving it. Behind the wheel, the hood went on for a mile in front of me. I could wiggle the steering wheel before it even got to turning the wheels. It went from zero to sixty in fifteen seconds. And the back seat could hold an entire Little League team. Or in my case, the rest of my cast members. I nicknamed it *The Seacrest*, in honor of the NBC series at the time, about a submarine. When going out to dinner and wanting to try a new restaurant, I'd hear, "And Noel? Could we take *The Seacrest*?" Sure kids, pile in; daddy's driving.

We shot the series in KCET's main studio, big enough to hold the whole raised set and room for any "swing sets" (the ones set up to be a restaurant; or Leon's living room; or where The Piece Police, the "adultish" monochromatic squad, who talked in gibberish, and maintained the Place, lived). We had several directors for seasons one and two, including "Savage" Steve Holland, who directed the John Cusack movie *Better Off Dead* and would go on to create the witty FoxKids series *Eek the Cat* ("Kumbaya!"). He was fun, funny, and great to hang out with.

He once invited the cast to his house for a party he was throwing. My mom happened to be visiting me, staying at the Universal Hilton, and I asked if she could come. "Of course," he said without hesitation. Savage's house was up in the Hollywood Hills with a stunning view of Los Angeles below. It had an inground pool … and a secret room behind a bookcase! This was something I promised myself to get one day (along with a swing in the living room I would add to my interior design list, based on another show I would get to work on).

Two of his guests still stand out in my memory. One was Gary Owens, the announcer for the NBC TV series *Laugh-In*, who always began each episode with "From beautiful Downtown Burbank…" The other was Kato Kalin, the guy who lived in O.J. Simpson's pool house. Yes. Take a moment to let *that* sink in. And these two charming men LOVED my mother. But of course, who didn't. She even charmed Gary Owens into saying her name as an announcement; he even cupped his hand up to his ear, as he did on *Laugh-In*: "From the beautiful Hollywood Hills, it's Edna MacNeal!" (Speaking of O.J. — you know that famous "ride" he took in his white Bronco? Well, on that June 17, 1994, he headed north along the 405. I was with my mom in her room at the Universal Hilton, and we happened to catch it on TV when, suddenly, we heard helicopters. We ran to the window that just happened to look down onto the 405 and — we saw the White Bronco roll by!)

On that visit, mom also came to the studio. That day, we had a guest star play Leon's dad, actor Terence "TC" Carson, from the hit sitcom *Living Single*. (Imagine the series *Friends* before *Friends*, with a black cast and funnier.) Having a human actor play his dad was just part of the weird aspect of the show — all the kid characters had human relatives. TC was great, funny, and totally game to be the father of a puppet. And *none* of the producers knew who he was. He was cast, but there was no Google, no IMDB, no internet to look up the guy. Not *one* of them had seen the show or knew who he was.

But Edna MacNeal did.

And she gushed and made him feel like a million bucks. One of the producers came over to me, as mom, seated in a director's chair next to TC in another, was laughing and chatting with him.

"Noel!" she said, "Thank GOD for your mother!"

I loved working on *The Puzzle Place*. And I loved writing for it. It was the second series I got to be a writer on after *Eureeka's Castle*. My favorite episode to write was "Dressing Up is Hard to Do" (the title being a take-off of the song title "Breaking Up is Hard to Do"). In it, the kids want to have a party and get excited about throwing a "grown-up party." "We'll act like grown-ups. We'll dress like grown-ups," Julie states. The Piece Police have turned the main room into a department store and as Leon proudly leads the boys to the "men's section," Jody can't find an outfit she likes. Julie decides to help her, but Jody ends up finding, and loving, a fuzzy pink sweater with a bunny stitched on the front, and a matching pillbox hat, with bunny ears. Julie is appalled that Jody would want to wear all of it and hurls the most offensive insult a seven-year-old can say to another:

"You look like a BABY!"

And she storms off vowing not to attend the party if Jody wears the outfit.

At the party, Jody does indeed show up in her outfit, and the others all love it, except Julie, who storms off to the kitchen. There, Leon in his purple crushed velvet jacket and bow tie (I told our costumer, the great Joe Self, to think "James Brown" for Leon) and sees Julie for the first time in her pink taffeta gown and matching crown and comments that she looks like "The Queen of the Planet of Very WIDE Shoulder Pads." Julie cannot believe he said that; she loves her outfit, and it was her choice and if he or anyone else doesn't like it — and *here* is our lesson of the day driven home. Respecting others' choices even if they clash with yours. And of course, there was a song, which our music director, the talented Steve Horelick asked what I had in mind and suggested I take a stab at writing the lyrics. I *loved* writing this song, inspired by those old 1930s MGM musicals, which I titled "It's You." The song wraps up with the kids singing:

KIKI: *It's my style.*

SKYE: *It's my flair.*

JULIE: *And if you don't like it...*

And here is where I gave Leon a line only he could get away with saying, while lying atop the grand piano:

LEON: *I don't care.*

Being a show full of diverse characters, we did have our moments of political correctness. For example, we did a photo on set with all the characters in a pyramid — Kiki, Skye, and Jody on the bottom, Leon and Julie in the middle, and Ben on top. Great.

Nope. Wait…

One of the producers asked if Ben, (aka the white kid) not be on "top."

"OK, how about Skye?" I said, "We owe it to his people."

To be fair, the production did try to find puppeteers who correctly matched the characters. Being African American, I matched Leon; Carmen Oshbar being Mexican, matched Kiki's Mexican American heritage; and Jim Martin being white, matched Ben.

"Oh, Ben's not white," one of the producers explained, "He's 'Euro-American.'"

Uh … Okay.

"Then what about Jody?" I asked. She was the other Caucasian puppet.

"Oh, Jody's Jewish."

Say what, now?

The producers felt Carmen and I accurately represented our characters, so, we got to do appearances, sometimes together, to promote the show. The best of these was when PBS needed Congressional support and she and I got invited to the White House, during the Clinton Administration, (along with Baby Alice from *Sesame Street*, played by the energetic Judy Slatsky). I remember Carmen and I were both given our puppets to take with us in the standard black box, around 27" x 18" x 16", and walking up to the security gate of the White House. Our names were on the list, we went through the metal detectors, and then the boxes needed to be inspected. Well, not really *inspected* as much as we opened the lids, the guard just looked down to see Kiki in her box and Leon lying in his box, each wrapped in clear plastic bags — the guard didn't touch a thing — and said, "Okay."

Seriously?! That's it?!?

I could have hidden a gun in the box — hell, there could have been one inside Leon's mouth that would go off when he said "hi!" I'd been frisk-searched at airports by TSA that lasted longer than this (once by an older man who I think was retiring that day and wanted to give one more "thorough" pat down for the road).

Carmen and I were escorted inside and then separated; I went to the room with men and she to a room for the women. And these rooms were on the lower floor where all the china, from past administrations, were on display. I saw the set from Jackie Kennedy's brief time and a set from Nancy Reagan (although knowing Nancy, I was sure this was one of many she had commissioned). The press event was to take place in the Rose Garden, with then First Lady Hillary Rodham Clinton. But before we were to go there, we were escorted upstairs to the Diplomatic Room (nicknamed the "Dip Room"), a round room facing the South Lawn and where diplomats and other special guests are greeted. We lined up with other guests representing PBS, including "Mister McFeely" from "*Mister Rogers' Neighborhood*" (played by David Newall, who was also Fred Rogers' agent and manager). I made sure Kiki and Leon would be last in line, with me as the last person next to Carmen. And then Mrs. Clinton came in and made her way down the line as someone made the introductions. When she finally got to me, she said, "It's so nice to have you here, Leon."

"Thank you," Leon replied, "And I love what you've done to the place."

Without missing a beat Mrs. Clinton replied, "Thanks. Not bad for public housing."

(A joke she would use again, many years later.)

Once, the entire *Puzzle Place* cast and I got to do an appearance together in New York City. All the puppets were part of the Macy's Thanksgiving Day Parade. The puppets were on the "Kaliope" circus wagon. Having done the parade many times before for Sesame's float, we knew what we needed to do: we were all inside the wagon, with monitors to view the puppets once we were on TV in front of Macy's. There were speakers for playing back the song we would sing, along with the theme, as we rode past onlookers. There were holes, cut out of the top for our arms to go through into the puppets, who all had their legs on to look like they were sitting, and dressed in their winter clothes; because it's November in New York. And it would be a while before we could put our arms down — from 77th Street and Central Park West until we got to 36th Street and Broadway (a distance of a little over two miles, which takes an hour). This was the designated "backstage" area, where floats stop and wait their turn to go on camera, while other floats or marching bands perform in front of Macy's, with the whole world watching. The parade is also made available to our armed forces, overseas. Millions of people line the route, with millions more watching from the comfort of their warm homes. It was going to be fantastic.

After we took the precious few minutes to put our arms down, we got the cue that the wagon would be rolling. We put our arms up, the song began to play just as we reached the front of Macy's and…

Cut to commercial!

Yep. The broadcast cut to commercial, the wagon kept rolling through, the song playing the whole time, as the wagon rolled on, never stopping, until it turned the corner out of camera range. What happened?!?

Well, …

You have to realize that the parade is just one extravagant commercial, not only for Macy's, but ANYONE in it. You *pay* for the privilege to be in it and for the insurance needed to ride on one of the vehicle/floats provided. But you also need to pay to BE. ON. CAMERA. Yes, a totally *separate* fee! And we all just laughed and laughed and laughed, and listened for the yelling from the executive producers, echoing all the way down from their Connecticut home.

We did, however, end up in The Tournament of Roses Parade, twice (both times sponsored by Southern California Edison). The first year was a float with all the kids, plus Nuzzle and Sizzle (the mischievous dog & cat played perfectly by Peter & Alice, respectively), larger than life and made completely out of flowers. The second year, we all got to be in it ourselves — sort of. There would be five vehicles driven by the giant kids and our pre-recorded voices would project from the appropriate vehicle, driven by that character. Leon got to drive a ginormous toy car towing a wagon with Kiki riding inside. I recorded the parade (as my mom and I were on our yearly New Year's trip to Walt Disney World, that began in 1986) and, playing back the video recording, loved seeing and *hearing* Leon and his friends greeting everyone.

The first two seasons of the show were the initial sixty-five-episode order, that was completely funded by Southern California Edison, the Corporation for Public Broadcasting, Sears, IBM, … and viewers like you –

"Thank you."

For a third season, funding was needed, and it took a while to finally get it. The scripts were already written (including the two I wrote), but by the time the season was ready to be shot, Peter Linz and I were already involved with *Bear in the Big Blue House*, and the schedules just didn't work out. Matt Vogel took over Peter's roles of Skye and Nuzzle the Dog, but there wasn't an African American puppeteer, other than me, for Leon. Or there *was*, but being 1998, there was no internet or social media to see who a black male was out there, able to do monitor puppetry. So, Eric Jacobson, who is white, puppeteered Leon, with my voice dubbed over his. And with my blessing.

I could not have thought of anyone more suited to take over Leon, at that time, than Eric. Of all the puppeteers I know (and trust me I know a LOT), when it comes to locking down a character, there is no one more dedicated than Eric Jacobson. He is so meticulous; he will analyze every single line of a script to make sure they are true to his characters. When he came over to my apartment to talk about Leon, he really wanted to talk *about* Leon. Not just his movement, but even when he was standing still and the poses for attitude, I created for him. Eric was, and still is, respectful of character and cares that characters stay true to who they are.

The Puzzle Place had a complete line of merchandise, mainly from toy giant Fisher-Price: clothes, books, games, playsets, dolls, and of course puzzles, which was launched and put into stores in June 1995. However, the show had only premiered nationwide in January 1995. The show was still new to viewers. Plus, there is one caveat I've learned about PBS: they don't air shows at the same time across the country.

I'll give you an example: for a period in 1999 here in New York City, *Bear in the Big Blue House, Eureeka's Castle*, and *The Puzzle Place* were all on at the same time, 10:00am Eastern. (I could literally switch channels and hear my voice range run the gamut from A to A-.) That's because Disney Channel (Bear) and Nickelodeon (Eureeka*)* were cable networks with a set schedule for their shows. But your local PBS station gets to decide for themselves when to air a show. So, Channel 13 aired Puzzle at 10:00am. Having attended many comic conventions as an invited guest, I discovered that where you lived meant whether Puzzle was part of your childhood. It could have been on before school, or during the morning, or after school, so some kids watched it, and some didn't.

Putting out tons of merchandise for a new show most people didn't know about was a huge mistake. The toys sat on shelves unsold, discounted, or sent back because no one was buying them. For years after that, within the toy industry, referring to not jumping the gun too soon on a product was termed, "don't pull a *Puzzle Place*."

It's a shame that the show is not airing anymore. It could totally air right now due to its timelessness, not just of themes, but the lack of dated technology that would showcase how old it was. This show of six diverse puppets coming together to play and sort out any problems, worked then, and it would work now. When it was still called *The Puzzle Works,*" I suggested the tag line be "When the pieces fit, the puzzle works." Now more than ever, living in America, our pieces need to fit together, for the puzzle to work.

Wow

Let me tell you about the seventy-two hours that changed my life, forever.

On Friday March 7, 1997, I went to an audition run by the Jim Henson Company for a new kids series in development. It featured a larger-than-life puppet. With my history of being Big Bird for parades and photo shoots, as well as on "the Street" if Caroll was doing Oscar in the same scene, plus my work on *Eureeka's Castle* as "Magellan the Dragon," it was suggested I come in and try out for the part.

The audition was being held at a space off the West Side Highway near Tribeca, in Manhattan, in what was once a warehouse. They had it there to accommodate the large puppet and the set pieces set up to simulate the locale. I walked in around 11:00am and saw the puppet, sitting on the floor, and nearby a few kids, brought in for the scene. This was a potential game show for kids and the larger-than-life puppet would be the host/MC. I barely remember what it looked like, but it was supposed to be an alien from outer space.

I climbed inside with the script and taped it inside the puppet. I sat down on the stool. The alien was one huge mouth, like the plant "Audrey II," in the musical *Little Shop of Horrors*. In fact, that's how you were supposed to operate it: pump the lower jaw up and down. And I sat there thinking, *"Why don't they just get Marty to do this?"* Marty is Martin P. Robinson, the *Sesame Street* puppeteer of Telly Monster, Snuffy (aka Mister Snuffleupagus), and Slimey the Worm. (His characters truly run the gamut in size.) But Marty is also responsible for the original design of the plants for Little Shop. He designed and built the plants that have since been the standard design for productions of the musical, even the movie. This alien *WAS* literally his design. *He should be doing this! Why hadn't they called him?* But I did some sort of deep, comical voice I thought would work, and that was that. I went home.

Around 4:00pm, The Jim Henson Company called me.

"Hey Noel." It was Rick Fernandes, the producer for this other potential show. "We have this other character we'd like you to come in and audition for."

Okay.

They faxed me (yes, kids *faxed*) the "sides," which are the lines from the script, and the sketch of the character. It was a black-and-white drawing of a large bear, with these little critters around him, and the smiling face of the moon behind them. Okay, this looked cute. I hailed a cab, reading the script and trying to think of a voice for this bear, and headed down to The Carriage House, a refurbished stable (hence the name), owned by the company, and used as a photo studio and studio for recording videos, and auditions. (It's where I was the Labyrinth Doorknocker for Jim Henson's pitch for *The Jim Henson Hour.* Remember?) As soon as I walked through the door, Peter Van Roden, an executive at the company at the time, came up to me and said, "Use your own voice."

"What?!?"

"Use your own voice."

"But we're The Muppets. We don't do that."

In this case, this character would be different. At this time, the popularity of a certain purple dinosaur was still high, so it was thought that this larger-than-life character should have a more soothing, normal, adult voice. Plus, all that day, they had heard performers do gruff, gravelly, deep, cartoony voices. So, for my turn, they wanted something different, something new.

This was going to be a body puppet, like Big Bird. In operating it, my right arm went up through the neck into the foam head and my left arm went into its left arm. There was no fur covering the puppet, so it was almost like operating its X-ray. I didn't have a monitor but because there was netting covering the hooped boning that shaped the body, I could see the large monitor next to the camera that was turned towards me.

As soon as I got in, I loved it. It felt so comfortable. As I moved the neck and tried out moves, I knew this bear would be so much fun to play with. But then it hit me:

Noel, it's quarter to five on a Friday; they've already picked who they want, and this is just a courtesy call to affirm they made the right choice, earlier. So, that's when I decided, "F@$k it; I'm just going to have fun."

And I did.

In the script, the bear, whose name was "Bear," was talking about water, and would show his friend, the viewer, a glass of water. But first, he realizes there's a "smell" coming from somewhere and he sniffs around until he discovers it's the viewer, whom he "sniffs."

Well, I had Bear sniff to the left, the right, turn around, and then realize it's the viewer. That's when I jammed his nose all the way into the camera, covering the view, and immediately pulled it back out. "It's YOU!" And then back in went the nose. I pulled it out again, telling them what they smelled like, adding, "Or maybe you smell this good all the time," with a little chuckle.

When it came time for the water, I had Bear look at the glass himself, and then hold it up, so close to the lens, that I lined up his eyes behind it, so that you saw them through the water. Every now and then I tried to do a more character voice, but Mitchell Kreigman, who created the show, kept telling me, "No, use your own voice!" which I called my "Uncle Noel" voice. Having friends with kids, whenever I visited, I'd take this tone, this attitude, of "what do you want to do; whatever it is, I'm in." It's similar to my own voice, just a little lighter in tone. And I'd follow their lead in whatever game they came up with. I thought that's exactly what this bear was like with his friends, both the ones with him and the one watching at home.

And that was that.

Around five o'clock, I got out of the puppet, said thanks to everyone, and left. And completely dismissed the whole affair once I was in the street.

The next evening, I was to go to see a friend perform. Wes, who lived across the hall from me for a while, was in an *a cappella* group performing at an *a cappella* competition (which I never knew even existed) at Symphony Space. His old roommate, Mike, told me that they were in town and Mike arranged for some of their old acquaintances to come support them. As Mike's goal in life is to meet and know everyone (and trust me, one day, you WILL meet him), I looked forward to meeting some of their other friends. I got to the Thai restaurant and there was Mike and company; four other people I had never met. There was a vacant chair and Mike said that "Susan is still coming."

Who?

Susan Elia was Mike and Wes's friend from college. Mike and Wes had attended M.I.T., and Susan went to Wellesley. Students at Wellesley could take classes and do theater productions at M.I.T., and that's how Mike and Susan had met, doing theater there. They never dated; they were just friends and had still kept in touch after college. When Susan was moving to New York City in the summer of 1992, her apartment wasn't ready, so she was going to stay in a women's hotel (which I didn't know still existed so close to the end of the twentieth century). Mike gave her a ride from Boston to NYC and pulling up to the building, Mike took one look at it, this less than desirable (aka safe) place and, without even getting out of the car, said, "No." He would not hear of it and told Susan that she could crash on his and Wes's couch, for the two weeks, until her place was ready. She accepted this kind gesture.

Now… the backstory.

In the summer of 1992, I had moved into this new building called The Monterey on 96th Street and 3rd Avenue. (The end of the line for the Upper East Side of Manhattan, at least to white people at the time.) It's also the beginning of Spanish Harlem. In fact, to entice people to live all the way "up there," there were ads on the sides of buses and in subway cars, with pastel colors and hints of palm trees, that read "The MONTEREY… California living in the New York Nineties." (You can't make up this kind of marketing.) And the building was gorgeous: a doorman greeted you and ushered you into the grand lobby of marble and wooden columns, with a concierge desk, before rounding the corner to the elevator banks and the health club, with an indoor heated pool. At the very top of the building was a rooftop garden with lounge chairs and a sweeping view of New York.

My apartment was on the 26th floor at the end of the hall. It was a "junior one bedroom," (meaning if you added water, it would grow into a full one bedroom). It was a fantastic apartment for one person … or two people who REALLY loved each other. The majority of it had six-foot tall glass windows stretched along the side of the living room into the bedroom. The view faced both west, with stunning sunsets, and to the north. Being so, high I could, with binoculars, not only see the Lenox Terrace building I grew up in, thirty-six blocks away, but once, when talking to my mom, I asked her to go to her living room window, which faced downtown.

"Wave!" I said. And I could see her!

Directly across the hall was Mike and Wes's apartment, a two bedroom (by converting the small dining area into a second bedroom). I moved into mine in June and they moved into theirs in July. Susan stayed with them for two weeks, before she left to move into her apartment in Chelsea (where she lived for about another two years, until she moved back to Boston). And during those two weeks I never met her or saw her, *not once* — heck, I still didn't know Mike or Wes yet! I didn't meet them and become friends until September of that year. That's when on a Monday evening, out of the blue, there was a knock on my front door, and naturally being a New Yorker, my guard went up.

"Yes?" I asked through the door.

"Hi!" came this incredibly chipper reply, "I'm your neighbor from across the hall."

I looked through the peep hole and thought …

Ok – if he tries anything I could probably take him. I opened the door and …

"Hi!" just as perky as before, "I'm Mike." And stuck out his hand to shake.

OK. I took it and he said, “I was wondering if I could borrow a cork screw.”

“Oh, … uh … sure,” I answered and got it, and handed it to him.

“Thanks. By the way, my roommate and I are going to watch ‘Northern Exposure’ later, if you want to join us.”

Seriously?! Who IS this guy?!?

“Oh, … um … sure,” I said.

And I did and Mike and I have been friends ever since, introducing me to his friends, and I introducing him to mine. But, not once, during the five years of knowing Mike, did he ever mention knowing a ‘Susan.’ Of course, Mike was proud of having a professional puppeteer for a friend, who worked on major TV shows like *Sesame Street* and *The Puzzle Place,* and would brag, via email, of my exploits to Susan. But never a photo. So, she didn’t know what I looked like. Being a puppeteer, she figured I had some form of facial hair, a ponytail, and t-shirts of various beer companies in my closet.

Now back to the Thai restaurant and March 1997.

I excused myself and went to the bathroom. Susan arrived while I was indisposed. She knew Mike but, that was all. She didn’t know anyone else, and when she asked about the empty chair, Mike said, “Noel’s in the bathroom.”

I come back and headed to the table and, suddenly, saw someone new was there and …

Wow.

Wow.

I saw the most beautiful brown eyes I’d ever seen and a smile that made me glow from within.

“Noelster,” Mike began, “This is Susan.” We shook hands and …

Wow.

I would later find out that Susan had a similar reaction, now seeing that "Noel" did NOT have some form of facial hair or a ponytail, and my collared shirt was not a T-shirt that advertised any form of beer. In other words, she was pleased to meet me.

We headed across the street to the theater, and I made a point of making sure I sat next to Susan. We laughed, chatted, and rooted for Wes, whose group came in second. It was a fun evening and wondered when I could see Susan again. By sheer coincidence, we were both going to the same engagement party the next day, for a friend whom we both had met through Mike (of course). At the party, I was primed to regale her with my many puppetry exploits and accomplishments, but she'd already known all of them from Mike. (*Great. Thanks Mike. This is going well.)* Susan was starting to work as an editor for Dance Magazine, the publication that covered the world of dance, but mainly ballet.

"Oh … I once saw Balanchine at a Nutcracker rehearsal," I said.

"Really!?!" was her response, eyes wide with intrigue.

"Y-Yes," I answered while within my brain, I'm screaming, *"Stats people! We need stats on Balachine! That rehearsal! Kermit Love! This is NOT a drill! MOVE! MOVE!!!"* I told her how Kermit was my teacher, but he also knew George Balanchine, aka "Mr. B."

I told her Kermit took our puppetry class to Lincoln Center and we sat in the audience to watch a dress rehearsal. At the moment the Nutcracker turns back into the young prince, the kid wasn't doing it right because, suddenly, from just a couple of rows in front of us, a small figure stood up, waving his arms, shouting, "No! No! No!" in this high, tinny voice. The silhouetted figure left the row, went through a door, and then appeared onstage, next to the kid. There was George Balanchine. And to help the kid understand the timing and the steps, first he did it, then "Mr. B" held onto the boy's shoulders and marched him forward, chiming out the beat of the music.

"He puppeteered him!" Susan exclaimed with a smile.

Oh, I like how this girl thinks.

I then told her more about the rehearsal. When we got back to the city, I asked for her number to call her to go out. And she gave it to me.

The next day was Monday. Just shy of six o'clock, my phone rang. It was The Jim Henson Company. "Noel, we'd like you to be Bear."

Hubba whuh now!?! "What?"

I had completely forgotten about it. I was too busy thinking about the girl with those brown eyes I had met. But here was the company that Jim started, Jim whom I knew and worked with, learned from, now offering me this incredible opportunity. Of course, I said, "yes, thank you" and started going to fittings that week. I also started dating Susan that week, who would marry me two years later. In those seventy-two hours, two amazing life-changing moments occurred that I still enjoy to this day. I look back and remember those days and everything that occurred, because I said "yes" to an audition and "yes" to a neighbor who wanted to borrow my corkscrew. And all I can say is…

Wow.

Welcome to the Blue House!

Jim Henson signed a deal with The Walt Disney Company to sell them The Muppets. Unfortunately, Jim died in 1990 and the deal got amended; the Henson Company would create three television shows for The Walt Disney Company. The first show was for ABC, a primetime sitcom called *Dinosaurs* that lasted several seasons. (When I visited the set of *Dinosaurs* in 1991, there was a scene that needed a fist to come out a peep hole in a door and punch a dino in the face. Steve Whitmire, who was on the show as "Robbie," called me over, gave me the glove – ACTION - and I did it, and – CUT - and I still get a residual check for ten cents.) The next show was another primetime series for ABC called *Aliens in the Family*. (In order for that show to work, their entire house was on a five-foot-tall platform with sections of the floor that could be popped off so that the puppeteers could comfortably stand and perform the baby alien.) It lasted less than one season.

Now, the Henson Company owed Disney one more show, but instead of doing something for primetime again, it was decided to create a show for The Disney Channel's new block of preschool shows. Mitchell Kriegman, the creator of the popular *Clarissa Explains It All* for Nickelodeon, was brought in to help develop one. I'm told he searched through files of old ideas and pitches that never went beyond the drawing board, when he found a description of a house, and a bear who lived in it. His gut told him this somehow had potential and …

Well, you know what happened.

At the time, I lived on the Upper Eastside, on 96th Street and Third Avenue. The townhouse, with all the offices, was on East 69th Street. The workshop started out there and then got moved to 67th Street, off Third Avenue. Getting the part of Bear meant that I'd have to go in for fittings. I knew this body puppet needed to be as comfortable as possible, while still being able to animate it. I remember the first time the shop called, asking when this week or next I was around for a fitting. "I'll be there in twenty minutes," and headed on down.

Before doing the episodes for the series, we needed to do a test, a ten-minute pilot to see if this concept of a bear owning a home filled with other animals would work. It was shot in the same space where I auditioned, The Carriage House, the studio just down the street from the workshop. And the set was so clever, given how small the studio was. There was the living room and kitchen with a wall separating them. But the wall was *hinged*. So, when Bear was in the living room, the wall was allowed the maximum space for dancing and singing (and of course sniffing), until Bear needed to go into the kitchen. I began walking towards the kitchen and then, as the hinged wall started to moved, I walked in place, the doorway passing through Bear, and exactly when the wall stopped, I took the last few steps. And it looked like Bear walked from one large room into the next! Genius design!

Speaking of genius designs, that was Bear. The builders at The Jim Henson Creature Shop are true artists, gifted with a talent to turn a drawing into a three-dimensional character. Bear was pieces all fitted together – the head and hands were attached to the neck/top half, which was attached to the bottom half, that had the feet attached. Except for the head, all the fur could be removed, and hand washed at the shop, while the understructure, of the neck and bottom half, would be professionally dry cleaned (at a shop that specializes in Broadway costumes). The feet were slippers (that fitted over sneakers) and were hand washed. This was to keep Bear fresh and not get, well, moldy. Because I sweat. A LOT. And fur is warm. VERY warm. I once put a thermometer inside and clocked the temperature at a cozy ninety-two degrees (but it was a dry heat; rim-shot). Which is why I was glad my dressing room had a shower (and I'm sure everyone else was glad, too). But part of the genius design of Bear was that the understructure had netting, and the fur was actually "amoebas," sort of like puzzle pieces sewn on, but just enough space to allow the heat from within to escape. Which is why, when you'd hug Bear, he was so warm and cozy. Because it would get hot inside, the air-conditioning in the studio was cranked up to full blast, thus, making it feel as close to Antarctica as possible. At the end of season one, the wrap gift to the cast, crew, and staff was a grey fleece jacket, with the logo on it. It was not only a great gift but also a way for everyone to not complain about the studio being cold next season. "Wear your fleecy!"

When test/pilot was shown to test/focus groups of kids it was a complete success. But even before then, Mitchell knew. Someone brought in their baby to watch the recording and see the puppets. Bear went up to the baby to say "hi." And Mitchell told me that THIS would be the real test of whether this character would work. Bear greeted the baby and talked and of course gently sniffed the baby, and – the baby smiled. And then gurgled a little laugh. WHEW!

Everything for the test/pilot worked … except for the names of the Otters would have to change. They were called "Pummel & Pop" but due to Disney's concern that "pummel" was too violent sounding, they were christened "Pip & Pop" And later, the lemur's name changed from "Treelio" to "Treelo" due to the show *Rollie Pollie Olie* being concerned it was sounding too close to their main character's name. (*Um ... O.K.*) Other than that, we were all set to go. We shot the first season (and the next two) on the third floor of Kaufman Astoria Studios, in Queens, and downstairs on the first floor was that little show I started my career on … *Sesame Street*. I'll never forget the day Caroll did a surprise visit and his wrangler, Lara "Lars" McClean (whom I love) brought up Big Bird. I got into Bear and Lars put Bird on Caroll for pictures together. But since Caroll didn't have the legs on, we did it from behind the couch (since it would have been weird seeing Big Bird in skinny GAP jeans). Then I got a picture half dressed, wearing the bottom half of Bear and my harness, with Caroll. I told him I'm using every trick he ever taught me, and he was so proud of me, and had no doubts I'd be great at it.

Again … thank you Caroll.

If you've ever watched the show, it begins with a model of the house that splits open to reveal the interior – a two story home with a kitchen, a bathroom, a living room, a bedroom, and an attic. Every room plus the Otter Pond was on a platform raised five feet off the ground. (Remember that platform for the show *Aliens in the Family*? Same one! Moral: never throw anything away.) There was a ramp at one end that you'd walk up and to the left was the Attic, with the balcony, and straight ahead was The Otter Pond. Then you'd turn right and there was this wide aisle that ran down the center of the platform. On the left side was the first floor of the house – the kitchen, the foyer, and the living room. And on the other side of the aisle, to the right, was the second floor of the house – the bedroom, the landing, the stairs to the attic, and the bathroom. And the center aisle was dubbed "Camera Alley" because that's where the three cameras were. Record Bear, in the foyer, climbing the stairs to the second floor – CUT – then turn the cameras around, reset Bear on the other stairs, to shoot him coming up to the second-floor landing, and – ACTION!

Now, performing puppets for TV, the way Jim innovated it, and how I learned it from him, was that what you see on a monitor is NOT a mirror image. It's "backwards." You wave with your left hand, but on the monitor, you see your other hand waving. I've done puppetry with monitors so long that it's second nature to me; my brain is hard wired to know what to do, and not be phased. Even inside Big Bird, I learned that the monitor inside strapped to my chest is my eyes, my only way to see what I'm doing. And I knew that would be true for Bear. So, the first day, before we shot a thing, I took a walk around the house, specifically the foyer. I walked up the stairs and then down. Then I closed my eyes and walked up the stairs and down, to get a sense of what my feet would feel, while counting how many steps there were. That's why there's the rug in the foyer and the thresholds across the bottoms of the doorways – this way I could feel where I was when I couldn't see Bear's feet (and even when I could). For scenes in the living room or kitchen, for example, portions of the floor were popped to allow the other puppeteers to stand and hold up the characters. But to keep me from falling onto them, wooden boards were screwed in along the edge, that I could then feel with my feet, and know *"Stop! Don't crush the cast!"*

I want to talk about the cast. There was five of us total: Peter Linz (who I worked with on *Sesame Street,* and *The Puzzle Place*) who was "Tutter the Mouse," "Pip" (of Pip & Pop) and puppeteered "Luna the Moon" and "Ray the Sun" (whose voices were the incredible Lynn Thigpen and Geoffrey Holder, respectively); Tyler Bunch who was "Treelo," "Pop," and "Doc Hogg;" Vicki Eibner who was "Ojo the little girl bear cub," "Grandma Flutter," and "Lois the Loon;" and finally Jim Kroupa (who I recommended join the cast) who was "Jeremiah Tortoise" and baseball legend, and Bear's high school buddy, "Ferret Jeter" (from a script I wrote and if you're a Yankee fan you'll get the pun's reference). We were all perfectly cast. This show was our chance to shine and create brand new characters, brand new Muppets. (Yes, Bear and his friends are Muppets in the Muppet universe just like you're a human in this universe. Bear is not one of *The* Muppets; he knows about Kermit and Miss Piggy, the way you know George Clooney and Angelina Jolie, because they're celebrities; but he's never *met* them.) And we loved every minute of it. We made each other laugh and cry (the song "Look at You Now" that Bear sings about when Treelo was a baby lemur, gets me teary more than ever, since becoming a dad). Brian Henson (chairman of the board of The Jim Henson Company and Jim's son) was in town and came by to visit the set once, during a particularly fun and silly afternoon and commented, "You all are having waaaaay too much fun."

And it was true. I learned from Mitchell that being the lead, I was the barometer for the set, so I was always cheerful. And why wouldn't I be? Look where I was and what I was doing? And I and everyone wanted a drama free, ego-free, no-need-for-tension-or-competition set. I worked on too many of those. (We didn't even have an official "Puppet Captain.") The crew and camera guys also told us that others in the industry were jealous of them working on the show. That's how fun the show was.

Bear in the Big Blue House premiered on October 20, 1997, and was an immediate success for Disney, and the launch of their new preschool segment, "Playhouse Disney." To celebrate, Disney invited Bear (and I) to the channel's holiday party in December, in California. My mom was going to stay over and pick-up my mail, so I invited her to ride with me to the airport – because I had an idea brewing.

When we got to the airport I checked in, while mom bragged to the desk attendants about who I was and why I was going to L.A. Then I asked if the seat next to me (in first/business class; thank you Mickey Mouse) was empty, and it was. That's when I turned to my mom and said, …

"Come."

"What?" she asked.

"Come with me."

"But I don't have any clothes."

"We'll buy a nightgown and a toothbrush. You got your meds?"

"Yes," she said.

"Well?" I said grinning.

I thought the attendants at the desk were going to cry when she said "yes."

When we landed, we were taken to the hotel, the Universal Sheraton, and after dropping off the bags, I asked my mom, …

"Wanna go to Disneyland?!?" Guess what she said?

I rented a car and, having memorized the route from my time living in LA for *The Puzzle Place*, we were there in forty minutes flat, and stayed until closing. That's when, on the way out, we went shopping on Main Street U.S.A., for a nightgown and clothes for her to wear, choosing the few subtle apparel that didn't have huge mouse ears printed all over them.

Next day, the party was in Tarzana, the city in the valley named after "Tarzan" because Edgar Rice Burrows lived there. And it was in a bowling alley! Bear came out during the cocktail hour and lead everyone in "The Bear Cha Cha Cha" and afterwards I got to join in on the bowling. I also introduced mom to Anne Sweeney, the then president of Disney Channel, who also was about to cry when I shared the airport story. The trip to Tarzana was the first of many trips and appearances for Bear and me.

In order to do more of these in-person appearances (or more accurately, "in-Bear appearances"), I needed to see out, and the Henson Shop came up with the perfect method. There was the primo head used for the show and a backup head. And for the backup head there was a *camera* in the left eye! It was given a lipstick camera; a thin wire with a miniscule lens at the end, and was imbedded into the left eye, with the right having a matching "glint." The camera was attached to a monitor on my chest. (Want to know what it was like? Close your right eye, make a circle with your left hand, and hold it up to your left eye. Now walk.) My first time on *Regis & Kathy Lee,* Regis Philbin asked Bear backstage …

"How can you see?"

"With my eyes," Bear honestly answered.

"No, really," Regis pressed.

"With. My. Eyes."

"Fine," Regis said, "Don't tell me."

Bear and I did many trips to promote the show and the merchandise connected with it. One time I went to Fayetteville, Arkansas to have Bear appear at the monthly Walmart meeting. Yes – once a month, Walmart broadcasts a LIVE meeting to all, ALL, of its stores in the U.S., to announce that month's featured items to promote. And the Bear merchandise was on the agenda. The meeting had a dais, with the corporate gents in their flannel shirts, regaling the in-studio staff, and the thousands watching, that this month's promotion is so good, that they all should be "fired up!" And each time they said this, a graphic of flames would appear on the screen. Well, I couldn't let *this* opportunity pass! Bear was introduced and calmly said, …

"Well, … I don't know about you … but this bear … is 'fired up.'"

And the room went berserk! This was followed by Bear leading everyone, including the flannelled execs, in "The Bear Cha Cha Cha." (Fayetteville also boasts the *worst* cocktail I have ever had – a Scotch Martini. I know, I know, but I have a morbid side and had to try it … and the first sip made me regret it. On the plus side, when I asked for Russian dressing and our server had no idea what Russian dressing was, I taught her, and she shared the recipe with the chef.)

I got to go to London, more than once, but that first trip changed Susan's life.

Bear was broadcast, not only on Playhouse Disney Worldwide, but also on London's Channel Five, during their morning block of shows, called "Milkshake." I was to spend the day with one of their hosts, Eddie Matthews (who met me to go over the logistics, and we're still friends), and the premise being that Eddie was supposed to meet Bear at "Bear Street" (yes, it exits; as does "Noel Street"), while Bear was traveling around on a double decker bus, trying to find it. It was so fun, with stops at Trafalgar Square, for Bear to cha cha in, and people smiling and waving as Bear rolled about London.

Meanwhile, …

My wife, Susan Elia MacNeal, was out and about having her own adventure. The night before, we had dinner with British friends, who had a Time Out London magazine, and gave it Susan to help occupy her time, while I was "bearing" it in London. (Hey, I warned ya about the puns.) One item, our dear friend James ("My darling James" my mom referred to him, completely in love with him and his British accent) mentioned was The Churchill War Rooms, the underground bomb shelter where Prime Minister Winston Churchill conducted the war against Germany, that were now open to the public. "Unlike what you Yanks might think," James said, "World War II did NOT start with Pearl Harbor." Seeing this as a challenge, as well as a suggestion, Susan was out to find the War Rooms.

The War Rooms had literally just opened and were not the slick, sleek museum, café, and gift shop it is now. Susan went in and down along the tunnels, the same ones used by Churchill as his staff, while the bombs rained down from the nightly raids of the Luftwaffe. At one point, she walked along and then … well, I'll let her tell it:

"I remember being there on a day when it wasn't at all crowded and doing a slow turn and realizing everything that I saw was exactly the same as it had been during the Blitz. And it was this very powerful, transformative experience — I really felt as though, for a moment, I had slipped through time, and I was there in 1940 — with the smell of cigarette smoke, the ringing of the telephones, the feeling of tension and dread in the air. I was doing the self-guided tour, with the accompanying audio recording, and when I reached the typists' room, an actress began reading from Mrs. Elizabeth Layton Nel's memoir of her time working as a secretary for Mr. Churchill — and I knew I wanted my main character to be one of the Prime Minister's typists.

And since then, Susan's first book from Penguin Random House, "*Mr. Churchill's Secretary*," the story of how young American Maggie Hope becomes typist to the Prime Minister, and helps foil a terrorist plot, as well as uncovers unknown family intrigue, spawned sequels and has become *"The Maggie Hope Mysteries"* series (the *tenth* book having come out in July of 2021 *"The Hollywood Spy").* I am so proud of her and this accomplishment few people on this planet can claim, including being a New York Times bestselling author *and* literary awards winner. And she credits the start of it all to a bear that owned a home and loved to dance.

Whenever Bear and I did an appearance, whether it was at a store or a TV show (such as *Hollywood Squares* or *The Walt Disney World Very Merry Christmas Parade*), I always asked if I could visit a children's hospital. These included … The Great Ormond Street Hospital in London (where J.M. Barrie bequeathed his royalties and rights to *Peter Pan*); Lurie's Children's Hospital of Chicago (with its own TV studio where Bear could do a twenty-minute show that was broadcast to rooms); and Give Kids the World, the resort in Kissimmee Florida for critically ill children and their families. This resort is an extraordinary facility, with rooms large enough to accommodate any piece of medical equipment; the onsite restaurant serves Christmas dinner every day; and a theater, where Bear did a show for kids and their families. One visit, there was a little girl, who had a wish (because Give Kids works with the Make a Wish Foundation) to meet Bear. So, she and her family were flown down to go to The Disney MGM Studios (and, again, it will *always* be The Disney MGM Studios, to me) to see the "Bear in the Big Blue House LIVE Onstage" show, with a meet-n-greet afterwards. It was just sheer coincidence that I and Bear were there the day they were going! She and Bear chatted and took pictures, and then Bear said, …

"Our show at the Studios is great, with so much singing, and of course dancing. So, after you see our show, I'll meet you, but I'll have to save my voice for the next show." As the way of getting around the fact that THAT Bear is not allowed to talk.

When Susan and I went to Mexico City, it was to promote Bear being shown on TV there, plus the merchandise that was being introduced. (It's where at lunch at The Four Seasons Mexico we got dared to eat one of the appetizers, - fried crickets - and we did. It was also the last time; they tasted like the smell of feet.) I got to go to a hospital there that was not state of the art. In fact, the nurses stations had computers and monitors from the mid-nineties. The beds had not top sheets, just fitted sheets, because there was no air conditioning. And as Bear was escorted around, I got the sense that this hospital and its children's ward was not going to be updated anytime soon, if ever.

In another building next door was the hospital theater. This is where I'd do the twenty-minute show with Bear, with the songs of the show dubbed in Spanish. Children who could come were brought in and there was a representative of the hospital who was the host (since I do not speak Spanish; again, that brilliant choice to study French in high school). When I got to the song "Baby It's You," about all the things Bear loves about you, Bear moseyed over to a boy in a wheelchair, in the front row. He was paralyzed down one side of his body, but when Bear squatted and held his hand while singing, the one side of his face that could still move, the corner of his mouth curled up. He was *smiling*. And nearby I heard sniffles while inside I am trying not to lose it. (*Keep it together, Noel!*) After the show, I got out of Bear, and, as I dressed in the bathroom, I cried and cried and cried. But it's why I loved doing those appearances. For those brief moments, kids weren't patients, they were kids; and it wasn't a doctor or a nurse coming for blood samples or to take them to a test. It was their friend … Bear.

Whenever I get emails and tweets thanking me for the show, I wasn't responsible; we all were. The puppeteers, plus the writers, composers, directors, the crew, and staff, plus the support from The Jim Henson Company and The Walt Disney Company, all contributed to this little show, that is now the cherished memory for so many people. I'm proud that Bear and his friends hold such a special place in people's hearts, and all those kids who watched who are now parents, introducing Bear to *their* little ones – first via old DVDs, what's on YouTube, even old VHS tapes. But as of October 19, 2022, one day before the twenty-fifth anniversary, *Bear in the Big Blue House* FINALLY was added to Disney Plus. (And the announcement came on September 15th – my birthday. Talk about an incredible surprise for a gift!) I've fulfilled requests on the Cameo app, and I am still shocked at the number of followers and likes on TikTok for my Bear puppet (made by the amazing James Wojtal, Jr., one of the original builders of Bear). People have asked me of all the shows I've worked on and characters I've created, which is my favorite. This show was fun and it's an honor to have been a part of something so positive and genuine and memorable.

How could it not be *Bear in the Big Blue House*?

“Ah… There She Is”

I want to take a moment to talk about Lynne Thigpen.

If you only know Lynne Thigpen as the soothing voice of “Luna the Moon,” then you don’t know who Lynne Thigpen was. Lynne was a consummate actress in movies, television, and theatre. Take the time to look her up on IMDB.com and the range of performances this woman did just for TV and film is amazing. Then head over to broadwayworld.com for stage credits. Lynne was a “working actor” — someone who isn’t the star but has a long and productive career earning a reputation of consistent quality, and the respect of peers, producers, and directors. That was Lynne Thigpen.

I had seen and always liked the surreal movie *The Warriors*, the 1979 film (based on the 1965 book by Sol Yurrick) about a street gang framed by a rival gang and their need to survive the night, getting back to their home turf of Coney Island. It’s a bizarre movie set in New York City at night, yet there is no one — and I mean NO ONE — other than The Warriors and other gangs. And these gangs are straight out of a comic book, dressed like baseball players and others wearing top hats. And the narrator is the voice of “the DJ,” a sort of omnipresence throughout the movie, but you never see her face. Just her lips and the microphone, but it’s her voice that captures your attention. It wasn’t until years later that I found out that “The DJ” was Lynne. When I asked her about it, she said that it was one day to shoot, and by one day meaning a couple of hours once the camera and lighting was set up. But “The DJ” is the character you remember the most.

Bear and Luna always had conversations at the end of the day — “the big picture moment,” as creator Mitchell Kriegman called it — but it wasn’t the first time a character of mine and a character of Lynne’s had a conversation. When I worked on the PBS series *The Puzzle Place*, my character was “Leon,” a precocious seven-year-old from NYC. (Once when we did a remote shoot of Leon at his school’s science fair, three little girls asked me how old Leon was supposed to be. “Seven,” I said. “No,” they said, having seen the show, “He’s nine. He *acts* nine!” As a dad, I now realize what they meant.) In the episode I wrote, titled “The Mystery of the Fabulous Hat,” Leon decides to solve the mystery of the missing hat just like his hero, “Sherlock Holmes.” The caretakers of the clubhouse, "The Piece Police," even dress him up, deerstalker cap and all. His best friend Ben (played by one of my dearest friends, Jim Martin) wants to help, so Leon hires Ben to be his "Doctor Watson" (and The Piece Police accommodate with an appropriate outfit for Ben). But when Ben does a better job of finding the clues, Leon's ego gets the better of him and he "fires" Ben. Now, working alone, Leon can't find any clues and needs advice.

The Puzzle Place had this contraption called "The Weebus," a huge computer with a large screen capable of contacting anyone in the world for a video chat. (Before Zoom, there was The Weebus.) He goes to the Weebus and says, "Weebus - (And yes, before "Alexa" and "Siri" there was The Weebus.) — please call 'The Chief' of the Acme Detective Agency." Instantly, on screen, pops up "The Chief," herself, from the PBS series *Where in the World Is Carmen Sandiego?* — played, of course, by Lynne Thigpen. "The Chief" then explains to Leon that sometimes everyone, including detectives, needs help. She remembers her first case and she needed help and called for some, just in time.

"Who was it?" Leon asks.

"I just told you," she replies, "Justin Time." (Did I mention I wrote this episode?)

Leon then thanks her and apologizes to Ben, and together they solve the mystery. It was very rare for two PBS shows to do a crossover. The only other time I remember is when Big Bird appeared in The Neighborhood of Make-Believe on *Mister Rogers Neighborhood* and Fred Rogers dropped by *Sesame Street*. We shot the Leon half of the bit first, then, when they were back in production that fall, Carmen Sandiego shot Lynne's half, with my playback as a guide for her timed responses. And it edited together perfectly.

So, how did this consummate actress of stage, screen, and television become the moon? Well, first, Mitchell Kriegman called me and asked me what a good name for the moon would be. Immediately, "Luna" popped into my head. When he was casting the voice of Luna, I instantly recommended Lynne, remembering her as "The Chief" and her voice of "The DJ" from *The Warriors*. I told Lynne about her Chief's chat with my Leon, when she came to the audition, and she remembered! We sat in an office at the Henson Townhouse and read one of the chats that occurs at the end of the show — and that was it. Mitchell and I both knew that this was not just the voice, but the essence of what you'd imagine the moon would be talking to you. That tone of warmth and wisdom you'd expect from an entity that has literally seen it all. Lynn and I would meet at a recording studio and record six conversations for six upcoming episodes at a time. I loved the time of those recordings because I got to have my own chats with Lynne. And not just about show business, but what was going on in her life, like the noise from The Limelight, the church converted into a nightclub in the Tribeca section of Manhattan, and right across the street from her loft, Friday and Saturday nights being the worst.

On *Bear*, we'd shoot six episodes in two weeks. The parts of each episode for Shadow's stories and the end of the show for the chats with Luna were all reserved for the Friday of the second week, dubbed "Chromakey Day" (what you know as blue screen or green screen). Lynne and I would record Bear's and Luna's lines prior to this. On that Friday morning would be all the Shadow stories, with Shadow shot against bluescreen (with Peter Linz manipulating Shadow's head to Tara Mooney's voice, the incredible Irish performer) and in the afternoon, move over to the attic set and shoot all six of the show endings, with Peter now lip syncing to Lynne's voice played back (and me lip syncing my Bear lines). Once, due to scheduling, we couldn't get the recording studio, so Lynn came into the studio and said the lines live, with Peter lip syncing in real time. Not an easy task, even after rehearsing. One fun shot that made it into the outtake reel was the first rehearsal scene. For rehearsals, I would step out onto the balcony with the top half of Bear off and I could see into the monitor strapped to my chest, Luna rising into place. Well, instead of the puppet, I saw Lynne's face slide up into the night sky. She, too, could see a monitor and mock-screamed seeing half a Bear, and I responded to camera, "Ah... there she is — No really, there SHE IS!" When Lynne got the role of computer expert Ellie Farmer on the CBS primetime series *The District*, she moved to Los Angeles where it was shot. So now, our recorded chats were scheduled with me in a studio in New York and her in a studio in Los Angeles. Still not as many miles apart as Bear and Luna were, but none of the intimacy was lost.

Bear in the Big Blue House wrapped production in March of 2002. Lynne Thigpen died, suddenly, on March 12, *2003*, of a cerebral hemorrhage. I was invited to speak at the memorial held for her at The Cherry Lane Theater, in Greenwich Village. Many people took to the stage to reflect on Lynne and her contributions to acting and share stories about her. The best was from actor Michael E. Knight, who portrayed Tad "The Cad" Martin on the ABC daytime drama *All My Children*. Lynne had a recurring part on the show, and he told of one of those rare times where every character is in the same scene, in this case a party. It's a scene like this that takes hours to shoot having so many characters and their storylines interacting. Lynne's character and another enter first and then make their way off-camera. Then, Michael's character, Tad, enters the party and makes his way towards the back, but still in view on camera. As the scene continues, holding a drink and smiling, he said he glanced over and saw Lynn sitting in a chair off-camera, and she mimed he had something in his teeth. Michael subtly turns his head away, so as not to use his tongue on camera, and then turns back, for approval that his smile is restored. Lynne, again, mimes he still has something in his teeth. This time, Michael turns completely around, to use a finger to wipe away whatever it is, all the while the scene continuing, characters saying their lines. He turns back to her with hope, only to see Lynn, once again, mime that something is still lodged in his teeth. "CUT," is called and "take ten," for a break, as cameras are reset for the next scene. Michael marches over to Lynne, points a finger at his mouth, and barks, "*What*?!?" And Lynne, calmly and quietly responds, …

"Honey, it's late. I'm bored. And I'm just messin' with ya." She explained to him that having done theater, and the same scenes night after night, sometimes, actors would play little pranks on each other to break the monotony. Michael, of course, laughed, and hugged her for what she'd put him through. I loved hearing this story.

I was the last speaker. I took to the stage to introduce the clip of the final show of Bear. The premise (which I suggested for this last show) was that Bear's friends think he's leaving, and they want to show him how much they appreciate him and do a grand *This Is Your Life* type of song called, "Thank you, Bear." It turns out to be a misunderstanding and Bear won a contest and gets to take five of his friends to stay at the grand Sequoia Lodge, in Sequoia City. The clip was from the last scene of the show with Bear stepping out onto the hotel room's balcony (what a coincidence) and sees Luna, who's surprised to see him not at the Big Blue House. He explains what happened and she tells him how nice that he feels so appreciated.

She then adds, …

"One life touches many others, Bear. We should make sure that each life we touch, we touch in as positive a way as we can."

I have heard and read more than once that *Bear in the Big Blue House* ended due to Lynne's death. And I am here to say (one final time) that this is absolutely **not true**. I even "dueted" a TikTok video of someone saying this and stating for the public record that the show ended in March 2002 and Lynne died the following year. In it, I also said that sometimes things just end. We often don't want something good and wonderful to end, like a beloved TV show, or even a gifted actress, and we look for a huge reason behind it as comfort, but it just happens. Just because. What we need to always remember is that some things and some people will live on in our memories and in our hearts. And as Luna said, …

"We should make sure that each life we touch, we touch in as positive a way as we can."

Lynne Thigpen did that in so many ways.

Thank you for our chats, Lynne.

Beyond the Sock

I've been puppeteering ever since I was a kid, but professionally since that first commercial I did, in Paris. Working on Sesame Street and seeing in person how Jim (Henson), Frank (Oz), Jerry (Nelson), Fran (Brill), and Carroll (Spinney) perform had me practicing and practicing and practicing at home. Their movements both big and small, their timings and pacing, were things I gradually began to absorb while doing it on set. And they did too. If you go on YouTube (the video junk drawer of the world) and watch some of the bits from the first season of Ernie and Bert, Jim and Frank's puppetry is not as smooth as it would become later, especially on *The Muppet Show* and the films they did together. They learned to become these "masters of manipulation" by trial and error: see what works, throw out what doesn't.

Sesame Workshop has "co-productions" of Sesame Street around the world. *Plaza Sésamo* is in Mexico and has continued for many years, along with other coproductions in Germany, the Netherlands, Canada, Israel, Palestine, Bangladesh, and many more. Some have come and gone (due to funding), but several remain airing, either in new episodes or reruns.

When a new co-production begins you need many elements, but the most important is the puppets. And for that you need puppeteers. But where do you find puppeteers able to perform these versions of *Sesame Street* characters on the same level as Jim and Frank, in another country and often in another language? Simple. You have auditions.

I remember when I was first asked to do this and was flattered, excited, and proud that I get to go and represent *Sesame Street* and help create a new Sesame for this country's children, a generation that will experience the same magic I did as I watched our Sesame as a child. And then it hit me …

"How the Fraggle do I teach this?!?"

As I said, I've been puppeteering since… forever… and the skills I know are so entrenched in me, that it's just second nature. When I "puppeteer," what my mind and body have to do is automatic. Now I had to break it all down and figure out the basics, the simplest steps needed to begin with, and add on more skills from there, without overwhelming anyone. So, I started with the most basic part: your hand.

Try it with me.

Hold up your hand.

Put your four fingers together and bend them, flat.

Now, tuck your thumb underneath them.

There — this is Kermit the Frog naked! (Thanks again for the joke, Bert Convy.)

Under all that fur or fleece is this: the puppet you have all the time - your hand. (Whenever I did appearances at schools, bookstores, and now comic conventions to promote my "how-to" books *10-Minute Puppets* and *BOX*, I ask the kids "What puppet do you have all the time?" And their answers range from "my dog" to "my foot," to two kids, who, on two separate occasions, said the same answer "my parents." "No," I said, "but that *is* related to 'puppeteering;' it's called '*manipulation*.'")

So now what? Well, Jim (again Henson) believed we puppeteers are actors; we just "act" from the elbow up. Thus, your forearm is the puppet's body, and your hand is the puppet's head. When I open and close my thumb in time to the words coming out of my mouth, that is called "lip sync." (*Ok, this is good.*) You want to just move your thumb, because your thumb represents your lower jaw, which only moves when you talk. You don't want to raise and lower the four fingers, because then we can't see the puppet's eyes. And in real life — now imagine me jerking my entire head up and down, as I say — We. Don't. Talk. Like. This!!! (In Caroll Spinney's wonderful book *The Wisdom of Big Bird and the Dark Genius of Oscar the Grouch*, Caroll tells of Jim Henson "amusingly bouncing his head up and down as he explained this point of manipulation" to him. I had no idea Jim did the exact same demonstration in 1969 that I've been doing for years! I'm still gobsmacked thinking that my mind thought along the same lines as Jim Henson's!)

You can help your hand's muscle memory for this by pressing your other hand down onto the top four fingers, and then just move the thumb when speaking. Or if you're sitting and there's a table in front of you, put your hand in the "puppet position" and place the four fingers underneath the table so that it prevents them from moving. (Check to make sure there's no gum stuck underneath before trying this.)

I continued breaking it down, all of it down, from head movements, to making sure the puppet was "grounded" and not floating to "sharing the frame," and everything else you need to know when puppeteering with a monitor. And not only did it all work, but this whole teaching process is also now second nature to me. The one thing I had to learn on the spot was looking for who to keep and who to let go. This is never easy. Everyone there came to try something they have never done before and put themselves out there. How do I determine who to train? It's a combination of several little things in rounds one and two.

Here's how it works, usually:

The production company of that country will contact casting agencies or place casting notices in local trade papers, asking those interested in puppeteering in a new children's series to show up on this date and time. Folks show up with their résumés and headshots. Oh — did I mention that 99.9 percent of the time these people are NOT puppeteers and have NEVER puppeteered at all, let alone working with a monitor, which is not like a mirror, with the monitor's image being backwards? Well, it's true.

A few are asked to come into the room, ideally a dance studio with mirrors, to see what they can do. They line up facing the mirror, hold up their bare hand in the "puppet position" (aka four fingers flat and thumb tucked under), and I ask them to count to ten. Then I give notes about lip sync, have them do it again; notes again; one more time; then, try it with a puppet (which are a few of Sesame's "Anything Muppets," the humanoid puppets that can be redressed into, well, "anything"), notes again; one more time; and "thank you" and "please wait outside." And depending on how many people, I do this a couple more times, all the while taking notes on who followed direction and who didn't, before lunch. Then I let them know who can go and who should stay after lunch, for round two. Round two has them saying *their* alphabet and playing "games." And giving notes and direction and seeing who utilizes the new direction, while still incorporating the previous direction, and so on and so on, until by day's end I tell those who didn't make the cut "thank you," and the lucky few "congratulations." And then the next day starts their training, which is less than a week before I leave and they are on their own, sending back rehearsal videos for me and Sesame Workshop to review.

One thing I look for is what I mentioned before: taking direction. If I give someone the note of, for example, just try moving your thumb, and then I see that their hand is now stiff, I'll give the note of "relax" and really drop the thumb, to get use to the movement. Then, if I see them tipping the head too high, I'll give the note of tip the head down, to keep the focus. Now… if they tip the eye focus down and keep the previous note of just moving the thumb, great. Now, let's add tipping the head from side to side, from the wrist up, while keeping the focus to camera, while just moving the thumb. I see who can keep and use *all* the notes. But anyone who concentrates on just the *new* note and throws out the previous one(s)… sorry.

I'm also, through all this, looking for "*it.*" "*It*" is that moment when this person understands, and I can see that they will be willing to put their arms and bodies through positions nature never intended. They get how it should work, that the puppet is an extension of them, and realize they can convey a full range of expression and emotion with this piece of cloth on their hand. With enough time and persistent practice, this person could get "*it*" in, maybe, three to six months. But I don't have that time frame. I need to start training THE NEXT DAY. And then, often, it's for only four days (five being a luxury).

I remember when I was sent to Nigeria to audition and train the two puppeteers for their *Sesame Square*. They needed a man for "Zobi" and a woman for "Kami." I had to conduct the audition in the lobby of the production building because studio space, even rehearsal space, is often not available in Lagos. (The top three movie-making capitals of the world are: Number One – Hollywood, U.S.A.; Number Two – New Delhi, India; and Number Three – Lagos, Nigeria!) So a couple of mirrors were brought in and lined up against a wall. All who came were actors and I remember one young lady who had a "'tude." Just her body language alone told me that this was a waste of her time. I had her and a couple of others do the exercises in the mirror, bare-handed. She literally stood with her hand on her hip, going through the motions. *"Well,"* I thought, *"this will be over quickly."* I handed out the Anything Muppets to each of them, including her. And then, something extraordinary happened.

"Miss 'Tude" looked at the puppet on her hand and quietly began to talk to it. And the puppet quietly responded. She was having a conversation with this puppet she had never seen before, let alone had on, but right then I knew. I had her do the same exercises in the mirror and… there "*it*" was. And she got the part of Kami.

On a few trips, the puppeteers were already chosen, and I had to go teach them or help them brush up their skills. In June of 2004, I got to go to Mexico to work with the new "Aberlardo," the giant green parrot and cousin to our Big Bird, and a couple of the new puppeteers for *Plaza Sésamo.*

Odin Dupeyron was "Pancho," their version of our "Oscar the Grouch," and he had chosen the puppeteers. Odin is one of the most charming people I've ever met, taking me and the production manager from Sesame Workshop to his favorite restaurants, including a tamale stand right around the corner from our hotel. He also interpreted for me when I was speaking to the others. (Once again, great decision in high school to study French, Noel.) I only had a couple of days to work with these guys, especially the one to play Aberlardo. They knew what to do, but I realized something was off: lip sync, eye focus, even just having fun with the material. It just wasn't clicking. And I was not happy.

First: a quick side note for context.

The first morning before working with the puppeteers, I woke up early, but didn't look at my cell phone. I left it plugged in and went to the hotel's fitness center to work out. An hour later, I came back, showered, dressed, and then looked at my phone. I had nine messages, and all from my wife, Susan. I listened:

"Morning! Hope you had a good sleep. Call me when you get a chance."

Second message: *"Hi. It's me. When you get a chance call me. Okay."*

But as I listened to more, they began to take on a more urgent tone:

"Hi. Call me. Bye."

"Please call me, I need to talk to you."

"CALL ME!"

I phoned home, apologized for taking this long to get back, and asked what was wrong.

"Nothing's wrong. I just have some news to tell you."

"What is it?"

"Are you sitting down?"

Immediately I thought she finally sold her novel that she'd been working on for so many years, *Mr. Churchill's Secretary*. Fantastic!

"No," she said, "That's not it."

"Then what is it?"

"I'm pregnant."

That's when I slowly sat down.

For the longest time, we thought about not having a kid. We'd seen the hectic life our friends with kids had and the amount of freedom that was now gone to them. We liked our life together and didn't want things to change. But then we began to think: what if, years down the line, we wished we had, and it was too late? Would we have regrets? We decided to leave it up to fate. We would try and if the universe decided, "They haven't killed their cat, so sure, why not," then that would be that.

And we did try, but the tests were always negative. I, of course, had bought the top-of-the-line tests, the ones that had the word "pregnant" appear and so we didn't have to decipher lines like a codebreaker. These cost more. My wife will admit to being "thrifty." So, she didn't use them because "it's just a waste of money now."

But that morning, after showering she noticed veins visible on her upper chest. "Oh," she thought, remembering that a friend of ours had a similar observation when she became pregnant and —

That's when Susan pulled out the expensive test.

"Meh," said our cat Mr. K (now immortalized in Susan's *Maggie Hope Mystery* series).

"Not now, K," she said to our ever-entitled feline, who wanted to be fed right then and there.

And then began the leaving of the messages to the husband, who was now thousands of miles away, with day one being the beginning and four to go.

"Are you all right?!?" I instantly went into concern mode and wanted to get on the next flight home.

I should be there. Right now!

"No, you stay. There's nothing for you to do here anyway. I'm fine. Go enjoy your day."

Yeah, with this huge amount of guilt I now had about being away. But I did go to the Televisa Studios (the home to all those "telenovelas") to begin training the guys.

Which is why by the afternoon of day two I was climbing the walls. These guys weren't even trying, they were actually goofing around, and I couldn't be home doting over my newly pregnant wife, but instead was stuck babysitting them.

And I had had enough.

After I had them run through a routine, that was so lackluster watching grass try to grow in a foot of snow would have been more exciting, I asked Odin to come with me into the hall.

"Odin," I began, "I just want to warn you that I'm going to go back in and it's not going to be pretty."

"Go for it," he said with enthusiasm.

He, too, had had enough. Afterall, he'd chosen these guys, and this was now embarrassing.

I walked back in and gathered them around.

"I. Have. Had it!" I said, feeling my voice, and blood pressure, rising. "With ALL of you! You guys are not even trying! I need to have footage to send back to Sesame to show them that you belong on this show, that this co-production can continue, and I CAN'T send this [pointing to the camera with footage of what they had just done] because it's *CRAP*!" I turned to Odin. I learned, during the time with Odin, to pause, to have him translate what I said into Spanish. But he was so upset with them, he started to yell at them too … in English! "Wait! What am I doing!" he realized and then proceeded in Spanish.

"Now here's the deal," I said, "We are leaving for ONE. HOUR. In that time, ALL of you will rehearse and record the bit AND rehearse and record the song. When I get back, I better be impressed because if not, we will all stay here. All. Night. Until. It's. Good. GOT IT!?!

And we both walked out.

Odin and I walked across the street, and he treated me to a coffee, while I calmed down. After an hour, we came back. They pressed "play" on the camera to play back what they shot and …

It was good. It was *very* good.

I turned to them, smiling, and said, "Thank you. Now… you're going to be even *better*." And they did get better from there. These guys needed to be pushed because the stakes were too high. They not only needed to be trained puppeteers, but trained to be professionals; you cannot pull this nonsense on a set where time is money and people expect quality.

Beyond the Sock is, per their website description, "an intensive educational experience that packs character development, design, physical manipulation of puppets, and acting with puppets into four and a half days." It was the brainchild of Professor James Martin of the Department of Media Arts for the University of North Texas.

He had this idea back in 2008, when he came to visit the set of the show I was currently working on, the PBS series *Between the Lions*. The final two seasons were being shot in Jackson, Mississippi, where Professor Martin also had relatives to visit, nearby. I had taken over the role of "Lionel," the precocious nine-year old lion who lived in a library with his mom "Cleo" (Jennifer Barnhardt), dad "Theo" (Peter Linz), and little sister "Leona" (Pam Arciero), plus an assortment of other characters, human and non-human. (Personal trivia: I auditioned and was offered the role of "Theo" when the series was starting off, but due to my commitment to *Bear* and appearances I was doing, I told the producers it wouldn't be fair to them to have to deal with my schedules. Funny how fate works.)

Professor Martin talked to Peter and me about this idea of having us as instructors for a master class in TV puppeteering, with the extraordinary puppet designer Pasha Romanowski teaching participants how to build professional camera-ready puppets, with supplies from his company, Project Puppet.

It sounded interesting and we said, "Yeah, sure, when you're ready let us know," and gave him the contact information for our mutual representative/attorney, Suzanne Phillips. I introduced Suzanne to so many colleagues she literally represented the majority of NYC-based puppeteers. Producers always said what a pleasure it was to work with her; she was polite, but firm in representing her clients (even when dealing with one production company's attorney, "Barbera," whom I nicknamed "Barbwire"). He thanked us and that was that.

Flash forward *five years later*. Suzanne calls me.

"Do you know a James Martin?"

"I know a puppeteer named 'Jim Martin.' Why?"

"He says he met you in Jackson, during Lions, and talked to you and Peter about teaching a masterclass in puppeteering."

"Wait," as I rattled my brain trying to remember. "Oh, *that* guy?! Yeah." I did remember because Jim Martin is white, and James Martin is black. And she went on to say what he was offering, and Peter and I both said (if the other agreed) we would both do it.

And give or take a global pandemic, *Beyond the Sock* was an annual thing for over five years. I loved my time there. Denton, Texas, where UNT is located, is an adorable small town; the food is excellent, as are the people I've met, who are now friends, starting with Professor Martin (and his wife, Denise, who always bakes us "welcome back cookies," ready for us when we land).

And participants who've come from, not only the four corners of the U.S.A., but Germany, New Zealand, Australia, and even the Arctic Circle. Some have been first timers, but most became repeat attendees, who would return to brush up on their skills. It all culminates with a last day variety show, made up of skits and bits created by the attendees, and hosted by Peter and me, with a group song for a finale. (And boy, those songs have run the gamut.)

Unlike the audition training process for the Sesame co-productions, no one is cut, everyone gets a chance, and everyone is made to feel that they've done their best. This isn't training for black ops; it's *puppets*. And people who came, for whatever reason and paid good money to take this class, got out of their comfort zone to try something new. Whether they continued puppeteering or not, it didn't matter. They did it. And if they were willing to try *this* (because even I will admit, it's a weird profession to be in), the only thing limiting them, from trying anything else, is themselves.

PART FOUR

"And Now… This"

I brag that my résumé is most people's childhood memory. The '90s had a LOT of shows for kids to watch. But I'm not just a puppeteer for kid TV.

Oh no, my friend. Far from it.

Every now and then, I get to go play and be something utterly ridiculous on a little award-winning HBO series called *Last Week Tonight with John Oliver*. Here's some backstory:

After triumphantly filling in as host for Comedy Central's *The Daily Show with John Stewart*, HBO offered John his own show, combining actual reported and thoroughly researched facts with humor. Halfway through the first season in 2014, John and the show wanted to do a piece about prison reform and parody a segment from *Sesame Street* that had a Muppet explaining that his dad was in jail. But they had never used puppets and puppeteers before. Puppeteer (and dear friend) Stephanie D'Abruzzio contacted me, asking if I'd like to work on the segment with her that weekend. (Half a nanosecond later, I said an enthusiastic "Yes!") The show would be taped before a live audience on Sunday (and aired later that night), but because this was new territory for them, John wanted to meet us (and James Wojtal Jr. and a puppeteer friend of puppet builder Bob Flanagan) Saturday afternoon, to read through the script with him, to see if this would work.

We met in a rehearsal studio at the CBS Broadcast Center in Manhattan. The puppets were there, and we tried them on and played with voices. And then John walked in. With a beard. I'd seen the show and John is always clean-shaven, but being not "show day," he was sporting his mountain man side. (Side note: I have never been able to grow a beard, let alone any facial hair that resembles a five o'clock-shadow. No moustache at all. My hair grows slightly along my jawline and under. I end up looking like a member of the Pennsylvania Black Amish.) We read through the script with him and started riffing off it, and John said, "Yeah. This'll work. Thanks guys." And left.

The next day when it was our turn for the segment, we got into position and then John came over to us. Now during the meeting on Saturday, I tried a joke: when the Alligator gets offended that John mistakes him for a crocodile, just before the racial profiling tirade the gator gives him, my monster character muttered, "Ah Jesus, here we go." And John laughed at it. So, then I saved it until the actual taping, not even doing it for the rehearsals. And when my monster said it, you can see John, on camera, trying not to laugh. (Go to YouTube; watch it.) The segment was a hit, and my monster, Stephanie's little girl, and James' boy got to be part of the season one finale, along with the rest of the odd assortment of characters used. Ever since that segment, I've gotten to go back and be many ridiculous characters:

Jeff the Diseased Lung in a Yellow Cowboy Hat

A Scottish unicorn (the front half)

A Moose getting a colonoscopy

A Polar Bear with the pain of a shrinking penis

A Funky Monkey mascot

A greedy seagull

A Lunar New Year Ram An inflatable T-Rex

The paws of a Supreme Court Justice Dog

Puppeteering the wax figure of President Warren G. Harding

"Gritty Cavanaugh" (the amalgamation of two heinous characters)

"Giant Baby with Hulk Hands"

The NBC Peacock

"Totes McGoats" the Recycling Mascot

And (as of this writing) the COVID Vaccination Cicada.

But of all these, there is the *one* character I've played that John has publicly said epitomizes the show.

For a segment about coal, it featured the machinations of coal baron Bob Murray. His mistreatment of his workers encouraged one to send back a "bonus check" in the amount of $3.22, with the words *"Eat shit, Bob."* But the one aspect of this man that was fascinating was this: according to legend, while Bob was sitting in a park, and trying to figure out what to do with his life, a squirrel came over and *told him* to get into the coal mining business. Murray denied it ever happened, but this tidbit was just too good to pass up. So, at the end of the segment, I got to dress up as a giant squirrel named "Mr. Nutterbutter," who came out with a giant check, addressed to

Bob with the same wording. And I got to say, "Eat shit, Bob" on camera. (Yeah, I can curse. Remember — it's not TV … it's HBO.) The beauty of the rehearsals with John is it's the first time he gets to see any of these creations. When I came out as Nutterbutter and scurried over to John, I immediately started jerking the head back and forth, like a squirrel would.

And John lost it.

He was laughing so hard he couldn't talk.

Yes! Score!

I was so proud. This is always the goal with these things: to get John to laugh. (By the way, a fan of the show on Twitter commented on how accurate my squirrel mannerisms were and asked if I studied their movements prior. Wow!) John is not only talented, funny, and smart, he is gracious and one of the nicest and most genuine celebrities I have ever met. In a February 2021 interview with *Vulture* magazine, he not only mentioned me specifically ("It's amazing because when there're just a costume and a decapitated head, you realize just how amazing Noel is" – now I'm blushing) to his legit respect for puppeteers and how hard it is to do what we do. He acknowledges that it's a skill not everyone can do. That is major props.

John has described wanting his show to be like *The Muppet Show*; I've described it as *60 Minutes* meets *Monty Python*. And it all mixes together to create one of the smartest, most entertaining half hours on TV, which I get to be a part of.

And with every Emmy Award they tweet winning, I respond with, "You're welcome."

Do the Write Thing

Being a professional puppeteer for children's television for over thirty years, I've worked on many shows, especially ones that featured puppets. After the first season and getting the tone and feel for the show as one of the principal characters, I'd ask to write for the series. And it was always rewarding, especially after wading through scripts written by people who had no idea how to write for puppets.

The first show I wrote for was the Nick Jr. series *Eureeka's Castle,* for the second season, and contributed towards the writing of is three specials. After performing for the first season of *The Puzzle Place*, on PBS, I became a writer for that show. I wrote six scripts: four for season two and two for season three. One thing I liked doing and was it's interesting to see were characters who normally aren't together. The caretakers of *The Puzzle Place* were a squad of four monochromatic "Keystone Cops" (Google it.), called "The Piece Police." I played the blue one which I named "Blu." Even though the four of them spoke gibberish, the kids could understand them and vice versa. They were always background characters performed by me, Carmen Osbahr (as "Fushia"), Allison Mork, and then Stephanie D'Abruzzio (as "Purple"), and Jim Martin (as the leader "Green"), but I had an idea: what if Julie (Alice Dinnean) arrived early and the other kids weren't there yet, but she ended up playing with The Piece Police? Titled "The New Adventures of Julie Woo," it was a way to illustrate the idea of meeting and making friends with new people, even people you've known, but never really interacted with. I loved describing where they lived within *The Puzzle Place* and the game, they introduce Julie to: "Fooda Da Moo," also known as "Hide and Sneak." (You read correctly; "sneak." You hide and then sneak around to find a new hiding place. If someone is already there, you're out, and the last one hiding, in this case Julie, wins.) The producers loved it, except for one caveat: potential "stranger danger." Yes. Even though Julie *knew* The Piece Police, the producers didn't want to seem like they *enticed* her to come down to their lair. (*Lord, give me strength.*) Fine. I had Julie return a ball she had borrowed from them, which meant she *knew* where they lived and had *been there before*. Problem solved.

When I became a writer for *Bear in the Big Blue House* it was easy, due to the format head writer Andy Yerkes had nicknamed "bearus interruptus." If you've seen the show, see if this sounds familiar:

Bear opens the door and welcomes you *("C'mon in!")*

Bear is about to tell you something, but then… *("Wait a minute — What's that smell?")*

Once realizing it's you, he then tells you, his plans.

Interruption #1 (by one of his little friends)

Bear introduces the theme of the day and the song to go with it

Then Bear asks, *"What do you think?"* (And footage of real kids commenting)

Bear tries again to do his task, but then Interruption #2 (by one of his little friends)

Bear then hears laughter *("Oh! Where oh where oh where is Shadow?")*

Shadow tells her story and then Bear tries, one last time, to complete the task

Interruption #3 (by one of his little friends or all of them at this point)

Bear can complete the task with friends' help

Time for Luna and "the big picture" review of the day

The Good-Bye Song

And Bear says bye to you and turns off the light.

Within this formula there would be adjustments, but the beats would all be there. And of course, we would add stuff that only made it funnier.

On the Disney Jr series, *The Book of Pooh*, I was not a writer, but I was familiar with Winnie the Pooh, in particular the animated series, *The New Adventures of Winnie the Pooh,* that aired on ABC Saturday mornings during the mid '90s. I was so familiar with that show that a few of our scripts for *Book of Pooh* not only *felt* familiar but *sounded* familiar. One script came through that was, word for word, beat for beat, an exact duplicate of one of the animated episodes. I told executive producer Mitchell Kriegman (who had created *Bear in the Big Blue House* and head writer Andy Yerkes. They told me that the writer of this script had also been a writer of the animated series. And that's when we realized this hack was palming off the same scripts he'd already written. And getting paid for them … again.

It was also his last script for the show.

But I haven't just written for puppet shows!

I got to be a writer for the last season of the animated PBS series *The Magic School Bus*, based on the popular book series. Since it was science-driven, "The Science Team" would come and conduct experiments and demonstrations with us, that one could do with children, to inspire us. For example, one topic for a script was "gravity" and the team had one experiment to show how much of a force gravity is. They brought in bathroom scales and we each stood on one to see our respective weights. Then we each held the scale against a wall and pressed on them with our hands, leaning against them as hard as we could, to try and match the weight. We suddenly realized how much force is being pressed down and pulling us down to the Earth every second. If you have a scale, go try it! (I also asked the team how gravity is created, and they said, "We don't know." *What?!? But doesn't the earth spin around and cause gravity?* "That's one *theory*, but we still don't know where gravity comes from or how it's created." Mind blown.)

When you write for puppet shows you write it the way you'd write it for a non-puppet show, with suggested stage directions and dialogue. Here's an example:

<u>ACT ONE-SCENE 1-KITCHEN-DAY</u>

(Julie, Jody, Skye, Leon, Kiki, Ben)

THEY'RE ALL GATHERED AROUND THE TABLE, TALKING AT ONCE, WITH JULIE IN THE MIDDLE, HOLDING A GAVEL. SHE SLAMS IT FOR ORDER; ALL ARE QUIET.

JULIE

Order! Order! Order!

LEON

O.K.: I'd like to order a hot dog and a large soda! (laughs)

JULIE

(glares at him; to others) Now, we have to decide what kind of party we're gonna have. Any suggestions?

BEAT; THE OTHERS ALL START TALKING AT ONCE, AGAIN. SHE SLAMS FOR ORDER; THEY'RE SILENT.

JULIE

C'mon. There must be one kind of party we can choose.

(to camera) Maybe you can help us.

What kind of parties do you like?

See? There's just enough here for the puppeteers and the director to know what to do. The director can create how she/he wants the scene shot, and the puppeteers have their lines and wiggle room for suggesting a bit more for the scene.

But when I wrote for *The Magic School Bus*, and animated series, I had to write *everything*! Not just the scene and the lines of dialogue, but the camera angles, the lighting, the sound effects; EVERYTHING.

Like this:

FADE IN:

EXTERIOR SCHOOL, SUNSET

CAMERA slowly PUSHES IN

KEESHA V.O.: Is it finished yet Tim?

TIM V.O.: Stop rushing me, Keesha.

CUT TO:

INTERIOR CLASSROOM, OVERHEAD CAMERA ANGLE, CLOSE UP

C.U. of Tim's hands working on a mechanical interior of the sun

KEESHA V.O.: How long does it take …

CUT TO:

INTERIOR CLASSROOM, OVERHEAD CAMERA ANGLE, TWO SHOT

Keesha watches as Tim continues working on the interior

KEESHA V.O.: To make a model of the sun …

CUT TO:

INTERIOR CLASSROOM, CLOSE UP OF KEEHSA

KEESHA: Play "Wait Til the Sun Shines Nellie"

CAMERA PANS OVER TO TIM

Tim closes the lid and winds the model sun with a key

KEEHSA V.O.: When you wind it up with a key?

CAMERA WIDENS AS OTHER KIDS ENTER FRAME.

TIM: There!

CUT TO:

INTERIOR CLASSROOM, WIDE SHOT

All kids stand around the model.

TIM: You think D.A.'s gonna like it?

PHOEBE: She'll love it!

And so on and so on and so on …

And when I saw the finished episode, it was *exactly* the way I had written it! All the direction and graphics and visuals I mentioned were all there! But writing all that wasn't really the hardest part of writing for School Bus. The hardest part was writing for the animated kids.

The Magic School Bus had a diverse cast of animated kids, each with their own specific personality quirks. "Arnold" was nervous about doing anything out of the norm. "Carlos" told bad puns. “Keesha” was confident. “Ralphie” loved food. “Tim” was level-headed. And … you get the idea. And with all these quirks came the bane of writers — they all had (… sigh …) “catchphrases,” such as…

“In my old school we (fill in the blank)”

“What do we do?! What do we do?! What do we do!?”

“According to my research (fill in the blank)”

“Is it just me or… (fill in the blank)”

“Oh bad! Oh bad! Oh bad, bad, bad, bad!”

“We’ve been ‘Frizzled!’” (Which sounds a lot more inappropriate than it should.)

In my script “The Magic School Sees Stars,” it explains the life cycle of a star. The premise I came up with was that it’s Dorothy Ann’s birthday, but she’s home sick. The kids want to give her a present and Tim sees “Horace Scope” (pun intended and also voiced by Dabney Coleman who costarred with “Ms. Frizzle” herself, Lily Tomlin, in the classic ’80s comedy *Nine to Five*). He’s selling stars on “SSH — the Star Shopping Network.” But before they buy one, sight unseen, Keesha insists they should see them, which cues Ms. Frizzle, taking them all into outer space.

Now, Dorothy Ann has lines, Tim and Keesha have lines, but I had to write at least *one* line for all the other kids *and* preferably use each kid’s catchphrase in the episode. But I made it work and the episode came out looking and sounding great. In fact, when I first pitched the idea to head writer Jocelyn Stevenson and the executive producer, I felt proud that it was the first story pitch they’d heard, during the entire run of the series, that didn’t require any adjustment, amendment, or reworking from them. A first for them and I’m still proud I hold *The Magic School Bus* record for it. (By the way… Jocelyn knew and worked with Jim Henson on creating *Fraggle Rock*. She told me that one day in London, she and Jim were sitting on a park bench, trying to think of a name for the always-building-busy creatures that lived alongside the Fraggles, when a construction crew pulled up across the road and began their work. Immediately, she and Jim turned to each other and, simultaneously said, “Doozers!” Meeting and working with such a gifted and giving writer as Jocelyn Stevenson, was the best part of writing for *The Magic School Bus*.)

For three years, starting in 2012, I wrote and produced three separate family musicals for New York City's Bronx Zoo, for their annual Halloween celebration, "Boo at the Zoo." The shows took place at the Asia Stage, a small outdoor theater located in the Asia section of the park. I loved creating these shows and performing them with talented (and patient) friends over the years, including James Wojtal, Jr., who built gorgeous puppets for the shows, and even my son (whose lip sync was better than most of my professional colleagues). With these shows, there was an underlying educational bent about animals and nature, but entertaining first and foremost. At least that's how I wrote them.

With the first show's script, I learned how I had to write for the zoo, specifically for the zoo representative who hired me. They had no sense of humor. They went through the first show's script, "Who Put the Trick in Trick-or-Trick," and cut the jokes out. I tried to explain that they would work, being puppets, but they couldn't understand how. So, Arlee (the other puppeteer that first year), James, and I started to subtly put them back in for the actual performances, and when they realized what we were doing and saw how the audiences loved them, they admitted they were wrong. But for the next two shows I came up with a strategy: I deliberately wrote in jokes I knew they'd take out, while ignoring the ones I wanted kept in. Yep, I wrote *decoys*! There were even two scripts: the one for them to read and approve, and the one for the actual show, with all the gags included.

When our son was little, I would make all sorts of things for him out of cardboard. Once, he asked me, "Daddy, can you make me a pretend fireplace?" I asked why he would need a pretend fireplace, to which he responded, "For my pretend fire." *Obviously*. What was I thinking?

It all started when he was a toddler and I'd take him to this indoor play space nearby, which had one of those three-foot-tall plastic, pretend kitchens. He loved playing with it, so I went online, to price it, to see how much, and — it's *HOW MUCH!?!?* My jaw dropped; it was priced at over *TWO HUNDRED DOLLARS! Are you kidding me?!?! I could make one of these*. And that's exactly what I did, out of cardboard. And it's included with other cardboard crafts in my second book, *BOX*.

The concept for *BOX* is the same as that of my first book, *10-Minute Puppets*. Whenever I was out with the boy (so my wife, Susan Elia MacNeal, could have the opportunity to write her books for *"The Maggie Hope Mystery Series*," starting with *Mr. Churchill's Secretary,* published by Penguin Random House — yes, this is a blatant plug moment, but I'm damn proud of her) I'd make puppets on the spot to entertain him. Remember when banks had deposit envelopes? Once when we were on line at the bank and he got squirmy in his stroller, I used one and turned it into a bird puppet that talked to him, and then he put it on his hand to talk to it. And with all this parent experience of quick and easy puppet making, Susan had an idea.

SUSAN: You know, you're a puppeteer and a dad. Why don't you write a book showing other parents how quick and easy and inexpensive making puppets can be?

ME: Wow. That *is* a great idea.

SUSAN: But — don't make it "*crafty*." Make it for people like me. You are not married to Martha Stuart.

In creating *10-Minute Puppets* (and later for *BOX*) I sat down and wrote out all the instructions step by step. Then I'd show it to Susan, who would take a pen and make edits, cutting it down and crossing out unnecessary steps. It got to the point where I'd hand her the papers and with one glance, she'd say, "Simpler" and hand it back to me. But she was right. It had to be user-friendly for *anyone* to use. And I designed the book to be one kids and their families could use over the years, as the child grew — even sections about creating puppet theaters and shows themselves. And every puppet has an "If you have extra time" sidebar for enhancing the puppet. To give advice on puppetry, I turned to my colleagues in puppetdom and used their sage wisdom in sidebars. Frank Oz (yes, the creator of Miss Piggy, Grover, and Yoda) talks about storytelling. Fran Brill (original Muppet performer on *Sesame Street* and originator of "Zoe") talks about character voices. Jerry Nelson (*Sesame Street*'s "The Count;" The Muppets' "Floyd Pepper," and *Fraggle Rock*'s "Gobo Fraggle" to name a few) was gracious enough to do the introduction. I'm still touched that they, and so many more of my friends, consented to give advice and share their experiences in puppetry for my book.

(Sadly, *10-Minute Puppets* is out of print. Workman Publishing had an exclusive deal to promote it heavily in Borders bookstores just weeks before the chain declared bankruptcy and closed. But you can find used copies on Amazon and maybe your local independent bookseller or library might still have a copy or two. I'm so proud of this book and the care that the late Peter Workman, himself, and my editor, put in to creating this book.)

During a holiday season, my then seven-year-old son was fascinated with the ballet *"The Nutcracker,"* specifically the battle scene between the Nutcracker and the Mouse King. A young neighbor from across the hall would come by to watch the ballet and then be Clara (or Marie depending on who's ballet it is), as my son was the Nutcracker, and of course, I was the Mouse King. (I did fantastic death scenes.) But then I began to wonder …

"Why are these two characters fighting? There's no story leading up to this; why do they hate each other so much?"

And it's true. There's this whole Christmas party, with dancing and celebrating, and the Nutcracker gets broken, and Clara (or Marie) comes to check on him, when, suddenly, this infestation of evil rodents just show-up, wanting to kill the Nutcracker. *Why?!?* So, I began to construct a story, a backstory of the relationship between the Nutcracker and the Mouse King, and how it could be done with puppets. We had friends over for dinner and our puppeteer/actress friend, Aymee Garcia, asked if she could bring her friend, Jim Camacho, who was visiting from Miami. We said sure and got to know Jim, who is an incredibly talented musician, composer, and songwriter. When he heard me describe my idea – it's the story of "The Nutcracker," but from the mice point of view, - Jim was immediately interested, saying it would be a great musical.

In March of 2013, Jim was back in town, and we met for coffee, and he asked again about my idea, which now had a title … *"Mouse King: The Untold Story of The Nutcracker."* Jim and his wife, Deen, are teachers at the Mandelstam School in South Miami and the school puts on shows in the spring. But Jim was interested in doing one for the holiday season and my idea seemed perfect.

"Great," I said feeling flattered. "So, for next year."

"No, *this* December."

Wait. What now?!? THIS December?!?

"Oh! All right!" *So ... I better start writing the script!*

And I did write the script, having done research by reading the original story by E.A. Hoffman. (Which is WEIRD! Let me tell you, read this and wonder exactly what E.A. was on when he wrote this.) I took some of the names and created my own original version. The Kingdom of Sweets is a haven created for, and home to, mice. The King and Queen are presenting their new son, "Mouserick," when the ceremony is interrupted by "Krakatuck," the spoiled nephew of the famous clockmaker and mouse-trap inventor, "Drosselmier." He wants to rule the kingdom but first, presents a "gift" – a clockwork cat that defeats the guards. The court astrologer and magician "Astrolog" says, ...

"Since you like toys so much, become one!"

And casts the spell turning Krakatuck into ... a nutcracker! The enraged doll orders the cat to attack the royal family, who hand the baby to Astrolog, before they are dragged away to their doom. The shadow of Drosselmier falls over the scene as Astrolog flees, with the heir to the mice kingdom, and finds refuge in the floorboards of a human house, with a mouse family – Mother Ginger and her mice children. Young Mouserick grows quickly, but is intrigued by the humans of the house, especially the girl Marie, who is kind - unlike her brother, Fritz. When a baby bird has fallen in the garden, Fritz releases his toy to run it over, but Mouserick jumps on it and steers it away. When her godfather comes to visit, she tells him what she saw happen, which intrigues her godfather. (And guess who her godfather just happens to be?)

Then it's that magical time of year for mice ... "Chrismouse!" It also happens the same time as the human family celebrate Christmas, and Mouserick scurries up to see Marie at the party, holding an odd "doll." Once the party ends, he returns to examine the doll closer, but Astrolog tries to stop him. The Nutcracker rises and recognizes Astrolog. Astrolog casts a spell to shrink the Nutcracker to a more harmless size, but the spell misses and hits Marie instead, and *she* shrinks! (Yes! This is why it looks like the Christmas tree is *growing* – it's not growing; she's *shrinking*!)

The Nutcracker orders the toy soldiers to kill them, but then Mother Ginger and her mouse kids arrive. And THAT'S why the Mouse King and the Nutcracker have their fight.

I'm so proud *Mouse King* has become an "annual holiday classic," according to local South Miami papers. And that kids, who see it, want to audition to be in it, for the following year.

And all this from my asking myself, *"Why are they fighting?"*

If you've ever wanted to write, do it. Seriously - Write. Just do it. A book is not going to write itself. A story is not going to magically appear. It's up to *you*. Could you sell it? Maybe. You won't know until you try. For the record, you may also fail… more than once. My wife is an award-winning, *New York Times* best-selling, author of a *series* ("The Maggie Hope Mysteries" starting with book number one - *Mr. Churchill's Secretary* available on Amazon and your local independent bookstore). And it took her *ten years* to get the right agent who knew the right person at the right publishing house interested in the first book. But it was worth it. I sent my memoir to my editor at the agency that helped me sell my first two books. But the one and only place he decided to pitch my memoir to, turned it down. So here I am self-publishing. So don't do it just to make money; that's not how dreams work. If you enjoy it and it's fun, that's all that matters.

(But if you *happen* to get some bucks from it, well, that's nice too.)

I Haven't Had This Much Fun in Years

Having been in a lot of shows over the years, I've worked with a lot of directors. They've all had their own style, some good, some great, and the occasional "how did you get this job?" On one show I worked on, there was a director who showed up so hungover (*"How hungover was he?"*), that they had a couch from the green room brought into the studio and a large monitor set up at one end, so that they could *lay down and direct the show.* (Hooray for Hollywood.) Another director, known for creating "pretty pictures," got those pictures because the performers, the cameramen, the stage manager, the floor manager – once, even the props department – would fix their (always unprepared) shot setups, all the time. However, I have had the good fortune of working with, and learning from, accomplished and creative directors, over the years. The first being Jon Stone.

Jon was incredible; a writer, producer, and, most of all, director of *Sesame Street*. He wrote and directed my favorite Sesame special, *Christmas Eve on Sesame Street* (that is still a Christmas Eve tradition with my family). And he was clever. On set was a lift used for adjusting the lights. You'd stand within the front part, and then, with a control panel on it, you could rise up to the light grid, and do whatever adjustments were needed. Well, Jon wanted a continual shot, with no cuts, for a scene that started on one end of the street (at the old Fix-It Shop), with characters emerging, and ends at the other end by the lamp post, with a glorious shot of the whole street, looking down from above. Well, to do this, the cameraman is backing up his camera (that's on a big cumbersome base) along the street until he gets to the lift (and the lighting guy waiting for him), slowly backing up the camera onto it. And then, the lighting guy slowly raises up the front end, as the camera tilts down and widens, to show the whole cast AND the whole street. Yep – before fancy "jibs" (cameras at the end of long poles) or drones, there was this little trick from Jon.

Another Sesame director I greatly admired was Lisa Simon, who started off as a production assistant. Lisa was also the producer for the show when I joined. Having been with the series so long, she knew how it should look and her direction proved it. Composing shots with puppets and humans is not easy. Then add in a very big bird and a snuffleupagus and you've got your work cut out for you. She always managed to do it. It's why she also directed other kids shows, three of which I happened to work on: *Oobi, Between the Lions,* and *Bear in the Big Blue House.*

On Sesame, first as the wrangler and then as an assistant/background puppeteer, I watched directors and how they worked through scenes; starting at the production meeting and going through what would work and what wouldn't, and what was not even necessary; reading through the script with the performers on set; the "shot sheet" for the camera operators (there are three used on Sesame in the studio); and readjusting a shot that isn't working. But also, being able to receive input that helps them. One example came with a bit Jon was directing during my wrangling days. It was at Oscar's trashcan, and in the bit, Oscar says to one of the humans, he has friends "dropping in." That's when he ducks down and four full body grouches, literally, drop into the can from above (thanks to the props guy on a ladder). And Jon felt the bit just laid there, no real payoff. That's when I suggested "feeding the grouches through;" one grouch drops and a props guy behind the can catches it, and tosses it, to another props guy, who catches it, and tosses it up, to the original props guy on the ladder. Jon liked the idea and was willing to give it a try. And it worked! The dropping, catching, tossing cycle kept going and going as the human wandered off. They played it back – "that's a buy!" Jon passed me, as I gathered up the grouches, and with his rolled-up script, tapped my arm, and said, "Nice idea." Who's proud and holding a bunches of grouches? *This* guy!

Another time a Sesame director needed help and didn't realize it. Emily Squires was to direct a bit with Big Bird and Snuffy, a spoof of vaudeville. (You can Google the word but basically, vaudeville was a variety show cities had, with different acts booked.) I rigged a cane in Bird's right hand/wing, and Caroll would hold a straw hat in his left hand/wing. Snuffy needed to wear this humongous straw hat (that was far too heavy, because, for some reason, automotive glue was used to piece it together, which adds weight). Against a curtain backdrop, each entering to do a little back-n-forth banter to music, while on the monitor, the shots continue to cut from a close up of Bird, saying his lines, to a close up of Snuffy, saying his.

There was also a monitor on the desk of our floor manager, Chet O'Brien. Chet and his brother, stage manager Mortimer (or "Snooks" as everyone called him), were an identical twin song-n-dance act back in the hey days of vaudeville. They traveled around the country for bookings at different theaters and knew *everyone* on the circuit (from Milton Berle to Bob Hope) and how vaudeville worked. (Quick trivia: the expression "Break a leg" originated in vaudeville. The parts of the stage include the side panels called "legs," the fabric that hangs down as scenery and blocks the view of backstage. And you only got paid if you got to go on stage; didn't matter if you were booked, cause sometimes houses would deliberately over book. So going past the "legs," onto the stage, meant money. Thus, for luck, you'd tell your fellow performers "Break a leg!" Now, back to the story.) When Chet saw the camera cuts back and forth, he got up, strode over, waving his arms, saying,

"No! No! No! THAT's not vaudeville! Keep it *wide*! You don't care what Bird is saying! You want to *see* Snuffy's *reaction* to what Bird is saying!"

So, Emily tried it as a wide shot with just one camera and … Chet was absolutely right. It looked and felt so much better.

Another director I worked with, and respect so much, is Hugh Martin. Hugh was the primary director for *Eureeka's Castle* and was great. He was receptive to our suggestions and totally got our sense of humor. When we stopped suggesting gags at the read throughs and decided to just do them during a take, we'd give him a heads up. "Do it!" he'd gleefully say. Hugh was the kind of director who genuinely enjoyed working with his cast and, because of that, we always wanted to make sure he was happy, and that, of course, makes his job easier. One time I even got to surprise him (and everyone else) with a last-minute gag.

The scene starts out in the courtyard and the door to Magellan's lair opens and he steps out. Now in order to do this, because the door is under the stairs, I had to crouch down inside. Then, as the door opens, I rise up walking, as if Magellan were climbing up his stairs to the courtyard. And to make Magellan look larger next to the other characters, a runway of platforms lead up to join the other characters. We rehearsed the bit, that ends with Magellan being the last one in the courtyard, looking baffled. And it just, kind of … laid there. When we did the take and the scene comes to an end, suddenly, I turned around, Magellan muttering about what happened, heading towards the door. That's when someone realized what I was doing, raced over, and from underneath, swung the door open. Magellan entered, and I began to lower myself, as if he was now walking *downstairs*, as the door swings shut.

Cut.

Once Magellan's head and neck were popped off, the other puppeteers told me how they frantically lined up on each side of the platform to make sure I didn't fall, then one racing to open the door to prevent me from slamming into it. From the control room, Hugh came out, laughing, and said to me, …

"Oh my GOD! How did you DO THAT?!?!"

For Bear, the two primary directors were the creator, Mitchell Kriegman (he was also the executive producer), and the assistant director, Dean Gordon. Both men were so creative with their scripts, with camera angles, understanding our pacing and energy, and trusting us; and we trusted them. For one song inspired by the stye of Tom Waits, Mitchell wanted it to start in the Otter Pond and end in the living room. To do this, Bear walks from the Otter Pond, through the back door, through the kitchen, entering and exiting the foyer, and, finally, into the living, onto the swing, before getting back up to exit camera frame. This was all ONE CONTINUOUS SHOT: no cuts. And we rehearsed a few times, because in order for Bear to walk and sing into camera, the camera operator had to walk BACKWARDS, holding a hand-held steady camera, with someone handling the cables (to keep him from tripping). Camera Operator Larry Solomon did it and it's still one of the most impressive pieces of camera work I've seen, let alone be involved with. (And I now understand Ginger Rogers' response when asked what it was like being Fred Astaire's dance partner; "Try doing it backwards – and in heels!")

The day would start with Bear opening the door, inviting the viewer in, telling them how good they smelled, then we'd skip to his monologue, about the day's theme, and the accompanying song. Mitchell and Dean trusted me so much that often they would ask me, "so what do *you* want to do?" Not just the choreography, but where I wanted to do the song, which meant where the camera should follow. "How about we start here in the foyer, to the kitchen, to the living room, and then, end back in the foyer?" I'd suggest. And it sounded good, and we'd rehearse, and then, record it. So, this was my unofficial moments of directing on Bear.

By the fourth season, I knew the look and feel of the show. That's when I asked Mitchell if I could direct an episode. I was already a writer for the series, so this was the next achievement I wanted. And, to his credit, Mitchell said, "yes." From asking me what good names would be good for the moon and the sun, to my appearances on other shows, he always trusted me to have the show and Bear's best interest at heart. I will be eternally grateful to him for picking me to be the embodiment of this incredible character. So, he knew he could trust me with an episode.

But, in order for me to direct, the script would also have to be a very special one.

You see, Bear was in EVERY SCENE of the show. It was very rare for him not to be. So, a script was written that has Bear, on the day he volunteers around town, hurt his foot, and needs to stay home. That's when his little friends cover for him; Treelo and Ojo go to the firehouse to clean the truck, while Pip, Pop, and Tutter do story time at the library. This way, I could be me – a human being with a headset – and direct my castmates. I am very proud of this episode, "Volunteers of Woodland Valley," pulling together so much knowledge I picked up from being directed over the years.

Of course, it was also fun to do a scene with everyone and then have Bear look to camera a say, …

"Cut!"

Shows such as Bear and Sesame are "union shows." Meaning, they are shows covered by the unions representing writers (the Writers Guild of America or WGA), directors (the Directors Guild of America or DGA), and the actors (now called SAG-AFTRA, the combining of the Screen Actors Guild & the American Federation of Television & Radio Artists). In 2019, Sesame launched a multi-episode arc called "Big Bird's Road Trip." In it, Big Bird wants to visit his cousin, "Little Bird," who lives in Los Angeles. Big Bird would visit a city and chat with a local kid, who would share knowledge about what was fun about that city, and their family. Ten cities were chosen: New York City (of course, because that where the street is), Pittsburgh, Detroit, Washington D.C., Kansas City (Missouri), Chicago, Denver, Dallas, Seattle, and finally, Los Angeles. Matt Vogel (who took over the role of Bird when Caroll retired) couldn't do all ten cities (because of commitments with The Muppets; Matt is also Kermit the Frog), so I was asked to do some (with Matt dubbing his Bird voice, later). But Matt also asked if I still had my DGA membership. I answered I did, and he and the production asked if I'd like to direct the Chicago shoot.

Say what now?!?

Immediately followed by, …

"YES!"

There was a formula for all the segments to follow, to keep all of them uniformed in appearance but, within that format, we shot great footage. I had a blast!

And … I wanted to direct, again.

I must have done a good job because I got to direct three segments for the Sesame YouTube channel in February of 2021, featuring Elmo (more adorable than ever, thanks to Ryan Dillon), Grover (voiced incredibly by Eric Jacobson; perfectly puppeteered by Peter Linz, for these segments), and Gabrielle ("Gabbi"), the new African American female Muppet (voiced so sweetly by African American puppeteer Megan Piphus Peace; and perfectly puppeteered by Carmen Oshbar). The three were different set-ups: one with a Muppet firetruck; one on a farm; the last one with Grover, driving a bus. And that's because all three segments had their version of that classic kid song "The Wheels on the Bus." Thus, "The Animals on the Farm," "The Firetruck Goes …," and, with Grover driving, "The Wheels on the Bus." But this was February of 2021 and social distancing, and masking and testing was at its height still, with no vaccines yet. The segments were to be shot at the studio within the offices of Sesame Workshop and the number of people in the room had to be kept at a minimum. So, Matt, as Puppet Captain (and we haven't heard this phrase for a while), asked if I wouldn't mind directing AND puppeteering. *Sure – two different paychecks, heck yeah!* I got to be the firetruck, an alligator on the bus, and ALL the animals for the farm. Which meant for the final shot on the farm, with all the characters, since it was against blue screen, we did three separate passes, with each character with an animal. And in post-production editing, they were all placed together. You'd never know unless I told you. (Go to YouTube and check out all the segments.)

Since then, for the show itself, I've directed the "Monster Foodie Truck" inserts (hysterically performed by Dave Rudman as Cookie Monster and Warrick Brownlow-Pike as Gonger) and an entire show. And not just any "show" – one of the shows of Season 53, has a new set (the Community Garden) that's raised and needing platforms for the humans. And, oh, did I mention Big Bird, too?!? Plus, with Abbey Cadabbey (performed with such genuine joy and magic by

Leslie Carrara-Rudolph) entering to help, I decided I wanted her to *fly*, (she has those cute little wings; use 'em) and she did … along with butterflies, a flock of Muppet birds, and a friendly Muppet cloud, to boot. And it all worked, and it looks fantastic.

There's an old joke with an actor professing the "process" and the "craft" of acting, and then adds, "But what I really want to do is direct." I know what that means now. For me, it's the natural progression of my career in show business, the next step. I know that eventually I won't be able to physically do the contortions and arm extensions for puppetry. (But that hasn't happened yet, so bring on those hot sweaty body puppets!). All those years of experience seem to have culminated into this new path. Having been a wrangler, I know what's needed for puppets to look good on camera. Having been a performer, I know what is needed for monitor placement, positions of bodies under the puppets, and what to do with props, costumes, and any tricks the characters need in order to look good on camera. Having written for puppet shows, I know what the characters can and cannot do, while still making it entertaining to watch (as in "*show* it, don't *say* it").

What has been the most gratifying about directing Sesame is the support from everyone, especially the puppeteers. My Sesame family of dollie wigglers have more than once shouted their praises of me to producers, how well I did, and requesting I direct more. After the "Monster Foodie Truck" inserts day of directing, I got home, and Susan asked how it was.

"Professionally speaking," I said, "I haven't had this much fun in *years*."

Odds & Ends

So far, you've heard me regale you with my adventures in front of the camera, whether it was for TV or film, blah, blah, blah. But I haven't just puppeteered in front of cameras. Movies and TV shows come and go; and I may get called in at the last minute to do *"Last Week Tonight with John Oliver,"* or *Sesame Street* (one former executive producer once introduced me to a visiting V.I.P. as … "This is Noel. He's our *'back-up Big Bird.'"* Wow! There's a job title you're not handed every day.) But I'm not their weekly salary as a principal cast member. So, I've had to take other jobs within my very limited skillset, to pay the bills and put food on the table. And they have run the gamut. I've been a teaching artist for an afterschool program and an instructor for making puppets at a summer day camp. But one of the most unusual puppetry jobs I've done is being a life size "baby" T-Rex.

Let me explain.

In the spring of 2012, in Secaucus, New Jersey, a new theme park opened: "Field Station: Dinosaurs!" The feeling was you entered an excavation site that also happened to have "living" dinosaurs in it, as if they never went extinct. It featured life size animatronic replicas of dinosaurs (built in China and shipped over) and an outdoor show (with one of two "baby T-Rexes" that were body puppets originally built and shipped over by "Erth," and their leader Scott Wright, from Australia, a company that specialized in bringing dinos to life on stage).

I went in to audition for the part at a rehearsal studio in midtown Manhattan. There I met two of the puppeteers that had been promoting the about-to-open-park with one of the T-Rexes, Miron and Sam. (I've become good friends with both guys and can say this because I've said it to them: Miron was around my height – six feet, one inch – and solid, so obviously he could haul around a ninety-pound dinosaur on his back. Sam, however, was not; he was around five foot ten inches, thin, and ridiculously handsome. Either the dino was *not* as heavy as I thought, or this guy is a *lot* tougher than he looks and I need to stay on his good side. The first time I told this to Sam, he laughed, and appreciated the compliment.) Miron conducted the audition (because he was the – here it is again – "Puppet Captain") and when I came in, I was expecting to see the T-Rex and to climb in and try it out. But there was no T-Rex in the room. But there was a table with these random "things" on it and Miron asked me to animate a few of them together, to create a character. *Oh,* I thought, *It's an exercise. Some sort of acting/puppeteer exercise.* I got flashbacks to the acting exercises in Oregon for TMNT3. (*I wonder if he knows Gordie.*) But, his house, his rules, and he was so enthusiastic, and a proud graduate of the UConn Storrs puppetry program, I went along with it, and then left and, per audition training, immediately forgot about it.

However, I did get the job and became one of the puppeteers for the new park and went to *finally* try on the T-Rexes. Scott Wright was there to consult and give pointers on how the "Ts" should move, and all of the inside gizmos that made it work, since his company built them. Scott, with his wavy greyish hair and a spark in his eyes, made me think *this* is the guy who Santa Claus consults with on what kids *really* want for Christmas. He has a natural exuberant energy that's infectious. We chatted and when he mentioned how much he loved "Bear" (having seen it on my resumé) marveled at the "mechanism" inside.

"The Mechanism?" I asked.

"Yes," he said in his crisp Aussie accent, "How you make the neck move so fluidly?"

"You really want to know the 'mechanism' I used?"

He nodded and I grinned as I slowly raised my right arm up over my head, and let my hand lip synch the words, "Like this."

Scott was genuinely shocked. He felt sure it was some elaborate system and tower inside because that's how his mind works; it's how the dinos worked. But no, it was just my arm and I felt proud that this creative genius thought it was something more.

Now, *this* is how the T-Rexes worked:

First, they weighed around ninety pounds. They had to be hung from the head and from the spine, in order for you to go under and up inside. There, you'd clip yourself inside of a harness so that the weight was balanced off your hips (similar to what I wore inside "Bear"), and the rest of the weight was counter levered between the head and tail. You held onto the metal structure that extended through the neck to the head, like a gunner in a fighter jet. You could coordinate the head and neck to tip, tilt, turn left & right, shake, rear up, and get low to the ground. One trigger made the mouth open and close, and the other trigger controlled the eyelids. Your feet were strapped in next to the dino feet. There was a small monitor inside, connected to a lipstick camera planted in one of the nostrils; this was the *only* way to see. And one last switch was for "the Voice." You wore a headset with a mike that was connected to a speaker in the neck and the pitch was way low, so that when you "growled" or "roared," it was amplified – and terrifying. You'd get unhooked and then you were free to walk and roar and scare the beejeesus out of kids.

I loved being "T." Looking back, it was hard, sometimes frustrating, especially on those heat advisory days, because the shows were performed outside. But it was never dull, and when it all worked, it *worked.* There was a team of around eight of us, four of us a day, and rotating; two puppeteers and two "handlers." We would do a show for families, six of them throughout the day, alternating between being the dino and being the "handler," who would lead "T" out and keep him from eating the guests, while doing "tricks." The "host" welcomed everyone, giving fascinating facts about dinos, specifically ones in New Jersey, and would introduce myself and another puppeteer who brought out infant dinos, swaddled, and we'd go through the crowd so kids could see them up close. These were incredibly cute and an easy precursor to meeting the T-Rex. Then the two of us would leave and one of us would then get into "T" and the other, now the "handler," would lead the "baby" T-Rex out to the astonished audience. One bit that was always popular was having a kid come up and bravely stick their head into "T's" mouth only to have it clamp down on them (which of course it didn't; all part of the show folks).

Oh – did I mention that the "host" had to speak in an *Australian* accent? Yes. You see the show at that time was sponsored by "Outback Steakhouse" and per the agreement (that lasted three years) the hosts had to speak with an Aussie accent. A dialect coach was hired to come and train the hosts in how to sound authentically Australian. I however did *not* get this training, nor did a fellow puppeteer. You see, he and I are African American, and look quite non-white, and it was just a given that *no one* would believe either of *us* could be from the Land of Oz, even though there are over *380,000 black Australians* (of African and some of Aboriginal descent). No; apparently *ALL* Australians are white, and the audiences coming just wouldn't believe otherwise. And that was that.

The best part of this gig was the incredibly talented people I met and whom I'm still friends with. The conditions were less than ideal, a park completely outdoors, with scorching temperatures or torrential downpours. Yet, we made it through the three seasons I was there, together. Dinosaurs may be extinct, but some friendships survive the test of time.

NBC started to televise live family-oriented musicals, starting with *"The Sound of Music LIVE"* in December of 2013. For December of 2015, it was to be *"The Wiz - LIVE."* With its all-star cast, featuring David Allen Grier, Queen Latifah, and Mary J. Blige, this was going to be spectacular.

Bob Flanagan is a remarkable puppet builder (who I met through Jim Kroupa in college) and made the puppet elements and props for *Saturday Night Live*, for over thirty years. He also made the head of "The Wizard" for Broadway's *Wicked.* So, the producers of *The Wiz - LIVE* came to him to create one for their production. And Bob has also been responsible for the mascots of *Last Week Tonight with John Oliver.* So, Bob asked me if I'd like to puppeteer the head. In fact, Bob insisted to the producers that it had to be *puppeteers* to animate it, not stagehands. It would require another puppeteer and I recommended Paul McGinnis (one of the best puppeteers I know as well as a dear friend). If I had to be trapped inside the pedestal of this ginormous head, I wanted someone who would know how, as well as get along with. And that was Paul.

The show was to be done at the same studio of the two previous, live musicals (*The Sound of Music LIVE* and *Peter Pan LIVE*), Grumman Studios in Bethpage, Long Island. A former airplane factory now used by movie and television productions. And it's a schlep to get there. I'd take a Long Island Railroad commuter train and then get picked up by the production van. And then having to coordinate when the next train was after wrapping for the day. But then, three days before the broadcast, the production put us all up – cast, crew, and staff – at the Marriott Melville. This way, *no one* could be stuck in traffic and miss the show.

The "puppet" was huge. It was the bald sculpted head and shoulders, a humongous bust on a pedestal, twenty-two feet wide and thirty feet tall. Paul and I had to sit inside the pedestal and coordinate our movements: I controlled the head, and the mouth, and Paul controlled the eyes and eyelids. And we had a monitor that gave us the same camera cuts you'd see at home. (Imagine trying to subtly animate a grand piano at the top of a flagpole and that's the kind of weight we were dealing with.) And we had to do this while Queen Latifah, as "The Wiz," spoke her lines … *live*. And her cadence was slightly different each time. But we made it work (and she was so appreciative of what we were doing).

There were two directors for the broadcast. There was the TV director, who worked out the camera angles and cuts. And then there was the "theatrical" director, who directed the actual actors … and us. Of course, many people still don't "see" puppeteers as actors, even though we are part of the actors union, SAG-AFTRA, and regarded as "on-camera talent," just like any other human actor. And in professional theater, it's often a battle to have puppeteers perform the actual puppet. (For the Broadway production of *"Shrek,"* John Tartaglia, Tony nominated star of *"Avenue Q"* was to puppeteer and voice "The Magic Mirror," a fantastic puppet that hung on stage and operated via remote control. But the teamsters union, IATSE, argued that the setup and operation of it made it a "prop." John could do the voice but only one of *their* members could animate it. And they won the argument. You don't mess with IATSE.) Whenever, the director wanted to convey a note to us, his assistant would come around back and give it. At one point the director, himself, actually happened to come back and began to give us an instruction. Rather than let him continue, believing we were two nameless prop guys thrown in, …

"Hi," I interrupted, extending my hand out, "I'm Noel." And once he shook my hand, "And this is Paul," shaking Paul's hand. Then, I said, "Now, what was it you'd like again?" (My mom raised me to believe there's always time for politeness, first.)

We got comfortable enough that we started experimenting with expressions. So good in fact that we were able to "throw shade;" the head and eyes turning away and then look back at the characters for the disdainful line "*You* wanna meet 'The Wiz?!?'" The first time we did it, the assistant came by and gave the note – from the director – not to do it. OK. But then after a few more rehearsals, we did it again to fineness it, … and the assistant, again, came back to give the same note not to do it. The day before the actual live broadcast, the final dress rehearsal was taped and then would be played alongside the live broadcast. This way, in case of something going wrong during the live broadcast, the control room could immediately cut to the pre-taped performance, no one the wiser. But the next night was the live broadcast, and everything was perfect so far so, when it was time for Paul and my scene, where the characters first meet the ginormous head, we set up, during the commercial break - back live in thirty seconds - I said to Paul, …

"Do the eyes. We're doing the movement." Because it looked SO GOOD; it was PERFECT. "Besides," I added with a smirk, "What will they do – *fire* us?"

And when it came time for that close-up, for that line, the head did the move. And "Black Twitter" erupted!

"The head threw shade!"

"OMG I just screamed at the synchronized head tilt! So, black LMAO"

"That giant Wiz head features are ethnic as heck!"

Because my Uncle John always taught me, …

"First make sure you're right, then, go ahead."

And we did … and we were.

"SO GO GIT IT!"

In February of 2020, I took my son to see the new Off-Broadway revival of the musical *"Little Shop of Horrors"* at Manhattan's Westside Theater. It's based on the 1960 Roger Corman film (and the classic tale of *"Faust"* who makes a deal with the Devil) about the nebbish florist-assistant, Seymour Krelborn, who nurtures a particular plant that feeds on human blood. It was more than wonderful: everything about it worked. The theater was just small enough to have the final effect of the ginormous plant be completely breath-taking and terrifying; the plants/puppets themselves looked and worked fantastic; but it was the cast, humans & puppeteers, that made it such an entertaining evening. My son loved it. And I happened to know one of the two puppeteers, Eric Wright, who then introduced me to his "comrade-in-vines," Teddy Yudain. And in the back of my mind while I sat watching the plant sing, gyrate, and devour, I thought …

THIS would be fun to do. I could do this.

Fast forward (through a pandemic and a lockdown) to October of 2022. The company Monkey Boys Productions, which had created the plants for the show, contacted me because the show needed a temporary "puppeteer vacation swing." A "swing" in basic theatrical terms is someone who can fill-in if a lead cast member is unable to go on, whether it be due to sickness or on vacation. Marc Petrosino (and his Monkey Boys partner Mike Latini) asked me if I'd be interested.

Hmmm ... Big puppet that's heavy, cumbersome, and sweaty? I'm your man!

On my first day of rehearsal, I met Teddy, who would work with me on how to manipulate each "pod" (the nickname term for the four puppets representing the four stages of growth the plant goes through). I'd seen a recent performance to refresh my memory and saw how absolutely amazing he and Weston Long (who took over for Eric) were. They made it look effortless, especially the last one the takes up half the set and consumes three people. So smooth, so articulate, so precise. And I so envied them. But even before I had touched a puppet, the production manager said …

"And we'd like you to go on next week."

Say what now?!?

Not only was I rehearsing how to be a carnivorous plant, but I was working with a new "Seymour." Matt Doyle (who'd just won the TONY Award for his incredible performance in the Broadway revival of *"COMPANY"*) was taking over the role from current Seymour, Rob McClure. It was fun not only working alongside this ridiculously talented man but also getting to know him. Matt is one of the most genuine and sincere people I've ever met. And we'd have fun onstage unbeknownst to the audience. You see, before Matt/Seymour places the small plant (aka "pod one") on the counter for it to interact and react with him (as in me puppeteering it), I'm under the counter … waiting. For over fifteen minutes from the start of the show. So, when Seymour first appears onstage and trips, causing the tray of flower pots he's carrying to crash across the floor, he has to clean them up. And that's when Matt would pull little tricks on me: balancing a broken pot piece on my shoulder; opening my hand to place a leaf in it. Once, he did something so funny I had to clap my hand over my mouth to not guffaw out loud.

And I thought … *Of course, you know, this means war.*

The next night, when he began doing his little tricks, he hadn't actually looked at me until he was centerstage with his back to the audience. And when he did, he had to immediately look away, trying not to laugh out loud. Because I was wearing a pair of glasses with a big nose, bushy moustache, and eyebrows. (It made me recall how Lynn Thigpen told me doing little pranks to each other is what stage actors do to entertain themselves. I was proud to now be a part of this tradition.)

Of course, Matt got this idea from Rob McClure. When I saw the performance to get an idea of how the show and the plants worked, it was with Rob being Seymour. During the song he sings with The Urchins (the three Greek chorus ladies who are beyond amazing; I love them), Seymour comes out holding the plant ("pod two," named "Audrey Two" after his crush, fellow shop employee, Audrey) and the four sing and do choreography while the plant takes on a life of its own. It even tries to take a bite out of each Urchin, who don't notice. And as I watched this, I knew it was a puppet but suddenly realized Rob was doing it. And it was ...*perfect*!

Who IS this guy?!?

I opened my program to discover Rob's extensive resumé that not only included his recent TONY award nomination for the lead in the Broadway musical *"Mrs. Doubtfire,"* but also ... *"Ave Q."* (*Ah HA!*) And he told me he was trained for Q by none other than fellow puppeteer colleague and dear friend, the talented Jennifer Barnhardt, who not only is an original Broadway cast member of Q, but she's also trained regional and touring companies of the show. And Rob is not only a good puppeteer but appreciates the art and those who practice it. To the point that this acclaimed star of Broadway fanboyed ME when he found out who I was. Because Rob grew up watching *"Eureeka's Castle."* Which is why for a farewell gift to him, I gave him one of the little rubber "Magellan" puppets that was part of a promotion through Pizza Hut, back when the show came out. And ... the man almost cried.

I was flattered that other members of Little Shop also were fans of my work, either watching Eureeka or Bear during their childhood. I've primarily done TV, followed by commercials and film. (My ignorance of theater terms came when the production manager mentioned a theatrical podcast whose host asked the guest "What are your three threats?" Everyone was thinking what theirs would be as in what three *talents* – acting, singing, maybe dancing. But I said that being a non-theatre performer, my three threats are 1.) Being pushed onto subway tracks, 2.) Getting a life-threatening disease, and 3.) Republicans.) But Little Shop was my first time doing legitimate theater and I ***loved*** it. I've watched the TONY Awards in the past and there's always the mention of the "community" within theater and the comradery among actors and their crews and staff, etc. etc. Well, I'm here to testify that it's all true. Never, and I mean NEVER have I been privileged to work with such a welcoming, supportive, inclusive group of people. Not an ego among them (and if there were any than they really are good actors in hiding it). I had the time of my life doing Little Shop. Teddy complimented me on how I picked things up so quickly and felt completely confident that, I could fill in for him or Weston.

(And thanks to COVID still being around, among other things, I did.)

“That Must Be So Much Fun!”

Whenever I’ve told people that I’m a puppeteer the usual reaction is …

“Really!?!? That must be so much fun!”

And it is.

Sometimes.

Ok, yes, the fact that I have been able to make a career from what I dreamt of doing since I was a kid, is no short of remarkable. Miraculous in fact. I remember one morning waiting for the van to that day’s location for the movie *Follow That Bird* and watching other people on the streets of Toronto pass by, some in business attire. And I thought, *Wow. I could not work in an office.* But then thought, *But maybe some of them* like *working in an office. Even* love *it. Working numbers all day may be someone else’s dream come true.* (Not me – I was terrible at math in school.) When I’ve done demonstrations of puppeteering in front of *kids,* I introduce myself saying, …

“Hi! My name is Noel. And I’m a puppeteer. That is my job. That is what I do for a living. Puppeteer. Who has ever heard of the word ‘puppeteer?’”

And lots of kids raise their hands. Then I ask, …

“Who knows what the word ‘puppeteer’ *means*?”

And maybe two or three stick their hands back up. And they’ll answer that puppeteers make puppets and I’ll agree, yes, *some* puppeteers do make puppets; and another says puppeteers work with puppets.

“Ok, *how*?” I ask.

After the pause of blank expressions, I tell everyone that “puppeteers bring the puppets to life; it’s called ‘animating the inanimate.’ It’s like a superpower or magic. And only puppeteers have this special power inside them. Now here’s a little secret I want to share with you.” And then I say very loudly, especially with a microphone …

"EACH! AND EVERY ONE OF YOU! HAVE THIS POWER! BECAUSE EACH! AND EVERY ONE OF YOU! HAVE BEEN PUPPETEERING! SINCE YOU WERE *BABIES*!!!"

It's the empowering moment of the day for the kids. (And for the adults, who've scrolled through their phone for the umpteenth time, it's also the "I'm-not-an-app-so-be-polite-and-set-a-good-example-and-pay-attention" moment.) Then I go on and ask, …

"Who has ever had a doll?" (Hands go up.)

"Who has ever had a stuffed animal?" (Hands go up.)

"Who has ever had … an action figure?" (Hands go up.)

"Now … who's ever made it walk? Who's ever made it talk? Who's ever made it sneak up behind mommy and go 'BOO!?' (Always a laugh here.) *That* is puppeteering! *You* made your toys come to life!"

And then I pull out puppets and show how they work, and have the kids try them out, all ending with a rousing version of the classic *Sesame Street* song, "Sing After Me." And these demos are 99.9% fun. But once in a while … you get *that* kid, that *one* kid, who interrupts and calls out (e.g., "I'm bored!") and won't shut up. So, when it's time for a kid to come up and try the puppets it's *that* kid … who I *don't* pick. In fact, I will be very "Willy Wonka"-ish and look at the kid and then – pick the kid right next to them. Or in front of them. Or behind them. Because I'm not going to reward, let alone encourage, rude behavior. And I don't blame the kid. I don't. When my mom once saw a kid not only talk back to the mother, but slap her, she said to me, …

"And *that* behavior did not start today."

Being a parent myself, I've come to realize that we have a responsibility to raise the next generation, properly. To prepare them, to not only take care of themselves, but to be able to join society as competent and positive entities. Legendary Disney animator Marc Davis created some of the most famous characters we all grew up with. But his standout, by far, was the villainess "Cruella DeVille." The story goes that in an interview, when asked why audiences responded so well to Cruella, he replied, "because at some point in life, we've *all* met a 'Cruella DeVille.'"

(Who knows – maybe little Cruella didn't get picked to try on the dalmatian puppet and, well, … the rest is history.)

Puppeteering is my job, and like any job, I have good days, great days, even extraordinary days. And then there are some days that are not. And in my job, I have worked with good people, great people, even extraordinary people. And then there are times when I have not. It's how I've learned to be professional, to rise above it, and carry on. But it's never easy. And fair? I once heard that "fairness was invented by humans." And my dear friend Matt Stoddart once told me his ninety-year-old, Irish grandfather would say, "Matt … you'll never be paid what you're worth."

Case in point …

I was hired by a show to be a puppeteer for a shoot, for another country. It was shot in New York, scheduled for the whole day, but we ended early. So, it was decided to use the time to do a pickup shot from *another* shoot, that I was originally not part of, and I was asked to stay and assist. Sure. And we did it. Then, when I got the check, I noticed it was only for the original shoot. I enquired why the extra added-on shoot was not included and was told it fell under the day rate for the original shoot. But my agreement only stated being paid for the original shoot. I brought this up to my entertainment attorney – the incredible Suzanne Phillips – and the union representative – the resourceful Michael Kinter (who always had our backs as puppeteers, and I wish the current SAG-AFTRA reps had this kind of genuine commitment). They were told by the production company that it loved the working relationship they had with me and would hate to have that *change* (aka … if this pursuit continues, Noel will no longer work with this company). Well, it did continue and eventually the company did finally pay me what had been owed me …

Seven. Years. Later!

This was a case of a bottom line needing to be met, which happens to all businesses, big and small, because it's business. Case in point:

Several years ago, I pitched an idea to one of the major – and I mean *major* – American kids networks. A live action show with puppets and hosted by my friend, the incredibly talented Aaron Nigel Smith. (Go check him out on YouTube.) It would be a show that introduced and explained the principals of music to young kids. I had cut outs of the characters; Aaron even created a sample theme song. And as I pitched it, I got the increasing sense that this was not going to happen. In fact, it began to feel like the last thirty minutes of the movie *Titanic*. Once I was done, I said …

"So, this isn't for you, is it?"

And they said it was not and then I asked, "So … what is it you *really* want?"

And they said …

"Noel, if you can create an inexpensive 3D, even 2D, animated show, where, during the course of the adventure, the characters have to collect items we can translate into merchandise the kids will want to buy, *THAT* is what we want."

I've told this story before, and every time I do the response is this shock at how blatantly crass and capitalistic this network "devoted" to children could be. But, as mom even knew, "There's a reason why it's called 'show *business.*'"

I've always enjoyed bringing family or friends to the sets I've worked on. My mom loved all the sets she got to visit and charmed her way with everyone. Muppet performer Richard Hunt would light up and yell "Mom!" whenever he saw Edna MacNeal on the Sesame set. Towards the final days of season one of *Bear in the Big Blue House*, I had my then girlfriend (and now wife), Susan, come visit. She'd never been on a set, let alone a set of a puppet show, and the lead character was a seven-foot-tall talking and dancing bear, whom she was dating. When I was in Bear, I called her over for a photo and I still have it – Bear and Susan in the foyer of the house, she looking up both in awe and surprise, pleasantly shocked at who was talking to her. (I've always said that it was true love for a woman to willingly marry a guy who dressed as a bear for a living.) My son loved the times I brought him to *Last Week Tonight with John Oliver*, mainly for the lavish craft service spread, which included freshly baked cookies or once, freshly baked apple pie. (This, of course, all pre-COVID.) When he was much younger, he and Susan flew to Jackson, Mississippi, where I was shooting *Between the Lions*. They both loved it and the little guy even got to be an extra in the library, in the background. However, when we were going to do live shows for two weeks, I got a call from the producer of it, enquiring if I planned to bring Susan and our son. I said "no," because they had plans for the summer: day camp, writing, etc. And then I asked "why," and was patronizingly explained that having my family might be a *distraction*. I asked if they were ever a distraction when they visited on set and was told "no," but everyone needs to be focused on their tasks and not be concerned with a child – this from the producer of a children's series. This was the most insultingly "professional" conversation I've ever had. But not every boss is as sincere and professional as Jim Henson.

Then there are co-workers. Ah – that merry team of comrades working with you towards that common goal of success. I've been lucky to work with some of the best, the most generous casts, crews, and staffs. When going to work was a pleasure and I didn't want the job to end. *Bear in the Big Blue House* is still the number one show where this happened. And people ask me "Noel if there was a reboot would you, do it?" And I answer, "In a heartbeat." Especially if the same people (or the same kind of people) were involved.

But some jobs also have some folks who make it a little difficult some days. I once worked on a job where one of the performers, before the end of every scene, had to have the last word. In every single scene. Always. Every… Single … Time. Or working for over a year on a fantastic show idea - for over *a year* - only to finally see how disrespectful, misogynistic, narcistic, and downright petty this "friend" turned out to be to others. You're not going to like everyone … and everyone is not going to like you. So, how do you figure out how to work with people like this? Sometimes, the answer is through television.

When my son was in middle school, he and his friends were obsessed with "The Office" (the American version). He'd watched seasons over and over and over again. When I was at the Rhode Island Comic Con in the fall of 2019, I met some of the cast of the show, who were there to meet fans and sign autographs. Lesley David Baker ("Stanley"), Brian Baumgartner ("Kevin"), and Catherine Tate ("Nellie") could have not been nicer to chat with when I asked for their autographs for my son. They said they've gotten more fans who are tweens, not just at conventions, but even at the airport and couldn't figure out why. I told them my and Susan's theory given our tween son's viewing; that the show reflects middle school. Think about it - you're stuck in this place five days a week with the same people; some of whom are your friends, some are not; the teacher can be clueless; and every now and then, the vice principal, and sometimes the principal, must come in to restore order. And they were amazed at how it made sense!

No job is perfect, but some are better than others. And when it comes to my career, the vast majority of it has been super fun. I've just learned that you roll with it when you can, stand up for yourself when you have to, and not only grab onto those good moments, but create them for yourself and for others, whenever you can. Case in point:

Over the years, I've gotten lots of fan email thanking me for *Bear in the Big Blue House*. Parents, grandparents, and the kids who watched who are now all grown up, have told me how lovely it was to watch a show as a family and that it's still a lasting memory of childhood. But I've also gotten emails from parents of kids with autism & special needs, saying how the show was such a comfort to their kids, some of whom, though grown, still watch the show on DVD and even VHS tapes. And now a whole new generation is visiting the Big Blue House on Disney Plus. But I realized though that there isn't a show currently on as sincere, genuine, and comforting as Bear was, especially for this demographic. And after that pitch to the major kids network that ended with them just wanting a cheap animated show to use to sell toys (remember that story?), I decided that if you want something done right, do it yourself.

Back in the early 2000s, I had an idea for a kids series based around putting on a show. All puppets and the guest star would be a number, a letter, a shape, or a sound. Sort of *Sesame Street* meets *The Muppet Show*. To show kids these concepts and help them understand them, I called my series *"The Show ME Show."* It was part of submissions asked by Noggin & Nick Jr. to creators. They wanted a new, original pre-school series and, after reviewing, it came down to mine and one other show. And … the other show got greenlit. (In case you're wondering, it was *Jack's Big Music Show* from puppeteer and colleague David Rudman and his company Spiffy Pictures.)

So, I still had my idea (and the rights to it) tucked away until I began to think how this might work for autistic and special needs kids. I reworked it, dropping the letter as a potential guest star and replacing it with an *emotion*. Having done research, including asking, one aspect of life that can be difficult for an autistic and special needs person is emotions. Recognizing them not only in others but within themselves. And there was one more component I changed.

Originally the host was also a puppet, a body puppet: an impresario named "Razzle," and I would play him. But then I began to think that maybe I could be the host as myself, as a *human being*. It would harken back to those shows I grew up with, that had human hosts with puppets. And I did have a brief stint as a human host in the fall summer of 2006. The previous year I had directed the first season of *"The Goodnight Show"* on the brand-new cable channel, "PBS Kids Sprout," a joint effort of Nickelodeon and Sesame Workshop. The head of the new channel was Andrew Beachum, who had been the head of Playhouse Disney UK when I would go over and do appearances in London. He remembered me and my mentioning wanting to get into directing one day. And he gave me the opportunity. Then the female host of the show left, and they were on the hunt for a new female host. But in the interim, he asked would *I* be interested in being the host – the *human* host. I was both intrigued, excited, and nervous: I've never acted like a human being. But Andrew felt I could do it having been a host before, only now with no fur covering me. He also asked my opinion about it. Would having a MAN in this role about bedtime and sleep be comforting and accepted. I told him yes: it worked for Mister Rogers. Plus, I'm a dad and bedtime comes every night and it's part of being a dad. So, for one month, I was "Leo the Gardner."

But then in 2020, after the shootings of George Floyd and Brianna Taylor (and sadly others), I decided that a black male figure who would be seen as a nurturing and supportive leader for this little troop of puppets was needed. Because representation matters. Now more than ever.

I've shopped the show around and pitched it to a few streaming services with no luck.

"It's too *niche,"* is the response I get.

But what show ISN'T *"niche?!?"* You create a show that teaches history, or a show that teaches science, or a show that teaches math skills, well guess what? Those are created for a specific target audience. Bear was a show about discovery. My show is the same concept, and *all kids* could watch it but, it would greatly help kids with autism and special needs (as this was the by-product of Bear). I've no doubt that it will be a full-fledged funded series one day. Because as my mom believed …

"Dreams do come true. Some just take a little longer than others."

(In the meantime, go to YouTube and check out *THE SHOW ME SHOW CHANNEL* I created and enjoyed the videos I've done so far.)

It's Hard Raising Parents

The moment I found out I was going to be a father, I vowed to be the best one ever. Not having one growing up, I made it my mission to always be there for my kid and go above and beyond the call of "dad duty." And having been one for many years, I have come to realize one significant fact:

We parents are braindead.

From the time that home pregnancy test is positive, all the way thru the pregnancy, the birth, and the years of raising a child, parents have little to no sleep, are constantly exhausted, nerves are shot, and patience tested, 24/7, with complete sentences often impossible to form. This is why *our* parents are the way they are – we broke them. And now karma is paying back.

I remember the early eighties Bill Cosby comedy special where he talks about his family life (which later inspired *The Cosby Show*), and how he walked into the kitchen, one morning, to find his mother and his kids eating chocolate cake – for breakfast. He asked "why" and his mom, who handed out the huge slices, replied, "It's got eggs. It's got milk." Well, one morning I walked into our living room to find this exact scene! My mom and our then toddler son on the sofa, each with a huge slice of cake. And she gave the *Exact. Same. Response*! She never would have allowed this for *me* as a kid. But for her grandson? Her "Pumpkin?" Absolutely. Cosby was right – "This is a woman trying to get into heaven!"

I did everything for my kid. Not just to support Susan's time to write in peace (her series "The Maggie Hope Mysteries" and her stand-alone novel, *Mother, Daughter, Traitor, Spy*, available on Amazon and independent bookstores – yes, another plug), but because it's what a dad is supposed to do. Walk the kid to school; pick them up; make snacks; host playdates; take them to the zoo; the park; the aquarium; read stories; sing songs; etc., etc., etc. When he entered elementary school, I became the volunteer parent for *everything*. School trips, class projects, bake sales, volunteering during gym time, co-hosting a book club for fourth and fifth graders, even being class parent, not once but *twice*. Even restarting the Diversity Committee (which was sorely needed in our quite homogenous school community). My wife nicknamed me "The Over Achiever Parent." And rightly so. I was doing a lot but wanted to show a good example to my son and be the dad I never had.

Being a parent is not easy. Having worked in live theater, having done appearances as characters for public events, I've seen parents run the gamut (from doing their best at the basic baseline level, to *you-shouldn't-be-allowed-to-drive-heavy-machinery-let-alone-breed*). One thing I have found true is this …

The most dangerous animal on Earth is an irrational parent.

An example:

Bear (and I) was doing an appearance at the huge toy store F.A.O. Schwarz when it was still located on 5th Ave and 58th Street, in Manhattan, to promote the new line of product produced. It was a meet-n-greet that was promoted and many people showed up, and Bear took the time to meet all of them and take a photo. Once it was done, Bear waved good-bye, and headed back to the dressing area, when I heard voices. One voice was particularly loud. I turned around and could see that a man was arguing with the staff and the organizers of the event. He had just shown up with his kid, having driven from Pennsylvania – *three hours straight* – to has his kid meet Bear. Bear calmly walked up to him and placing his "paw" on the dad's shoulder, said, …

"Hello. You made it! I'm so glad you two could come! Hi there," Bear said to the kid who smiled, and Bear asked how they were and was it a long drive and, of course, they smelled good, took the photo, and got a hug.

"Thank you! Thank you, sir!" the dad said shaking Bear's hand. It was so easy to turn around what would have only gotten worse.

When I worked at Field Station Dinosaurs, I shared my brain-dead theory with my co-workers who witnessed it. Some parents, again who've been on duty since the pregnancy test was positive, walked in thinking we were a team of babysitters. They would generally look the other way while their kids would wander and completely misbehave during the shows. Which is why, whenever I was in the T-Rex, the dino would have fun with this; slowly walking by and suddenly turn and roar right at them. (Good times, heh heh heh.)

My son has seen firsthand puppets and characters of all shapes and sizes. When he was three months old, he and my wife came with me to Los Angeles for the second half of shooting the Bear spinoff series, *"Breakfast with Bear."* I was twenty-one years old when I first flew on a plane and this little guy already had his first flight under his belt (or back then, diaper). He even charmed the flight attendant! I came back from the bathroom to see her happily sitting in my seat holding my smiling son. (By the way, I swear, babies have more luggage for a trip than Cher. Diaper bag, stroller, car seat, pack-n-playpen, extra carryon with extra outfit[s] in case of "spittyups.") We got to stay at a lovely extended stay hotel off Sunset Boulevard, The Montrose. There was a king bed, a living area, and a small kitchen, complete with fridge, oven, sink and microwave. Perfect for storing away all those bottles of formula.

While was I off with Bear in actual homes of families, Susan took care of our son. She and the baby would take walks, the kid is his stroller, with a bright, multi-colored blanket (one of the many birth gifts given) wrapped around him. And being located in West Hollywood, a lovely area and known for its LGBTQ+ acceptance, she got lots of smiles due to this rainbow blanket. (One morning, to let her sleep in, I took the baby out for a stroll and seeing me *and* the rainbow-colored blanket around the kid, well, I, also, got A LOT of smiles.) For one segment out there, I had to go Fort Irwin, the military based located in the middle of the Mojave Desert, and a fourteen-hour drive from the hotel. So, I had to stay overnight halfway there. Susan and the baby were alone for the night and as the little guy was on the bed, happily cooing, and Susan lying next to him watching, he suddenly swung his little fist outward and clocked her right in the eye! She said she literally saw stars – the kind cartoon characters would have, circling their heads. Luckily there was no mark, but she knew, from then on, to watch out for his right hook.

As a "thank you" for doing the spin-off, Disney Channel treated us to a weekend at the Disneyland Resort. We stayed in Disney's Grand Californian Resort & Spa, and it did not disappoint; it is stunning! Our favorite Disney restaurant became The Napa Rose, located in the hotel. The food and wine were superb, but the true highlight was the staff. At one point, when I was in the restroom, and Susan was trying to eat, the baby got fussy. I came back from the restroom to find our server holding him, to his delight (such a little flirt), to allow Susan those precious seconds to chew and swallow. (I go to the bathroom and free childcare. Win, win!)

Of the two parks, the second being Disney's California Adventure, the hotel had a direct entry into it. But we decided our son's first Disney Park would be the original – "Walt's Park." There is a true rite of passage for kids who grew up loving Disney, to now take their own kids to discover "the magic." I've been to Walt Disney World so many times I've lost count; to Euro Disney (before it became Disneyland Paris); even Tokyo DisneySea. But Disneyland is … *perfect*, especially for little ones to enjoy. The size and layout and scale are so cozy and welcoming for families of young kids. And you get the sense of what Walt Disney had in mind: a family park.

Of course, we had to take our son on the Mecca of rides – "It's a Small World." My mom took me to the N.Y. World's Fair when I was a baby, and I rode it (and apparently loved Cleopatra and her "wink"). As we headed towards it, off to the side in this little pavilion like area was … OMG! *The* Wicked Queen!?! From *Snow White*?!? But it was really her and she was doing a meet-n-greet with a family. And it was just her by herself. Friends of mine who work for the parks explained it this way: Walt Disney World has "handlers" when the characters come out, and then create and maintain the line for guests to meet the characters. And there's a cutoff; once a certain time passes; they close the line so that the character can finish up and then head "backstage." But Disneyland is different. It's a "neighborhood park." Smaller and more casual. So, characters will come out on their own and then decide when to leave. "We HAVE to meet the Queen!" I told Susan. I held my son and walked towards the Queen, who immediately threw her hand forward, indicating I stop at once. She trained her eyes on my son and asked, …

"Will he … *burp*?"

"No," I answered and took another step when the hand came up again, commanding I stop.

"We he … *spit* … *up*?" she asked coolly.

“No,” I answered again, with a chuckle. Having passed this test, she bade us to step forward.

She signed our autograph book and I asked …

“Your majesty, may we also have a picture with you.”

“Of course,” she said, and folded her arms together with a flourish, in that classic move from the animated film. I thanked her and she gave a slight bow before she turned her attention to the next family with a little girl.

“How old is she?” the Queen demanded.

“Six,” the mother said proudly.

“And what *chores* do you have her do?” the Queen enquired as the family laughed. But the best part was when the little girl handed this villain her autograph book and a “princess pen,” colored pink, with feathers and sparkles. The Queen stepped past her to others waiting and, holding up the pen as if she were a dead rat by its tail, she declared, …

“Does anyone have an *actual* pen I could use?” After the laughter and no other options, she growled, “Fine …”

“It’s a Small World” at Disneyland is the same one from the N.Y. World’s Fair. Yes, it’s been refurbished, and new additions have been added (like the holiday makeover and the kid versions of Disney characters) but essentially, it’s the same. Approaching you see this massive white structure that seems to get bigger the closer you get (which is the exact opposite of the castle, which actually gets *smaller* the closer you get). You board your boat outside and sail into the building for your “trip around the world.” As the music played and the dolls danced, Susan and I were smiling and both got misty eyed, being the generation that was introduced to this experience and now passing on the joy to our child. However, our three-month-old son was not so impressed. He didn’t cry, he didn’t smile. His eyes were wide, his head was turning from side to side, his little mouth open, and he had this expression of …

“What … the heck … is going on?!?”

To be fair, it’s a LOT to take in, at any age, but for a baby, this was over the top entertainment.

(He then recreated this same expression/reaction when meeting Mickey. I’m smiling, Mickey is “smiling,” and the kid is looking at Mickey in shock, with the expression …

“Oh, dear Lord … it’s a mouse!”)

There are many more stories of my adventures in fatherhood (like my son saying his fourth-grade class was going to recreate "The Boston Massacre" for a project and he volunteered me to make all the tri-corner hats and muskets – for the next day!) and they run the gamut. There are highs and lows and moments to cherish and moments you want to fling yourself out of a window. Taking care of kids is not easy. (Like that myth of bedtime and it being the winddown of the day with songs and stories and cuddles. It can be that … and some nights it can also be the seventh ring of hell.) But it's all part of parenting. And I wouldn't have traded it for anything. My greatness achievement and true honor is being a dad. What can make it even more difficult for my generation, though, is doing the same … for our own parents. Our generation is handling the difficult task of caring for the people who cared for us.

During the last six years of her life, my mom began to have health issues. She always dealt with arthritis in her legs and hands during the nineteen-nineties, but then, her calves began to retain fluid, swelling up. UTIs would frequently send her to the hospital, more than once a year, with anemia and dehydration detected, compounding things, and resulting in relocating her to physical therapy centers to recuperate. And then go back home … and the cycle would start all over again.

My mom and I would chat in the morning and in the evening, mostly to make sure she was OK. I was working the first day of the Sesame special *"Elmo Saves Christmas"* when I called, and she didn't answer. I contacted the management office of the Lenox Terrace, who had to break the lock to get into the apartment. They found my mom on the floor, conscious but unable to get up. They contacted me and I left to meet her at the ER of St. Luke's Roosevelt on the Upper Westside of Manhattan. Another time, I called one evening and she sounded odd, and I told her I was coming up, much to her objection. It took an hour to get there and when I unlocked the door, I found her on the floor of her bedroom. I wanted to call 911, but she didn't want me to, so I helped her back into bed saying I'd be by in the morning. I left saying I'd call when I got home and an hour later when I did, it was that same tone again. I headed back up and, yes, she had fallen, again. This time I did call 911. I rode with her to the hospital, and we waited in the ER for (no joke) *eighteen hours* for a bed. And this cycle went on year after year until Susan (bless her) said that Edna should move in with us.

We gave Edna our son's room of our two-bedroom apartment, because the bathroom was right next to it, and I put up a makeshift wall in part of the dining area to create a new smaller room for him, who was nine years old now. Once we fed him breakfast and he was washed and brushed, he'd kiss "Grandmama," and he go off to school. Now it was time to pretty much do similar things for my mom, who'd then settle in with her books and the TV on for her court shows (with hosts "Judge Cranky," "Judge Loud," "Judge No-Patience," as my son nicknamed them). We'd joke …

"We have two kids; only one goes to school."

Years earlier, whenever I went on those long far away Sesame International trips, my mom would stay over and help out; clearing and loading the dishwasher; doing and folding the laundry; and helping to entertain her grandson, to give Susan time to write and rest. She loved being useful as well as getting to spend time with her "pumpkin." But those days were over, and I could tell she felt bad about not being able to contribute the way she used to.

"I hate being a burden," she once told me.

"You're not a burden," I reassured her.

"You took care of me, now it's my turn."

"Once a man, twice a child," she lamented.

Then one day while our son was at school, we had to call the paramedics; she was weak and couldn't get out of bed. They took her to our nearby hospital where she stayed for a week to (again) get rehydrated and the swelling in her legs go down (and even "drained"), followed by admitting her at a rehab center for physical therapy.

While she was there was when we decided that she couldn't live alone anymore … or with us. She felt bad taking our son's room and I started to look into how to set her up in an assisted living facility. I also began to clean out her apartment, the place I grew up in. To this day I am eternally grateful to my friends Alex, and Michael Schupach, and James Wojtal, Jr (both incredible puppet designers, builders, and puppeteers). I don't know how I could have done it without their support, patience, and muscle. I even let them take some of my old stuff. And I took photos of some of those early puppet attempts I made, before letting them get tossed. (But a couple I did save for old time's sake.)

October 20, 2014, was the seventeenth anniversary of Bear premiering. At around five o'clock, I got a call from the rehab facility, and they told me that Edna was having trouble breathing and was being taken to the hospital, luckily the one near where we lived. I went to the ER and there she was, on a gurney, with an oxygen mask on, and a blanket tucked around her.

"We have to stop meeting like this," I joked, and she smiled and squeezed my hand.

They moved us into a side area with a curtain. I told her about my day and how Susan and Matt were. And I knew the routine – we wait until a bed is available upstairs and she's admitted, which will take several hours, because it always did. Knowing this, I brought a phone charger with an extension cord, and a book. I would glance up from sitting at the foot of the gurney and see my mom dozing in and out of sleep. When I had visited her the day before at the rehab facility, she told me she was "tired." But not in the normal way. She meant she was "ready" to move on. And she told me she requested and signed a DNR (Do Not Resuscitate) form.

As I was reading, I suddenly heard a sound. It was an alarm coming from the machine that had been hooked up to her to monitor her vital signs. Her eyes were barely open, but she was looking at me, her body trembling, and I stood up and came round to the side and held her hand. A staff member rushed in and began to do something, but then, suddenly, another staff member came in with a clipboard, and said, "There's a DNR." And the first staff member stopped and stepped back. And I was at the side of the gurney, and I looked at my mom, whose eyes were looking up at me, and I held her hand and her body slowly stopped trembling, but her eyes were still looking at me and the staff member checked her pulse and, …

"I'm sorry."

And at that moment I let out this sound that I cannot describe or think I could ever recreate, but this sound burst out of me, from my gut, from the depths of my soul, and I bent over her body and started balling. I have never cried that hard or that long in my life. As a slowly straightened up, I looked at the staff member with the clipboard who said, …

"Take all the time you need," and left us, re-closing the curtain behind her.

I sat down and thoughts started going through my mind. Not a jumble or any of them rushing through, more like when you walk into a room and things are there that you notice and acknowledge – there's a chair and a table and two windows, maybe a mirror on the wall and you take it in, while noticing little things – should I get a new chair; I need to wipe down the table; I gotta clean the windows; do I look fat? Then the thoughts of everything I'd done for so many years – getting the meds; picking up Fixodent and Depends at the drugstore; prepping meals – with the new thoughts of needing to find a funeral home to come get her and telling everyone she'd known (and she knew a LOT of people). And telling Susan. And telling our son. Oh God … telling our son "Grandmama" died. (When we told her we were having a baby, we asked what she'd like to be called – "Granny" was definitely out – and she asked could it be "Grandmama." I think she got it from watching the classic sitcom *"Bewitched,"* and Endora wanting to be called "Grandmama." And you can't get more fabulous or flamboyant than the incredible Agnes Morehead. It's good to have role models.) I was probably sitting there for an hour when I got up, and very gently closed her eyes.

"I have to go," I began, "Thank you. Thank you for everything. And don't worry – I'll be fine." Then I kissed her forehead, and said quietly, …

"I love you. Bye."

In the back of your mind, you sort of prepare for that day when the person in your life that took care of you, was always there for you, is suddenly gone. You prepare for that, but you don't think to prepare for *after*. *After* the service and condolences and sentiments, it's *after* all that you need to adjust to life as you go along without them. I'd have knee-jerk reactions to want to call my mom to tell her what her grandson just did; immediately head down the aisle at the drugstore for her supplies and her meds; or schedule my day around visiting her. Nope. All done. But those "firsts" – first holidays without her, first birthday without her – it's those you're not fully prepared for.

I like to think that if there is an afterlife for us, that we get to design it, to choose how we'll spend eternity, and wait for our loved ones to join us. For my mom, it would be based on the last time I and Bear was invited to be part of the *Walt Disney World Very Merry Christmas Day Parade* (always taped in November, not Christmas Day). Disney flew me, Susan, and mom down and put us up on the Concierge Level of The Grand Floridian. So, her version of heaven would be this trip from Disney World; staying on the concierge level of the Grand Floridian and listening to their orchestra play while sipping her red wine, followed by a Bailey's Irish Cream as a nightcap. I am glad that when she did die, she wasn't alone, at the rehab facility or the ER. Edna MacNeal, the woman who believed in me, encouraged me, and put aside her own dreams so that I could have mine; the woman who held down two jobs to get me the best education; the woman who was the best mother-in-law and the most loving "grandmama" ever, wasn't looking at a doctor, or a nurse, or a paramedic.

It was me.

Too Black or Not Too Black? *That* Is the Question

I am an African American male. I am the son of two African Americans — a man and a woman — born and raised in Central Harlem, New York City. Both my parents were dark skinned, yet I am lighter than either of them. My mom always told me it was because of the "Italian blood" in me, but she didn't know that it was the *Scottish* blood in me. My great-great-grandfather, who was white and emigrated from Scotland, married a woman named "Parthenia," who was white, and their son eventually ended up in New Orleans, and married a Creole woman, named "Pelomina." I learned that it's the mixing of those Caucasian genes that has played a huge part in my African American family's history.

When the MacNeals lived in New Orleans, it was during the height of the Jim Crow Laws, the racial and completely legal reaction to blacks freed from slavery and making strides in society. The laws were so condemning of being black that if you even had a drop of "black blood" — the "one-drop rule" — you were discriminated against. Or the "paper bag test" – if your skin matched or were darker than a brown paper bag. That's why some blacks could "pass" as white, while others could not, driving wedges between family members. The legal oppression became so intolerable that my family and thousands of others left the South. "The Great Migration" began in 1916 (and is brilliantly chronicled in Isabel Wilkerson's book *The Warmth of Our Suns: The Epic Story of America's Great Migration*). Within the MacNeals, those who could "pass" settled in Denver and Los Angeles, while those who could not, my father being one, settled in Chicago.

All this is to say that I am African American. I am not white. But if you were to look at me, the term "black" would not immediately pop in your head. I've been told more than once, …

"You don't *look* black," or in disbelief, "You're *black*!?!"

"Nice tan! Where'd you get it?" a white neighbor once asked me. To which I responded… "Birth."

One time I was sitting at a bar in Queens, N.Y., waiting for a friend, when I saw out the corner of my eye, this old white guy staring at me.

"Hey!" he called, "What are you?"

"Really thirsty," I said as the bartender came over.

"No," he said, "What nationality are you?"

"American."

"No!" he said, "Where are you from?"

"My mom, who's very proud of me," and picked up my drink to join my friend, who'd just snagged a table for us.

Another time, Susan and I spent part of our honeymoon in Indialantic, a town on the Atlantic coast of Florida. One evening, while walking their boardwalk, we passed two old white codgers on a bench.

"Hey!" one called (which seems to be the universal old white guy greeting to others), "Are you 'Eye-talian?'" (Because that's the way he pronounced it.)

"Nope. But I could go for a pizza. Thanks for the suggestion." And we walked on.

Even in our building, I and my wife and son have been the victims of racism. Case in point:

I am in a bi-racial marriage: I am black, and Susan is white. We have a biracial son as a result, who, if you saw him, you'd say he's "white." Another biracial couple lived in our building (also a black husband, and his white wife), whose three kids all "looked black." After dropping off our son at elementary school, a neighbor — let's call her "Karen" — asked Susan how our son was doing in school but used the name of the son from the *other* biracial couple (one of our son's best friends, FYI). Susan explained she was mistaken, and "Karen" couldn't believe it.

"It's ok," Susan said, smiling, "All biracial couples look alike."

And Susan laughed it off.

We shared the experience on Facebook, without using any real names of course, and our friends were rightfully shocked, angered, and giddy over Susan's retort.

Well… somehow "Karen" got wind of this and sent a private message to Susan. The most offensive, profanity-laced tirade we'd ever read. Ultimately, "Karen" said she just couldn't be friends with (and this is a direct quote) "our kind" and "people like you" and to (direct quote again) "stay the f%$@ away from my family."

Once in the courtyard between our building and the other, I was talking to the black husband. I mentioned to him that I had found out that my last name, MacNeal, was not a slave name after all. For many black people in the U.S., their last names are the names of the owners who owned their ancestors. A way of branding (though often branding with actual branding irons were also used as a mark of ownership). I was proud and still am that my great, great grandfather MacNeal emigrated to the United States in the 1800s. I've seen pictures of him. Yet another white neighbor, who was Scottish herself (and who had the good fortune to move), happened to be near us, and said to me while passing, "Oh, your family most likely worked for mine." And strode on.

By today's standards, I suppose I am under the umbrella of a "POC" — Person of Color. Or in my case "Puppeteer of Color." From the late '80s into the '90s and the 2000s, the most well-known African American television puppeteers were me and Kevin Clash (who originated Elmo). We were the only two black puppeteers. Or more accurately, there *were* other black puppeteers out there, but you couldn't find them the way you can now — there was no internet or widespread social media; no platforms like YouTube or TikTok for puppeteers to showcase their talent (no matter what level). The fact that we two black kids — one from Baltimore and the other from Central Harlem — were influenced by Jim Henson, and have circumstances fall into place for our careers into puppetry, meeting and working alongside Jim on *Sesame Street*, *The Muppets*, and beyond, is still remarkable.

As I mentioned before, I was cast as Leon (MacNeal) for the PBS series *The Puzzle Place.* Leon was black and so was I (aside from the sheer coincidence of our first names being backwards versions of each other, which is why the producers gave him the last name "MacNeal"). To promote the first season which was premiering in January of 1995, I went on a press tour with one of the executive producers, culminating in the "upfronts" — the couple of days twice a year when networks present new shows to the press — held at The Ritz Carlton Huntington (now The Langham Huntington) in Pasadena, California. Now, normally, if a puppet is doing an appearance on a morning show or midday show, even a live event, you try to hide the puppeteer. (This was before the *Avenue Q* style of puppetry, of seeing the puppeteer with the puppet.) The puppeteer would hide behind the couch or a set piece, with only the puppet being seen on camera. However, *The Puzzle Place* was all about diversity and tolerance of other people and their cultures. So, if you've got an *African American* character being performed by an actual *African American*, you sure as heck ain't gonna to hide him. I sat on the couches and chairs, with Leon right next to me, on my hand.

When The Muppet characters "The Whatnots" took over *The Today Show* with Muppet versions of the hosts, and then years later for *Sesame Street*'s 50th anniversary promotion, with *Sesame* Muppet versions of the hosts, I played Al Roker. He even remembered me, not just for portraying him, but when Bear appeared on the show years earlier. Because how many black puppeteers had Al seen come through the show? Especially playing him … *twice*!

When *Bear* took off, I wasn't available for the third/last season of *The Puzzle Place*. Had the producers or I knew of a black puppeteer who could puppeteer Leon, and do the voice, it would have occurred. But again, no internet, no social media, not even word of mouth. Puppeteer Eric Jacobson (pre-Grover, Fozzie Bear, and Miss Piggy) was hired to puppeteer Leon, while I would go back and dub in Leon's voice over Eric's, and it worked out great. Eric was very respectful of performing Leon, even coming to my apartment to talk to me about mannerisms and style, to keep the character consistent, physically. But one time, having a white performer and me being the voice for a black character didn't work out.

I once traveled to a foreign country. A predominantly white country. I had to go there to potentially be the voice of a black character for a series. A puppeteer, who was Caucasian, was puppeteering the character, but the network executives were concerned about a white guy doing the voice of a black kid. My schedule and commitments at the time didn't allow me to do the show, so they asked me to go and meet with the production, to see if I could be the dubbed-in voice.

The production itself was quite impressive. New state-of-the-art studio; all in-house editing and postproduction capabilities. And the puppets themselves were impressive to look at — but not to operate. They were huge and needlessly heavy. I still applaud all the puppeteers for the phenomenal job each of them did. I saw the black character's homebase, which was highlighted with computers and keyboards; he was supposed to be very techy, loving gadgets. That was his "thing." (Remember this.)

When I met with the producers, I read a couple of his lines in a character voice. Now, keep in mind, again, this is a predominantly *white* country, not known for their wide diversity and melting pot history. So, their collective knowledge and exposure to non-whites was limited to TV and the movies (and this was before YouTube and all the other social media platforms). They were all lovely and quite genuine in wanting this to work out. But the notes I got were…

"He should sound like one of those guys from Harlem."

"Well, … I *am* one of those guys from Harlem, and this is how *I* sound."

"But he loves electronics and should make 'bleeps' and 'bloops' in his speaking."

I took a moment to fully absorb what reference this was and finally said, …

"You mean…" I began, "like the guy from the *Police Academy* movies?"

"YES!"

I thanked everyone … and got the next flight home. (And they eventually did hire an African American voice actor for the voice.)

Now, these people by no means were "racist;" as in deliberately setting crosses on fire, wearing sheets, or suppressing voting rights. They only knew from what they saw on TV and in the movies. Which is why representation matters so much, to those being represented, and to those seeing it. It has an effect, and it can last. That's why we need to make sure it's good ones.

Case in point:

I've gotten to direct segments for the Social Impact division of Sesame for the YouTube channel. One I loved directing stars "Elijah & Wes," the Muppet African American father & son duo perfectly played by African American puppeteers Chris Thomas Hayes (as "Elijah") and Bradley Freeman Jr (as "Wes," who is also the energetic "Tamir" on the show). This one takes place in a barbershop, with Wes getting his first "very special haircut," and featured an African American human as the barber, several African American Muppets (performed by African

American puppeteers, Jimmica Collins, and Brandon Smith), AND "Gordon," himself, Roscoe Orman. A friend of mine, also black, saw it online and said, …

"Damn! Sesame hasn't been this black since 1974!"

I'm glad I wasn't drinking anything because the resulting spit-take would have been glorious. But what he meant was, the Sesame that he and I grew up on had a set completely based in reality. Looking at those early seasons it, and growing up in Central Harlem, I loved the sense that *Sesame Street* was right outside my door, in my neighborhood. Now, here was a barber shop, a central point in black communities, on Sesame. And the setting and the bit was suggested by Chris and Bradley, themselves. (And in the waiting area, there are two human portraits hanging on the wall. And they are my great-grandfather and great-great grandmother!) I even found out that the segment was shown to the South African co-production team of *Takalani Sesame* and that went nuts over it. Especially Kwame, the very dark-skinned Muppet who enters the barbershop.

"HIM!" they declared, "We want Muppets like HIM!"

I told this to Chris and Bradley saying they should be proud and that representation matters, everywhere. Even all the way back to "The Motherland." As an African American, I am so proud Sesame did this segment (and can't wait for the shop to come back in future segments).

Oobi was a show on Nick Jr., with Tim Lagasse (as "Oobi"), Stephanie D'Abruzzio (as his little sister "Uma"), Tyler Bunch (as their grandfather "Grampu") and me (as best friend "Kako"). The puppets were literally our bare hands with glass taxidermy eyes over our fingers, who only spoke one or two words at a time. "You." (Oobi pointing at the camera) "Oobi. Friends. Bye!" (And then waving the way you'd wave good-bye.) I auditioned and got the part of Kako, and it was a fun show to work on, particularly the musical episode. Yes, these characters who only spoke one to two words at a time would be *singing*. And it totally worked! Before it became a series on Nick Jr., it was interstitials, two-minute segments in between shows (to keep the viewer interested and not change the channel). However, there was concern in the beginning that it would be hard for the kids at home to tell my hand apart from Tim's. So… I was given a couple of tubes of *tanning creams*, to see which worked best, to help "enhance" my natural shade. I brought them home and Susan was appalled, while also impressed —

"These are expensive. They paid for the good stuff."

I didn't use any of them, so Kako got a little red hat, rakishly tilted to one side of his "head."

During the summer of 2014, I began to clean out my mother's apartment, up in Central Harlem. There was a LOT to go through and clean out, not to mention it had been a while since the place had been cleaned up. I put on a pair of faded jeans, a t-shirt, and a hoodie and was about to head out. Whenever I head out to a meeting, Susan gives her "eye of approval" in what wardrobe will work, given the occasion to make a good impression. (Which is also why she picks out perfect wardrobe items for me.) However, seeing her African American husband, in his hoodie and jeans, about to get on the subway to head up to Harlem, she said, …

"No."

And why would she say this? Because she didn't want to see her hoodie wearing husband the potential victim of police brutality. And she was right because, it could happen. Because it still happens, with no end in sight.

When it comes to auditions, they can run the gamut. If you've ever done one, you know what I'm talking about. You put yourself out there, do your best, and (should) immediately forget about it, until you hear from them, one way or the other. (Or not hear from them. Which isn't "business" or "professional;" it's rude.) And auditions are so arbitrary. It's up to "the-powers-that-be" behind the table or at the receiving end of the video you just sent. Roles will be denied you for any number of reasons, and it's happened to me. What is interesting though, are some of the reasons *why* I haven't gotten a role.

I auditioned three different times over a couple of years for the Off-Broadway production of the Broadway musical *"Ave Q"* and it wasn't until I ran into my neighbor, Q co-creator Bobby Lopez, that he was surprised nobody bothered to tell me that it was out of my vocal range. But, they did fill their quota of asking a "Puppeteer of Color."

I once auditioned for the voice of a character. Just the voice; not a puppet, just a voiceover role. And the email described the character and all its foibles. Great. And included lines from the script to use for the audio audition. Okay. But the email also stated, "no ethnic voices." *Excuse me?!?* "No *ethnic* voices?" I was taken aback reading this because why would you need to say this? Because the majority of people you've sent this too is *white*? Then, why did you send it to *me*? I'm not white. So, is it a heads-up to not sound too … "black?"

"Blaccent" is the combination of the words "black" plus "accent." Presto! "Blaccent." It's the verbal version of "blackface;" jargon, colloquiums, and slang spoken by non-African Americans. And it's been around a long time; from minstrel shows & Al Jolson; to the radio show "Amos & Andy;" right up to comedian/actress Awkwafina. My mom, having taken acting lessons (from Sydney Poitier, remember), always said, "Play your voice like an instrument." Meaning to speak clearly; to enunciate; and to project. But I now think it was her way of making sure I didn't pick up too much from my friends in the neighborhood, in Central Harlem. Mom was from the generation before and having lived through the Civil Rights Movement. And she appreciated and applauded the advancements made for black folks, while still conscious of being able to "fit in" (white society, the dominant society). Thus, I've heard all my life …

"You don't *sound* 'black.'"

But I do. Because I am African American, and *this* is also how an African American sounds.

I've done many auditions (as I've said) and sometimes not gotten the part (as I've also said). But once, not only did I not get the part, but I also found out why.

I once auditioned for a non-puppet role, aka a human being! (Gasp!) And went in prepared and came away with the rare feeling of having nailed it. I mean I was so certain that I had gotten the part and imagined the fun of doing this show. But when I hadn't heard back and knew production had started, I asked a friend on staff (and the one who recommended me) why. I mean, I really nailed it. And they agreed with me I had.

But ...

The (white) producers were looking to cast, not only an African American, but a *younger* African American, to show how progressive they were being in supporting the "next generation" of talent. And I didn't "look" as *black* as the others. And, of course, I am older. So, for the first time, I was on the receiving end of racism, colorism, *and* ageism. "The Trifecta of Prejudice." (I know I can be an over-achiever but ...)

I am an African American male in the United States. I never had a lot of cultural refences to our black heritage growing up at home, so it's funny that I'm now embracing it so late in life. I remember when Susan was pregnant that I thought this was definitely something our child should be aware of. The baby would be bi-racial, so I wanted to educate myself on things I never learned to pass on to him; all those black inventors left out of *"Schoolhouse Rock"* (like Mary Van Brittan Brown, who invented the home security system utilizing a camera in 1966); that the author of one of my favorite books, *"The Count of Monte Cristo,"* Alexander Dumas, was black; how to properly do "The Electric Slide" (which happened on the set of "The WIZ – LIVE;" with the broadcast over, cast & crew partied on set, including doing the dance). Susan even caught me trying to Google the African American holiday between Christmas and New Year's, with no results.

"Sweetie … 'Kwanza' isn't spelt with a 'Q - U.'"

I will continue this journey as a black man in the U.S.A. I am proud to be African American. It is part of who I am, and I will continue being who I am. I will continue to uplift, support, and encourage whomever I can, black and otherwise. It doesn't take much to do that.

(Which is also my way of setting up the next and last chapter.)

"Be the Person You Needed"

As I've said, over the years, I've had the good fortune to meet a lot of people, so diverse in their backgrounds, talents, and personalities. And, the majority have been great, even exceptionally fun, to work with and just be around. And I've learned so much from those fun people, those supportive people, some of whom I'm still in contact with, and consider true friends. But I've also met a few who were definitely *not* fun to work with, be around, or supportive in any way, shape, or form. And yet, I've learned a lot from them, too. I've learned from their treatment of me and others and attitude towards themselves how *not* to act. I know I'm not the only one — maybe you'll recognize a few similar experiences you've had with certain individuals in *your* life.

So here we go…

NUMBER ONE: I *HATE* pretentiousness.

I hate the deliberate effort to make oneself appear better than everyone else around, especially when in a position of authority. You already got the job, you're in charge, why do you need to *remind* everyone of it? Are you that insecure or was narcissism actually a job requirement in the application? Don't talk down to people; don't belittle people; don't deliberately set up an atmosphere of rivalry amongst others in order to get your attention. Don't mislead people with promises you never intend to keep but was just an exercise in stroking your own ego, with how many hoops folks are willing to jump through for you. Don't give yourself a made-up title that screams "There can be only one — and I'm IT!" Whenever I've come across another iteration of this persona, I remind myself, …

"Pack your bags kids; we're going on an ego trip."

NUMEBR TWO: Sucking up.

That black hole of attention I just described? They only remain that way from encouragement around them. My advice?

Don't.

Just… don't.

Don't laugh at everything they say. Don't be at their beck and call, and then wait anxiously, by the phone, hoping against hope, you'll get called. I once was brought in to do a character on a show and their "Puppet Captain" (there's that phrase, one last time) came over and, while I still had on the puppet, holding it up in camera, actually reached up and grabbed the puppet, by the neck, and began to reposition it – pulling *me* along. I immediately stopped, reached up, and grabbed *their* wrist and said, …

"Don't EVER do that. You want it moved; you tell me."

"I can't tell you; I have to show you."

"No. You use your *words* — like a grown-up."

Sucking up is something I've never been able to do. I guess reading "*Cyrano de Bergerac*" in high school did have an influence on me. My favorite speech of his begins:

What would you have me do?
Seek for the patronage of some great man,
And like a creeping vine on a tall tree
Crawl upward, where I cannot stand alone?
No thank you! Dedicate, as others do,
Poems to pawnbrokers? Be a buffoon
In the vile hope of teasing out a smile
On some cold face? No thank you! Eat a toad
For breakfast every morning? Make my knees
Callous, and cultivate a supple spine, —
Wear out my belly groveling in the dust?
No thank you!

NUMBER THREE: Don't be unprofessional.

Don't show up late. Don't come unprepared. Remember I told you about that director who always relied on the camera crew, performers, *anyone* else to make their shots, not just look better, but actually work? Or that other director, who was so hung over, they had one of the couches from the green room brought into the studio, the monitors placed at one end, and directed an entire episode, while lying on the couch?

Yeah. Don't do that.

Be on time. Be prepared to work. Be prepared to be part of the team, even if you're the lead character. Especially if you're the lead character. Set the tone of professionalism and comradery to help make it a productive environment.

NUMBER FOUR: Be open to constructive criticism and willing to learn something new.

"Be water, my friend" — Bruce Lee

I practice the Korean marital art "Hapkido," which means "the way of coordinated energy." In the school handbook, one piece of advice is, "The only thing that gets in the way of someone knowing their true power and being free of their weakness is their ego. (Your ego is not your 'amigo.') This is the main reason a person will be or become uncoachable, untrainable, or unteachable."

And it's true. In my training, I must be open to critique and learn not only how to listen when advice is given, but also how to respond to it. This is something I've passed on to puppeteers I've trained for the Sesame co-productions, because it's something I've also learned in the world of puppetry. For example, if Bear director Dean Gordon (a true mensch of a man) asked, within a scene, could Bear do such-and-such, I would feel comfortable saying, …

"No."

Then immediately add, …

"BUT … Bear can do *THIS*."

And that's the difference in being a "diva" to being a "team player." I had the right to say "no," because Bear and I both knew what "we" were capable of, but I always would suggest an alternative (that nine times out of ten was something not thought of and turning out better for the scene). That's what I've passed on to others; you have the right to say "no," but only if you have a better idea.

The quote "be the person you needed when you were younger" is one I try to live by each day, not just on set, but with everyone who asks to interview me for their podcast; for advice on how to become a puppeteer; sharing a friend's post, to help advertise their business or project. Just little ways, each day, that I can help encourage, whenever I can. My mom, my mentor Caroll Spinney, my wife Susan, and my son are four people whose words of encouragement for me have helped me be the man I am. It's not that hard to pass it on. Plus, I'll always remember this conversation I once had with my son.

I was walking him to school, when he was around seven years old, when out of the blue he asked me, …

"Daddy? Is there such a thing as 'karma'?"

I asked how he had heard of the word, and he explained that a friend had heard it.

"Do you know what it means?"

"It's when you do good things and are nice, and nice things happen to you. But if you're not, then you get punished. So, is there 'karma'?"

I thought for a moment and then said,

"Oh yes. And she is very … very … *very* … patient."

Now, *you* go be the person *you* needed.

"Seems Like We've Just Begun"

This last chapter title is, once again, a lyric from "The Goodbye Song," from Bear.

I've been racking my brain on how to wrap this up. You've been so patient and attentive of my droning on about my life, that I wanted to give you something special, something that would last beyond this book. But how do you wrap up a memoir. I mean, I'm still alive (knock on wood).

So, what do I write here?

This is whole book is definitely a check off the bucket list, one I didn't even know I wanted to do. But that's life, right? Sometimes you end up wanting to do something you didn't realized you wanted to do. For example, two summers ago my family and I were having a weeklong summer holiday with our friends Mike (remember him, cause one day you *will* meet him) and his lovely family – his wife Heather, and their daughters, Alexa, and Kia. (And their dog, "Callie," one of cutest little puppers, ever!) One of the perks of their place is that they have a pool, from three feet to around nine feet deep. And as I was floating in the shallow end, with Mike, who had cannonballed into the pool, and my son nearby on a chair, I suddenly said, …

"By the way … I don't know how to swim."

There. I confessed it. Fifty-nine years old and nothing to lose in finally admitting, it out loud.

And both their faces dropped.

"But" my son began, "You chaperoned us (him and his third-grade classmates) for our swimming lessons!"

"Yes, I chaperoned, as in *took* you to the YMCA pool.'"

"But you *taught* us how to swim!"

"No, … I took you to *other people* who taught you how to swim."

"But you were *in* the pool!"

"Yes," my devilish grin increasing, "in the *shallow end* … with the beginners."

I floated closer to the side of the pool towards him.

"All those years, I was with you for your swim lessons. All those pools we went to at Disney World and other hotels. Think. Did you *ever* see me in the *deep* end?"

He didn't blink for thirty seconds, taking it all in. And realizing - Yep, his dear old dad had fooled him, and everyone, for years. But especially myself. But seeing Mike just jump in and Susan, who is a natural born mermaid, I finally wanted to get it off my chest – and do something about it.

"When we get back, I'm going to look into swim lessons at the Y."

However, Mike's girls had taken a junior lifeguard course that summer and their instructors also gave swimming lessons – to adults.

"I'll call and see who can come by," Mike offered.

Oh. That soon?

But he called, and for the next two days, two different instructors came by, and I got a one-hour private swimming lesson, in a private pool. (Have a mentioned life can be good? Here's the secret – the goal is not to have a pool; the goal is to have *friends* who have a pool.) And I learned how to swim and any hesitation I had about the deep end, and you know, … drowning …, was gone. (Plus, I had two junior lifeguards in the house so …) But I never thought it would ever happen, but it did. Sometimes, it really is never too late.

And that's the thing about life – it keeps changing. We all keep changing. I'm a fan of the BBC series *"Doctor Who."* It's a great show and the premise they use to change actors to play "The Doctor" is brilliant: being an alien, specifically a "Time Lord," just before The Doctor dies, he/she gets a whole new body and personality. (Yes, I'm a proud "Blerd" – Black + Nerd.) And that's us too. We keep changing and growing each day. We even get a brand-new year to our lives to celebrate the day we were born. Of course, my mom took the Disney Parks approach to celebrations – *year long*.

"Why limit it to just *one* day?"

And if you think about it, she was right. Don't limit yourself. You get a whole new trip around the sun. So many adventures waiting for you. Try to enjoy each and every day, every way you can.

So, for me, this is only the end of this book. I've still got a lot more I want to do (like another season of my podcast *Noel's Booknook,* available wherever you listen to podcasts) and open to any surprises along the way (having done Off-Broadway's *Little Shop of Horrors* I do like theater now). The fact that *you* took the time to spend it with me is very flattering. I hope you enjoyed hearing some of the adventures I've had. There's still many more I haven't mentioned. (So … maybe this is book is "volume one?") In the meantime, I'll keep living by what Edna MacNeal would say, …

"Too blessed to be stressed."

"Bye, now."

ACKNOWLEDGEMENTS

Once again & forever after, I thank the two people who mean the most to me, who are the most beautiful part of my life. The idea to jot these stories down was the idea of Susan Elia MacNeal (Penguin/Random House award-winning & New York Time best-selling author of the *"Maggie Hope Mystery Series"* – beginning with *Mr. Churchill's Secretary* – AND her stand-out novel *Mother, Daughter, Traitor, Spy*. This last proud shameless plug was brought to you by love). Without her faith, love, and support, I wouldn't be where I am and who I am. And the other person is my pride, my joy, my reason for being a better person and the best dad I could ever be, my son. Matt, you continue to inspire me. Your talent and your big heart make me so intensely proud of the man you are becoming.

To you both, now & always, … thank you.

Next, I need to say that every reference I made to any production or any characters, were just that. I do not claim any rights or ownership to any of them. They just happened to me and around me.

When you're writing about your life, there are a LOT of people who contribute to your experience here on this earth. Some people I've named, some names I've changed, and some I've omitted, for various reasons. So, to every single person I've ever met, … THANK YOU.

Now, here a just a few specific folks who helped with this book:

To Marshall Salazar (and the team of Amazon Publishing), for his eternal patience and support in getting this done (including the gentle prodding), thanks Marshall.

And lastly, thanks to *everyone* who contributed to the Indiegogo campaign and helped make this book a reality. Specifically (in no particular order, including dear friends & colleagues):

Judith Bobalik, Kara Dymock, Jerome Black, Lilly Beards, Noah Sunday-Lefkowitz, Sophia Rodriguez, Zoe Lowe, Dante Amo, Sally Poutiatine, Adam J Bougher, Tanya O'Keefe Limb, Elana Halberstadt, Brian Ó Broin, Abigail Maughan, Rory Galvin, Matty Hawke, Elizabeth Loredo, Jonathan Penland, Rebekah Bundang, Jason Mateo, Alex Graudins, Wayne Dawson, Shane Keating, Celeste Ainsley, Peter Atsaves, Crystal Kendall, Chris Palmieri, Chase Woolner, Pagatha Christie, Olivia Fouts, Alex Patton, Tom Mace, Sascha Pollok, Glenn Kane, Janet Kim, Hannah Ward, Camille Carino, Jacob Persily, Jason Lee, Dalton Jetter, Allison Ozark, Olivia Daniels, Justin Brown, Mike Walsh, Cana Vaught, James Gallagher, David, Julia, and Nick Bradley, Andrew Cuevas, Hannah Lunt, Rivkah Pettry, Molly Cady, Jon Brangwynne, Donovan Gaffney, Joshua Gillespie, Jack Thomas, Ian Sweetman, Micaela Clark, Michael Maschio, Jan Themann, Tori Schmidt, Eric Sweetman, Chris Stulz, Jean Marie Keevins, Matthew Soberman, Chris Jones, Sean Carter, Keith Conod, Erin Gray, Howard Scully, Charlotte Achen, Jennifer Stock, Kimmerie Jones, Kiearon Devlin, Frances Serchia, Andrew Brown, Blaine Mitchell, Edward Minnix, Zachary Snyder, Sandra Johnson, Daniel Bessels, Jon Bristol, Scott Armstrong, Melissa Forbes, Leonardo Delvage Garcia, Brandon Croker, Kit Mcconnell, Meredith Gomes, Cheryl Goldman, Stanley Levine, Ann Biegan, Arthur Esposito, Marcelo Bottaro, Jeremy Wilcox, Michelle Sontarp, Paige Estep, Jared Herr, Kevin Temmer, Heidi Levine Gonzalez, Lee Thompson, Matt Vogel, Jordan Koch, Kurt Hunter, Jessica Galicia, Liliana Reyes, Lucy Parat, Kathy Haworth, Sebastiano Ricci, Helen Pritchard, Danielle Connolly, Dustin McClain, Christopher Chabot, Abbie Slaman, Andrew Vesci, Michele Alogna, Troy Murphy, Fiona and Jason, Erika Reed Myers, Jeffrey Pittle, Lynn P. Hippen, Leila Ghaznavi, Kate Alice Taylor, Brianah Bellamy, Judith Rycar, Megan Hudgell, Megan Hudgell, Joanne McBride, Melissa Satterley, William Carroll, Anneliese Huntington, Dominic Kinsella, Josh Jones, Michael Nixon, Joseph Bradley, Corie Lawson, Isabella Perry, Sammi Carillo, Marissa Blake, Chris Buttkis, Emma Young, RJ Dodd, Brock Bucklew, Cameron Fowler, Vanessa Rodriguez, Kelly (kmbarnefiher), Charles Lyons, Brody Atchley, Shane Laguna, Catherine C Tidwell, Shelby Goodwin, David Solove, James M Ditto, Andrew Crane, Chad Blankenship, Rachel Deering, Michael Rohan, Christian Frates, Emma Kennedy, Katherine Beck Fey, Aidan Drury, Elijah Bailey, Samantha Brave, Brandon Croker, Michael Nally, Maxwell Vaughan, Idria Barone Knecht, Dylan Jackson, Arlee Chadwick, Dalton Krum, Peter Lurye, Tom Nesler, Jimmy Anthony Hayden, lckilbane, Katie Jane Amanek, Christian Celey, Rachel Parker, Joey Ammons, Brett

Hansen, Matt Krygier, Merideth Norris, Peter van Roden, Annemarie Kennedy, Andrew Williams, Leigh Aufenanger-Udice, Eric Pahl, Adele Soto, Dano Johnson, Alexandra Weiher, Charles Pillsbury, Karen Bierman Hirsh, Matthew Spadaro, Erica Perwitz, Andy Clinton, Joe Apel, Chris Thompson, Steve Knudstrup, Christopher Harris, Dru Ann Love, Marsha McKeever, Scott Hanson, Chris Patstone, Kevin Coffin, Kevin Hansen, Ryan Sullivan, Scott Joy, David Wright, Abby Carson, Christina Coombes, Kenny Durkin, Lynn Roberge-Ligay, Stacey Weingarten , Jana Riess, Robert Balton, Fergie L. Philippe, Aaron Ratzan, Emily Copp, Desiree Garrett, Ryan Roe, Timothy Ryan Griffin, Kimberly Aglipay, Joe Hennes, Eve Cunning, Liam Geraghty, Tagen Marshall, Scott Traylor, Matty McDonald, Sara M Dariotis, puppetclass, Lauren Marchisotto, Kynan Barker, Mike Raab, G W Rigters, Riley Soderquist, Erica Crooks, Kelli Ann Blodgette, Emilia Leonetti, Gayle Horowitz, Jonas Riley, Nancy Kogel, Alvaro Monserrat, Ty D'Olimpio, Hannah Gordon, Danny D, Luke Macy, Jen Seggio, Michael Gleason, Alex Simmons, Kristen MGregor, Trystin Otero, David Isetta, James Byrne, Joe Zigila, Alexandra Velazquez, Noel Harper, Padmé Bruce, Nathan Danforth, Michael Lopez, Brogan Simons, Matthew Kraut, Dara Zwemer, Noah and Jacob Martin, Ashley Tilbury, Erin McGee, Angela Kurzawa, Livia Beasley, Kallysta Panagakos, Terry Tucker, Rachelle Cade, Katie Devlin, Mackenzie Marrow, Nathan Pattinson, Frankie Cordero, Jason Seck, Kyle Hirshon, Austin Costello, Stacey Gordon, Traci Lawson, María Garrido Manzano, Raymond Carr, Bradley Freeman, Jr., Amanda Avery, Kathryn Guarino, Katie Abbey, Peter McNally, Justin H Piatt, Kimberly Trefz, Amy Foltz, Joyce Gabbert, Matt Sides, Frank Simpson, Chris Steele, & Henry Greenberg

To all of you (& to anyone else who simply shared the link to the campaign):

THANK YOU! THANK YOU! **THANK YOU!!!**

And finally, to my mom, Edna MacNeal.

You helped start me on this life's journey – literally – and your support and the faith you had in me, I will always carry in my heart. You always told me, …

"Don't get a job – get a *career*."

And thanks to you, I did.

Made in United States
Troutdale, OR
11/18/2024

24968995R00153